Hallelujah! IN HOLLYWOOD

Mary Anne + Roger —
Thank you for your
support! May the blessings
of God be with
you ALWAYS

By
SHAYTEE GADSON

ISBN-10: 0615588093
EAN-13: 9780615588094

To Mama, Daddy, Reggie, Telley, Quati, Qynn and Felisha; thank you Hollywood for allowing me to show the world that, every now and then, that which does not glitter may still be gold...

TABLE OF CONTENTS

INTRODUCTION

Hollywood, South Carolina, my home, is a wide spot in the road between Charleston and Edisto Beach. We have one traffic light and forty-six hundred residents. We are, for the most part, poor, black and as a consequence, undereducated. There are also white people here that fit that description (poor and undereducated). Hard times in Hollywood don't discriminate-even if we the people do. The rich white people that live in Hollywood reside in Stono Ferry- a ritzy gated community. It may as well be on another planet. Think Beverly Hills.

We're not outwardly a real friendly people. If you're white and not from here, we don't like you. If you're black and don't sound like us – and we know what we sound like – we don't like you. If you're white *or* black and sound educated, we don't like you. But that shouldn't bother anyone. Everybody here is related to everybody else, and many times we don't even like each other.

My family's history in Hollywood extends back as far as memory goes, and everybody here knows we are lunatics. My brother, Reggie, is a crack-dealing, crack-addicted, thieving degenerate. My sister, Telley, is an ordained and highly sought-after minister in the United Methodist Church. My mama, the Divine Linda Gadson, is a Jesus freak to whom Jesus seems to listen intently. And my daddy, Herbert Gadson, is an alcoholic, a whore-monger, a recognized genius and a peerless politician.

A little more than a decade ago, Daddy told my brother, after Reggie nearly killed him, "You aine shit. I run dis fuckin' Hollywood show, nigga! Um da star uh dis here flick. Yo' ass aine nuttin' but uh damn extra." Somebody almost succeeds in precipitating your untimely demise, and you tell him you still run the show? You are still in control? You still hold serve? Marvelously delusional, you might say. Well, you get to be delusional when you're the Mayor of Hollywood.

And Daddy was that. Delusional to the point of diabolical arrogance. He lacked any awareness of any chinks in his political armor. He was too charismatic to show even the slightest hint of weakness- political or otherwise. My Daddy would often tell me, "Boy, dey can't tell me shit 'cause dey can't outthink me."

And he was right. From 1989 to 2003, nobody could outthink him. He was always two moves ahead of his political enemies and four steps ahead of the law. He was the game in Hollywood. He was human chess. He was the Pawn. The Rook. The Knight. The Queen. Burglary. Banishment. Rape. Attempted Murder. The Mayor fought the law and the Mayor won.

He would hold court in our den on Friday evenings and I'd see and hear this man quote facts and figures on the phone to the people in Charleston County government when he was trying to procure water and sewer services for Hollywood. If I were to be completely candid, with regard to our infrastructure, we'd been in the Dark Ages before Daddy came along and saved us. He'd be as drunk as Cooter Brown and still verbally disengage any county official who would try to dispute him. He didn't need a computer in front of his face. He didn't require a pen and pad or book in his hand. And yet, his facts and figures were always dead on. I know this to be true because when the conversations would commence, more often than not, there would be an unhealthy discourse rife with acerbic and specious sentiments coming from the other end of the phone. After Daddy worked his analytical and profanity- laced mojo, there would always be a litany of conciliatory, "All right Mayor," "You're right Mayor" and "We'll get right on it Mayor" that would spill from his eardrums.

Daddy told me once, "Even the craziest nigga can beat uh smaht man if dat smaht man brain aine as big as his nuts. An' I got da biggest nuts in Hollywood, boy. 'Cause I da craziest somebitch in Hollywood. I just so happen nah be da smahtest one, too." And he was. Checkmate.

What kind of woman could deal with this man who was an enigmatic, dogmatic, pragmatic and erratic ball of beautiful confusion? She would *have* to be a woman like King David, who was modeled after God's own heart.

Enter Linda Dingle Gadson. The Divine Miss G. Mama and Daddy were married for thirty years, but were together long before that. She ran a non-profit for more than three decades that fed, clothed and sheltered those who couldn't do it for themselves. She stood by Daddy during more affairs than you could count. I think after a while, she did stop counting. She was by his side after he raped that girl. Or didn't rape that girl- who knows for sure? She was in court with him after he burglarized a home.

She even managed to create *Hallelujah! Oil. Hallelujah!* has cured diaper rash, the worst kinds of sunburn you'll ever see and has stopped breast cancer in its tracks. The local CBS Television affiliate even came to Mama's legendary prayer room one day to run a story on *Hallelujah!* and the women whose breast cancer it brought to a screeching halt (www.youtube.com; video name: "Hallelujah Oil Halts Breast Cancer"). Doctors even testified to it. Mama makes it in an Igloo Cooler. Amazing, right? Yeah, I know. She's an amazing woman.

But hell, she's crazy too. You would have to be crazy to stay with a man like Daddy for as long as she did. At least that's what everybody whispered, murmured and hollered in Hollywood. Mama said she couldn't love Jesus and not forgive the Mayor for being the Mayor. He ran Hollywood, remember? Nobody chastised Spielberg for being innovative and being able to capture the magnanimity of a movie moment, did they? They didn't castigate De Palma for being able to make gore glamorous, right? So, Mama left him alone. In Hollywood, the Mayor was a force just as irresistible as Scarface. All he had in this world was his balls and his word and he didn't break 'em for no one. Pacino was acting when he uttered that iconic phrase. The Mayor *lived* the phrase. So, Mama just told God all about her troubles.

Reggie, my older brother, was a hustler. He was a ladies' man and he sold dope during the '80s. Crack cocaine would get him in the '90s. It took him to the brink of death too many times to count, and he never blinked. Several stints in state prison hardened him. But, because he and Daddy never got along, he was free to live his own life and choose his own path unfettered by any pressure to live up to any expectations that being the Mayor's son may have bound him to. Criminal Domestic Violence was the law of the land in the Mayor's house. The Charleston County Police Department knocked on our door so often, it was almost our own personal Avon Lady.

Now I know Reggie loved Daddy; he just didn't like him. And for as much as Daddy knew about love, he loved Reggie too; he just regretted having him. They went to jail too much together not to have loved each other. As sure as fat meat is greasy, Reggie would try to maim and kill Daddy when Daddy and Mama started fighting. What good son wouldn't protect his mama? But when law enforcement authorities detained the Mayor and his son, the inmates in the Charleston County Detention Center knew better than to attack Reggie's father. Reggie made it very clear, to any who would listen in jail, that he'd kill for his daddy. Now that's love.

Dynamic. Gifted. Spiritually Talented. Authentic. Obese. My sister, The Reverend Telley Lynnette Gadson, is a spiritual stalwart in the United Methodist Church. She has been bruised by growing up a Gadson; and, she is just like Mama. She's unsullied by the ways of the world but battered and bruised because of Daddy. My sister is the most awesome preacher I think I've ever seen. She's fiery and she's engaging. And I am convinced she chose the ministry because of Mama's example. But, I know my sister spent high school and college being ridiculed because of her weight. It didn't matter. Once people saw that her heart was as big as she was, her conviction and principles as uncompromising as Mama's and her gall as sheer and unmitigated as Daddy's, the jeers turned to cheers. And because she saw, up close and personal, just how loose of a cannon Daddy was, I know her concept of men is skewed. Wouldn't yours be? She thought she found love once, but it wasn't to be. I know that still haunts my sister more than a decade later, but she still soldiers on. And on her shoulders she carries so much of the pain of the past, as well the responsibility for saving lost souls. Because upon this rock she built her church. The gates of hell didn't prevail, either.

No matter how much the Mayor continued to push the gates open, the fires never torched her soul.

Hollywood, South Carolina, is my town. It's not anything like the town of tinsel, glitz and glamour on the other coast. No stars of stage and screen reside here. We're not anything like Charleston, either.

Ahhh, Charleston. Our big brother, just a few miles away from us on the map, but a world away from us in every other way. Rich Charleston, with its expensive tastes, culture and history. Charleston, the Antebellum darling of these United States. So near we are, but yet so far. We're a small town with a huge name and the Mayor made us famous. In our minds, people and though we may not have the copiousness of our famous and star-studded father, we've got the grit and the spunk of the unrecognized and invisible son. We're not the prom queen. We're her fat best friend. Hell, Daddy made us so schizophrenic around here that he turned us into Sybil.

I'm not sure what I am. I'm the Mayor's son; that much I know. I've always been smart, but I'd be lying to you if I told you that I've ever really been proficient at anything. I witnessed the hell in my house and it played out live on TV, because any time something happened in Hollywood, it made the local television news shows. Well, those lights and cameras turned me into an insecure, depressed and at times suicidal alcoholic. I'm the father of two little girls and maybe fate played a cruel trick on them by making them my offspring. If they had gambled in Vegas to pick a father, they would have crapped out by getting me. Most times, I'm scared as hell. What am I going to do with myself? I'm as unremarkable as they come. If you passed me on the street, I doubt you'd notice. I tried for a time when I was in college to create this Tasmanian devil of a character. He was my alter ego who was a livewire act that was irresistible to women, irreverent to everybody and everything and funny. And would you believe, it worked? I became a whoremonger too, just like Daddy. I also realized, during my four years in college, that I liked to drink – just like Daddy. Okay, it was closer to seven years in college. I can't tell you for sure because most of those semesters were a Crown Royal induced haze, okay? I left college with no degree, two children and a life plan so feeble it would be classified more along the lines of a wish.

I wish I liked myself. Maybe I hate myself, I'm not sure. Telley wasn't the only one who was teased, you know, although for very different reasons. I wish I were more than what I am. Somewhere, I wandered off the cliff of hopes and dreams and landed in the valley of aimlessness and despair —the valley of the shadow of death. Every day I fear its evil. I wish I could tell you that I had a rhyme or reason for doing some of the ridiculous things I've done, but the truth is I'd be being disingenuous if I told you that. And I wish I could tell you why fright flouts the joy out of my days and nights now. I wish I were still that fearless guy from yesteryear. I wish. Hollywood is the place where you can wish upon a star. It makes no difference who you are. Thank God for that. I'm the Mayor's son, so I pray that when it comes to wish-granting time, the powers that be in Hollywood don't hold my title against me. I hope now that I've let you peek into my soul, you won't let the fact that I've grown addicted to the lights, camera and action affect how you feel about me, about us, about Hollywood. I wish.

But, I digress. A dollar and a wish, in this world, will only get you a hot cup of joe and a dream. And just as in the well-heeled, time tested and tried and true tradition of our just slightly better known namesake, in my Hollywood, some of the names and details have been changed to protect the innocent. As well as the guilty.

The following is based on a true story. A True Hollywood Story.

CHAPTER 1

Great Expectations

Mama says the only person who ever called her grandmother by her name – Tammalee, or "Miss Tamalee"– was the gangling, skinny, white insurance man with the pitted face and black hair. But after awhile, and after he had eaten many a Sunday dinner consisting of collard greens, fatback, hog maw and cornbread, even he felt comfortable with calling her Doozy.

Her real name was Tammalee Pinkney. She was Mama's maternal grandmother and she raised Mama because Mama Clay, Mama's mama, had to go to the big hotel in downtown Charleston, to work to make a way for the family. Mama Clay was a salad maker at the Francis Marion Hotel, at Calhoun and King streets, during the 1950s and '60s. Mama said she used to love going to work with Mama Clay because the Francis Marion Hotel was like "mini heaven." The hotel was twelve stories tall and it engulfed the famed intersection. It was a huge black and coral, brick and stucco building. It had a palatial lobby complete with primrose Italian marble floors and French crystal chandeliers. Mama said that every time she walked into the building she felt like she was entering her own kingdom. The place had

24-karat gold-plated elevators. She said she would pretend that the elevators were carnival rides, and she would go from floor to floor just to hear the bell ring as people came on and got off of them. Mama Clay may have only been a salad maker, but she so charmed the rich white people who came and went with her stories and jokes that they treated her as if she owned the place. She was the Queen of The Francis Marion. Mama was the princess. Everybody loved them.

Mama Clay's birth name was Annabelle Pinkney. I don't think anyone knew that except for maybe her doctor, and that was only because he wrote her prescriptions. Even he called her Mama Clay. Almost since the day she was born on June 11, 1911, she was called Clay. In an attempt to strengthen the muscles in her legs as a baby, Doozy dug a hole in their yard and buried Mama Clay in it up to her mid thighs. Everyone referred to Doozy's yard as the "football field" because it was just that mammoth. She would bury Mama Clay right next to their Sycamore tree. The football field had only sparse amounts of grass. It was a dirt field and the tree sat in the center of it. Doozy ensconced Mama Clay in that same spot every day because most folks believed that tree had mystical powers. Doozy would dig a small hole and water the dark brown earth until it became crude oil-colored mud. She would then get on her hands and knees and scoop the mud right back into the hole forcing Mama Clay to have to climb her way out of it. Eventually, after two months of repeating this absurd action, a thirteen-month-old Annabelle Pinkney managed to walk herself right out of that black hole. At thirteen months old, she walked out of the clay of the earth and into a new pseudonym that she would carry for the rest of her days.

Mama Clay was Doozy's heart. She knew that Mama Clay was slow, though. In today's jargon, Mama Clay would be labeled as developmentally delayed. Older men took advantage of that. Mama said that as a child, she often wondered why Doozy never let Mama Clay transact any business. Mama would always see Doozy on the porch painstakingly pouring over bills. One day, as a very young girl while she was ironing clothes and Doozy was sitting in her chair looking them over, she asked her why.

"Doozy, why my mama dough nevah (don't never) have tah pay da bills? I know you always struggle tah have tah fine uh ride downtown an' mama work downtown every day."

Doozy looked up from the bills at her confused granddaughter's face. Mama could see that she was looking for the right words to use to explain Mama Clay's shortcomings. After a short pause, Doozy did her best to elucidate.

"Linda, ya (your) mama do da bess (best) she kin wit' whah (what) da Lawd (Lord) done give she. Clay gah (is going to) make it. She jess (just) gah have tah make it diff'rnt dan (than) everybody else. God jess make my chile tah run uh lil' slower race dan everybody else is all."

Mama Clay was the chief breadwinner of the family. She was just a hair over five feet tall, cinnamon colored and solidly built with huge breasts and kind eyes. Her eyes were so kind that they hid the fact that something unspeakable happened to her as a child. It was so horrendous, in fact, that Mama could never quite muster the gumption to tell me exactly what it was. I have my suspicions. I only mention her breasts because in her later years, after she retired from the hotel, it was Mama Clay's breasts that nurtured me. Many was the day that, as a baby and a little boy, she would rock me to sleep on her more than ample bosoms.

We watched *The Price Is Right* at 11 a.m. and the Channel Five midday local news at noon. The "news" was anchored by a pearly toothed, fleshy faced and chubby cheeked brunette with perfectly coifed hair named Bill Sharpe. Bill Sharpe's hair did not move. It was immaculate. It was thick on the top and shorter, but even, on the sides. His mop was shellacked with the chemist level prodigiousness of Jerry Zucker, with what appeared to be a masterful combination of Breck, Grecian Formula and Consort, to a high gloss. I was enamored with his hair. His tresses and his ability to clearly and succinctly relay the facts of a story as if he were there before, during and after it occurred, combined with his folksy and homespun wit, was flat out the epitome of the "Charleston bubba." As a little boy, I felt as if Bill Sharpe was my uncle who came to watch Mama Clay and me eat Oscar Meyer Hot Dogs and drink White House Apple Juice everyday just because he loved us enough to keep us informed about what was going on in the world. He just happened to be white, but he was my uncle nonetheless. "Uncle Bill" babysat Mama Clay and me all during the 1980s. After he went off the air everyday at 12:29, we would watch *The Young and The Restless* at 12:30.

I became addicted to *Y and R* as a little boy, and I watched in a sexually curious trance. Victor Newman taught me how to kiss. Victor Newman was the resident ladies' man and tycoon of the show's fictional Genoa City. Somewhere along the line, I guess I internalized what I later dubbed the "index finger slide" technique. This was where Victor would take the object of that episode's affection into a deep embrace. He would gaze deeply into her eyes and cup both sides of her face. Victor would then take his left index finger and gently slide it down the right side of her face. The enchantress would then melt in his arms as she folded into his torso. He would cup her face in the palm of his hands again so that he could control the angle in which he wanted to go in for the kiss. He would exhale deeply and, in that melodic and hypnotizing Victor Newman voice, tell the object of his desire how beautiful she was. He would then exhale passionately once more and kiss her. If you ask me, Victor Newman should have been voted Time Magazine's Man of The Year every year of the '80s. Whoever said that TV wasn't an invaluable teaching tool was a damned fool. If they'd ever employed that index finger slide technique, they'd be singing a different song – I'll bet you that.

While we watched TV, Mama Clay would sit on the pea-, forest- and Kelly-green argyle-colored couch in the den of my Mama and Daddy's brown brick house. The den was the center of our home. It was the size of the three bedrooms in Doozy's house combined. It had tan fir-paneled walls and ceramic tiled floors that were copper, canary and India green. I always envisioned the interlocking assorted colored rings in the floor pattern were what tigers jumped through at the circus. We had a twenty-four-inch floor model 1970s style television that was a big oak box with a huge glass in the middle of it. I would rock back and forth in my rocking chair for hours watching that oak box. I was the king of my little world. During the day, I was the supreme and undisputed ruler of the den. The characters on television were jesters sent from Hollywood and New York City specifically to entertain me, King Shaytee. That was how I viewed it, at least.

Mama Clay was sixty-seven years old at the time. I was five. Sometimes while we were watching soap operas – she called them "the stories" – and sitting on that comfortable cloth sofa, she would fall asleep before I did. Then, Victor Newman and I would be watching her. I would always laugh at Mama Clay when I saw her head bobbing up and down in her futile attempts to stave off sleep. I'd look over at her sitting on the couch and scream at her: "Hey! Mama Clay! Wake up! Why you always goin' nah sleep?!" We'd go through this exchange daily. It was fun and it never got old.

"Boy I aine young like you; Mama Clay gotta get her rest. How else you think I 'posed tah get da enah'gee (energy) tah run ba'hine (behind) you? Ole people gotta sleep, Shaytee." She would constantly remind me that she was old and that I was young whenever I tried to pester her into staying awake with me. Mama Clay loved being old. "Ole people done earned da right tah be sleepy. I done earn da right tah sit right cha (here) an' go sleep." And she did. She more than earned it.

I, on the other hand, at least most of the time, could only fall asleep when she placed me on her breasts.

The year was 1982. Ronald Reagan was President of the United States and kindergarten was only a half-day. Every single day, almost ritualistically, Mama Clay would walk down our one hundred-foot graveled driveway to the gap to pick me up off the school bus. In our town, everybody referred to the beginning of a driveway as "the gap."

But long before President Reagan and half-day kindergarten, the force that held Mama and Mama Clay together – held the whole family together, for that matter – was Doozy.

Doozy earned her name. She was just south of six feet tall and slightly north of two hundred fifty pounds. She was amber hued and her hands were massive. Nobody – man, woman nor child – trifled with Doozy. She was the mother of the Pineland Community in Hollywood. Because, even as a very young child her resolve and will proved to be indomitable, people in and around Pineland would often quip *"Dat gal dey!...Dat gal is a doozy of uh gal!"* The name became intertwined in the fabric of Pinelanders' lexicon.

They called it Pineland because of its plethora of pine trees, which were stacked against a deep wooded mosaic akin to a Thomas Kinkade painting. The dirt road that led there ran under a ceiling of moss-laden tree limbs that seemed to haunt the darkened path at night, ominously warning all who dared to walk there after sunset that they were on a forbidden trail. Tall and imposing grass insulated the road. A conglomeration of lush brown and green shades carpeted it. Dogs, children, men, women, horses and cars all shared the track. They didn't need a stoplight there; life was just that slow. Living in the Pineland was just simple country living.

Doozy was a mother to the fourteen grandchildren and great-grandchildren who she shared her home with at various points in their lives. Her house was a soup kitchen to anyone in the neighborhood who found themselves hungry and in need of a meal. It was a daycare center for most of Pineland's children who were under school age because during the day their parents had to work in the fields. It was also a battered women's shelter to many of Pineland's women whose husbands and boyfriends went upside their heads with punches, kicks, the butts of axes and switches off trees.

One such woman was Miss SayJane. Whenever Miss SayJane's husband, Allister, would get drunk and want to "twirl", she would always end up hurt. (Her name was actually Sarah Jane, but when you said it in our Gullah-Geechee dialect, "Sarah Jane" became "SayJane". Gullah-Geechee was the language spoken in Charleston by most black folks and some white, because of the influence of the West African slaves that were brought from places like Sierra Leone and Liberia. It was the combination of their native languages and the English that they were forced to learn here. The King's English was most assuredly our second language. Because of our unique linguistics, Miss Sarah Jane was "SayJane" and Mr. Allister was "Mista Allistah".)

Miss SayJane was a smallish honey-colored woman with dough eyes and an easy but fearful smile. Her eyes had seen more pain than they should have in their thirty-four years of watching. Sometimes Mr. Allister would get so drunk that he couldn't even eat the food Miss SayJane had prepared for him. He'd fall asleep, and when he woke up from his drunken stupor and found the food cold, he'd blame her. He'd say, "SayJane, my goddamn food cole, you no-good, lazy-ass wench – you mussy (must be) wanna twirl da'night (tonight)." Sometimes he'd beat her with his fists and feet. Other times he'd make her go out to their pear tree and pick a pear for him to eat and a switch for him to beat her with. And he'd beat her bloody.

One spring night, after years of taking his beatings, Miss SayJane got fed up.

"Allistah, I aine one uh dese damn chern (children) in dis house dat you kin beat wit' uh switch. On dis night cha, you gah have tah bury me 'cause ya ass doggone sho' aine gah beat me."

Then she spit in Allister Jontiss Hull's face and took off running. She sprinted out of that two-bedroom, tarpaper matchbox house and headed straight for Doozy's house. She was seeking not political, but insane asylum. Mr. Allister was so drunk that he couldn't take off running immediately after her, and that was all the time Miss SayJane needed.

When women came running up to the front porch of Doozy's three-bedroom, brown-board shotgun house at dusk or dark on Friday evenings, she knew before they swung open the squeaky brown splintered door of the porch who the woman was just by the inflection of the screaming. Doozy was the philosophical and moral queen of the Pineland and her front porch was the queen's court. She settled disputes and dispensed her brand of wisdom, tough love and common sense from that fourteen-by-twenty-foot space. The sepia board floors creaked like those of a haunted house when you walked on them. The floors were swollen in the summer and frigid in the winter. The walls were wrap-around mesh screen. Some sections were torn and tattered; other sections were as strong as the day they were installed. Doozy's throne was a discarded but refurbished school bus seat that sat on four Payne's gray cinderblocks. When she sat on her perch, it really did appear that this woman was much more than the neighborhood sage. When she ascended on high, she appeared exactly like what she was: The Queen Mother of the Pineland.

You could hear Miss SayJane screaming bloody murder all the way down the dirt path. By the time she made it to Doozy's porch door, panting, sweating and out of breath, Doozy was standing on the other side of it ready to let her in.

"Doozy, I tie'ud (tired) uh da man beatin' on me like I some mule. I tie'ud of it! Doozy, you da one gotta keep him off uh (of) me da'night."

"Chile, I been waitin' seventeen yazz (years), since da very day you play fool an' marrid dat monsta, fah you tah tell me tah keep Allistah Hull off uh you. An' I bet chu he think he bad enough tah fallah (follow) you to dis porch 'cause he know whay (where) you done come runnin' to. Well, I tell you whah SayJane, when he cross dese ya porch steps da'night, he gah wish he had stay tah y'all house an' enjoy da lass uh dat drunk he been on. I kin gan'tee (guarantee) you dat."

As Doozy held Miss SayJane in her arms rocking back and forth with her, she said, "Chile, dis gah be da lass night you have tah run from yo' house whay you ress yo' head at night. Yes Lawd. Da'night, big time gah bring him down an' his sin gah fine (find) him out."

Doozy looked over at Mama, who was sitting on the Ash gray block cement steps of the front porch, and said, "Chile, go look in da back room an' git my thing fah me ya (you hear)."

"Yes ma'am."

Mama said that Doozy was just thinking aloud when she made her statement, but she started running toward the back room anyway. She ran to the back of the house to Doozy's room and got her "thing" out of the middle drawer of Doozy's burgundy cherry wood three-drawer nightstand. She knew exactly where Doozy's "thing" was because she used to play with it when Doozy went downtown to pay bills. Mama would pretend that she was Little Annie Oakley, the title character of the television western that ran in the mid 1950s, as she pretended to shoot robbers with it. The "thing" was hidden under some old newspapers and her great-grandchildren's baby clothes. Doozy had a maple wood grain-handle sawed-off shotgun and a box full of shells under the papers and the baby pajamas. Mama grabbed the gun and the shells and ran back onto the porch. She gave them to Doozy and watched her carefully load the cannon. Doozy, Miss SayJane and Mama then waited on the dimly lit brown-board porch as the single sixty-watt bulb swung precariously in the middle of it by a beaded metal string.

"You aine gah have tah pick no switch off uh no mo' tree like uh chile afta da'night SayJane," Doozy said. "Oh, no ma'am. He be ya duh'reckly (in a short time), an' I gah be *waitin'* on um."

The knock at the door sounded like thunder. Mr. Allister, all six-foot-three inches and one-hundred ninety pounds of him, and as black as the dusk that had fallen on that humid evening, was a ball of fury at Doozy's porch door. He pounded so hard on that brown-boarded splintered wood door that the paint on it, which was already chipped, seemed to jump off. He pounded it almost completely off the hinges.

"Come on out cha (out here) SayJane! We gah have us uh twirlin' good time da'night. Oh, yes suh! Come on out cha so I kin ca (carry) you on home."

Miss SayJane was lying on Doozy's chair with her head buried in Doozy's lap. Doozy rose up slowly from her throne to confront the Gordian knot at her door.

"Allistah, you mussy done take leave uh all uh yo' good sense bammin' on my dough (door) like dat. Now SayJane aine leavin' my house dis night cha."

"Doozy, dass my wife! You aine got no cause tellin' me whah I kin do wit' my ownt wife!"

"Oh yes I is, an' I tellin' you Allistah: SayJane is stayin' right cha da'night. Now you got two choice: you kin leave my house down dat same dirt road dat you stumble down tah git cha (get here), or Mr. Sam Baker gah come ya, call da bus (ambulance), an' you gah git carry off my porch."

Now everybody in Hollywood knew that if you brought Sam Baker into an argument during those days, the person that uttered the name meant business. Sam Baker was the only police officer that patrolled Hollywood back then. He was white and he was mean. He was a heap of a man who was muscular and fat. When you made him angry, his Terra cotta-tinged skin that perennially appeared as if it was in one stage or another of healing from wicked sunburn, turned the shade of his carrot colored hair. Mr. Allister had to know that Doozy was ready to kill or be killed because she uttered the two words that were feared by most of the black men in Hollywood, law abiding and law breaking alike: Sam Baker.

"But three things I know Allistah: Number One: SayJane aine leavin' my house 'til she dough have tah pick no switch off uh no tree fah she da git whip wit' like she some chile. Number Two: SayJane aine leavin' my house 'til she staht (start) gettin' betta treatment by she husband in she ownt house. An' number three: You leavin' dis front porch dis night cha. Dem da three things I know. Now you kin take yo' damn choice."

Allister Hull then did the single most ill-conceived action that any man could have done at that particular juncture: he entered Doozy's house, uninvited, after being asked to leave.

Mr. Allister used his right shoulder under the force of all of his weight and broke open the porch door to confront Doozy. She uttered five words as she pulled that double-barreled shotgun out of her omnipresent, faded, floral print yellow, orange and blue housedress.

"Oooh, you bad 'ey Allistah?" She always asked people if they were "bad" right before she had to, in her words, "put uh nigga in e (his) place." Doozy had Mr. Allister's chest in her sights and before he could walk the three steps over to where she, and by this time Miss SayJane were standing, she pointed the sawed-off at his chest.

"Allistah, please make one mo' move tawd (toward) dis gal an' dey gah be able tah drive yo' hearse through da hole dis thing gah put in yo' chess. Please, come on ovah ya Mista Hull. I want chu (you) to. I beggin' you to."

"Doozy, now all I want is mah wife an' you aine gah have no trouble in ya da'night."

"Allistah, you da only one on dis porch 'bout tah have da trouble! Leave ya, Allistah, fo' I see to it dat you kan' (can't) leave!" Mr. Allister didn't move a muscle, but he started to flash those ivory white teeth of his in the manner that he always did when he was nervous or angry.

"Doozy, we always was able tah git 'long," Mr. Allister said weakly. "Please ma'am, gimme mah wife back."

"Allistah, when you learn dat God give you dis woman tah love on an' not tah box on, you kin have she back. 'Til den, I suhgess (suggest) you leave."

Mr. Allister, up until this point, had been perfectly still; but in trying to reason with Doozy, he made a step toward her and Miss SayJane. That's when the shotgun blew the porch door to kingdom come.

"Now Allistah, I mean tah shoot da dough dat time. Next time, I gah mean tah shoot chu."

Doozy said all of this as she cocked the gun for the second time with it aimed squarely at Mr. Allister's chest.

"You got five seconds tah see yo'self off uh my porch, sir. Four. Three..."

"I gone, Doozy! Please, dough shoot me Doozy! I gone!"

Mama said that she knew that Mr. Allister had departed because she heard him running off the porch. He was moving so fast it was impossible to see him in the ebony night.

Mr. Allister brutalized Miss SayJane just once again after that night, and then the Lord stepped in and stopped him. Mama said that's how Doozy characterized it anyway.

Mr. Allister was an anal-retentive man. His floors had to be spotless. His beds had to be made. He even made Miss SayJane scrub the windows because he enjoyed seeing his reflection in them.

About a month after Doozy fully intended to blow a hole through Mr. Allister's chest, Miss SayJane came down with a urinary tract infection that left her debilitated. She could barley walk after about a week of suffering, much less perform her normal chores and "wifely duties." Of course, back then, medical technology being what it was and poor black peoples' access to health care being what it was, Miss SayJane didn't receive any treatment for her sickness save for home remedies.

One Sunday evening, while Miss SayJane was preparing dinner, Mr. Allister hit the gin bottle a little too hard one and demanded sex from Miss SayJane. He said that it wasn't some "piss infection" but a "nasty woman's infection" which occurred as a result of her "cocking yo' legs open fah some outside nigga." As Miss SayJane stood over her stove, listening to Mr. Allister accuse her of being the worst kind of whore imaginable, he charged toward her and grabbed her. He shoved her face to within inches of the hot stovetop and told her that if she moved a muscle, he would burn her exquisite face. He tore off her frock and panties, dropped his pants and disengaged his erect penis from his underwear. Miss SayJane mentally prepared herself another brutal rape at the hands of her husband.

But then she heard Mr. Allister's breathing become labored and he gasped for air. He let up off of her as he continued to gasp and gurgle, losing more and more oxygen with each wince. He dropped to his knees as he clutched his left arm. By this time, he'd fully loosened his grip on Miss SayJane. She turned around and saw Mr. Allister lying on the floor in the middle of their small kitchen, frothing at the mouth like a rabid dog. He was slumped over on his knees, then slumped further onto his left side.

He was having a stroke, which made his cries to his wife for help incomprehensible and undiscernable. Miss SayJane said the last thing she heard her husband say, that she could decipher, was, "Help me, Jesus. Ahh Lawd, help me Jesus. Lawd, dough let me die in ya." Seconds later, Miss SayJane said his eyes rolled to the back of his head. He was dead. She was free.

Shortly after the funeral, Miss SayJane hightailed it to Newport, Rhode Island, with her four children in tow, to live with her aunt. She never came back to Hollywood. Doozy said she remarried an older man who owned a construction company and reportedly had ties to the Kennedys. She had another two children. She spent the rest of her days happy, far removed from her Hollywood nightmare.

But that was an entirely different time, fifteen years earlier. Mama wasn't the scared skinny seven-year-old pecan-colored girl on Doozy's porch from that night. She was Linda Dingle: a fully grown woman who was quite capable of making her own decisions. Mama was twenty-two years old and she wanted Doozy to understand that she was serious about her love for Herbert Gadson.

They met at Baptist Hill High School, the all-black high school in Hollywood, in 1964. Daddy was a sophomore and Mama was a freshman. Baptist Hill was a small, African-American, rural school of the '60s South. It was an underfunded afterthought of the district. It was a minuscule, vermilion-lacquered, single-story wood building about ten years behind the times in its curriculum. According to the city leaders, it was as good a place as any to warehouse the "good niggra chill'ren" in Hollywood who wanted an education. The district expected that education would be applied in the service of the white people of Charleston no matter what station in life these black kids decided to undertake. At best, some of them would learn a trade that would somehow be used to benefit the white folks of Charleston proper. Decades later, the pervasive undercurrent of racism that was a vestige of the bigotry of those days would lead a Charleston County School Board representative to refer to the African-American children in Baptist Hill's district as "brain dead."

There was another school close by, St. Paul's Parish High School in the neighboring town of Meggett, but it was all-white and reputed to be full of racists. It was a two-story, coconut-colored brick building that lacked centralized heating and air. In the summer, all the windows in the classrooms had to remain open to combat the sweltering Lowcountry heat. In the winter, the big oil furnace had to operate full blast to keep the school even quasi-warm. St. Paul's wasn't a modern facility by any means, but the curriculum was better than Baptist Hill's, the books were newer and it had an aura surrounding it because it was the "white school" where blacks were forbidden. That made Linda Dingle even more determined to obtain an education there.

Mama forged Doozy's signature on the consent form in order to enroll, in her sophomore year, along with six other blacks. By the time Doozy found out what she'd done, school was already several weeks old. She was hell bent on getting that white man's education, so even if Doozy had tried to intervene, it wouldn't have worked.

White kids at the school did all they could to get rid of Mama. They spat on her, threw eggs at her as she walked to the bus, put gum in her hair and called her nigger. These were almost daily occurrences. Sure there were good white kids at St. Paul's, but most of them did their best to make her life miserable. Their efforts to get rid of her failed. There was no way that they were going to break my mama.

My daddy was average height. He was a thick-framed and chubby football player who was the color of a fudge brownie, smart and wore thick black cat eyeglasses. My mama was a few inches north of five feet, size twelve and had a smile that would light up a room. Mama said that although Daddy wasn't what she considered "cute", he was attractive because he was highly intelligent, funny and charismatic, all character-istics that he would use to become the first black mayor of the Town of Hollywood. He would use every ounce of all three of these attributes to stay there.

The genesis of Mama and Daddy's courtship didn't come from the pages of a story book or romance novel. It would have made an excellent caution-ary prologue to a novel wrought with melancholy and woe.

When Mama and Daddy first met, he virtually hobbled into her life. He was walking down the hall and Mama was standing at her locker when she looked up and saw him struggling with trying to walk on crutches while carrying his books. She ran over to him after she saw that he'd dropped them. She picked them up and proceeded to walk him to his classroom door. She handed him his books. He didn't even thank her as he turned and limped into class.

I can remember asking Mama several times, as a little boy, what her cogitation was about Daddy in the beginning. Her tale was always morose. And foreboding.

"Shay, your daddy broke his leg playing football during practice. I don't think da man evah actually played in uh game. Herbert was uh nerd. He was uh brainiac. He was always academically gifted. He was by no means athletically inclined. He used football as uh way tah git da girls. Between his pseudo athletic abilities and his real ability tah think two steps ahead of any objection any girl may have given to him, he did well wit' da ladies."

converted school bus seat, her de facto prayer altar, for patience and understanding. She prayed not for herself, but to help a young Linda Dingle understand why they were afflicted with all the "whys" in life.

Mama never stopped with the deluge of questions for her grandmother. "Doozy, why we so poor? Why we dough have uh taulit (toilet) or runnin' water in our house? Why do I have tah chop so much wood tah heat dis house, Doozy? Doozy, why we have tah go outside tah use da taulit? Why we aine got nuttin'? Why aah (our) life so hard?"

Doozy would pray to the Lord, asking Him to give her the answers to tell her granddaughter when she asked these heart-wrenching questions. Her answer from on high was always the same:

"Chile, pray. Pray fah long life so dat da Lawd will give you da strength tah git all dem things ween got. I know ya want uh taulit in ya house. I know ya want runnin' wah'dah (water) in ya house. I done did da bess I kin do fah ya, an' I kan' git it. Gal, I want you tah pray da Lawd give you long life so you kin git all dem things. If you pray, da Lawd gah bless sha (you); an' I bless sha chile. I give you mah blessin' 'cause you gah be somein'. You aine gah have tah worry if you gah live betta dan whah we livin' now 'cause da Lawd done already fix it fah ya. E (It) dough matta dat I kan' git dem things. E dough matta 'cause you gah git um. Jess put cho truss (trust) in da Lawd, chile. *Man might pint, but God quart.*"

My mother wanted a better life for her son than the one she had. She didn't want to raise this child alone. Sometimes, she would lament to me, or maybe she was just thinking aloud on those Friday nights as I combed her hair, that "If I had listened to dat ole lady, I might not uh gone thu' all da hell I been thu' wit' cho Daddy." Doozy's words were my mother's "soundtrack of regret" for many years to come.

On paper, Daddy looked good. He got his undergraduate degree and Master's Degree in Industrial Arts Education from South Carolina State College. He flourished in college because the greatest asset that a college student has is freedom. Daddy was free from the constraints of any parental control and he was unobstructed to formulate and articulate his own worldview. My daddy was drawn to teaching because of its autonomy – its freedom. He hated authority in any way, shape or form. The older he got, the deeper his resentment of rules festered.

One day, shortly after Daddy came back to Hollywood from his teaching job in another city, and as he and Mama sat on the long Phthalo green wooden bench on Doozy's porch, Daddy said, "Linda, I aine got no place tah stay. I aine got no place tah go. Mama let Chitney stay in my room 'til I got back for da summer, but now the nigga whoa (won't) let me have my goddamn room back."

Mama was floored. She knew how close Daddy and Chitney were, but she also knew that four walls, a roof and a bed were enough to turn poor people against each other.

"Whah you gah do, Herbert? You kan' live on da skreets." She could tell that Daddy was afraid of what was looking more like his inescapable eventuality. "Da whah I tryna tell you Linda; if I dough find uh place tah stay, da jess way my black ass gah en'nup (end up). If he aine bin my mama sistah son, I'd fuck his ass up. He only my mama sistah son now 'cause afta dis shit he done pull, he damn sho' aine no kin tah me no mo'. Anyhow Linda, da school year is ovah an' I kan' even go back home. I need you tah help me."

Mama said that Daddy slumped his shoulders and dropped his head. He was utterly defeated. She knew what she had to say. She knew what she had to do. She put her right arm around him and cupped his face in her left hand. She dropped her head so that she could look him in his eyes.

"You know O'wl (I'll) help you, Herbert. I promise, I gah help you." Now Mama knew full well that the only way that she was going to be able to "help" Daddy was to let him stay with her in Doozy's house. There was but one problem: she and Reggie were living there. Doozy was not going to allow Daddy to reside there and them not be married. Believe you me, my father was in no rush to get married. He was, however, in even less of a hurry to live in a cardboard box. If he didn't do some fast talking and some even swifter thinking, that's exactly where he was going to be relocating.

In the nearly four years after my brother was born, Daddy had never seriously considered getting married. He and Mama even broke up for a time because of his reluctance. During the hiatus, he became engaged to a United Methodist minister's daughter, but he eventually repossessed the engagement ring because he realized he didn't want to marry into a religious family. But now he was out of alternatives.

He gave the usurped ring to Mama on June 16, 1972 – three years, five months and twenty-six days after my brother was born. And on that same day Herbert Gadson and Linda Dingle, two of Hollywood's best and brightest rising stars, married in a small ceremony in the home of a dejected Tammalee Pinkney. It was a marriage that would form a supernova, one so hot and so highly combustible that it would nearly burn Hollywood asunder.

CHAPTER 2

Mama Gone...Daddy Long Gone...

When Daddy got drunk, which in the 1980s was just about every Friday night, he would mesmerize me with harrowing stories about his life when he was young. As he talked, all I could muster was an occasional "Fah real, Daddy?" or a "You gotta be lyin'!" I would interject every few minutes, just to keep the rhythmic timing of his semantic cadences going. Every now and again he would respond with a "Shitch'yeah, boy!" But mostly, he just talked; and mostly, I just listened. Nobody disturbed Vincent van Gogh as he cut off his ear, did they? Sometimes, it's just best to let a tortured genius bleed.

I was only a kid- eight, nine, maybe ten years old at the most. I didn't know that once blood drips onto your consciousness, no amount of cold-water soaking or dishrag scrubbing can remove it. Even if you immerge your soul in Crown Royal, you can never completely wash that blood away. I watched Daddy try. Years later, I would try, too. We both failed.

Daddy remembered as far back as my great-grandmother, Ma (pronounced as in "math") Bally. According to Daddy, she was "one-third black, one-third Edisto Indian and one-third hell raisin' shit talker." She started having children when she was a teenager, and she didn't really care what her offspring did. She was trying to survive herself.

The depths of her wanton disregard for her children reached levels hard to comprehend. For example, when one of her daughters, Kayvass, was eleven, Ma Bally locked her in a closet for three days, allowing her only grits and water, because Ma Bally found out that she and Kayvass were having sex with the same man. Ma Bally didn't care that Kayvass was having sex; after all, she was just using her "womanly tools" for survival, just like Ma Bally had taught her to do. Ma Bally was just angry that she was using her "tools" with one of Ma Bally's many male companions.

When Kayvass, who would become my biological grandmother, was twelve, she started having sex with a twenty-three-year-old man named Murray Gadson. When she was fourteen, she married him. In those days, the 1950s, in poor towns such as Hollywood, there was nothing wrong or immoral when an older man took an interest in a child. People would just say that the older man was "raisin' da young gal fah eself (himself)." Conversely, marriage was considered a good thing because it gave the girl some hope for the future. Ma Bally was ecstatic because it left her with one less mouth she had to feed.

According to Daddy, Murray Gadson was a coal black, diminutive and bitter man. After his children were born, he joined the Army and fought in World War II. But he didn't join for any heroic reasons, feelings of unabashed patriotism, or because his black skin limited his opportunities. He joined because he loathed the idea of fatherhood and responsibility. He just didn't want to deal with a wife and kids.

"Da somebitch just cun (couldn't) wrap his mind 'round da fact dat raisin' chern an' havin uh wife was uh everyday routine dat would require work and sacrifice. An' Murray aine nevah sacrifice shit fah nobody 'cept Murray. Mothafucka was uh selfish bastid. Evah been selfish. ALL things wit' da nigga was always 'me, me, me.' Wudda (What the) fuck Murray kin get outta da deal, ya see. Da was da mothafucka credo: wudda fuck Murray gettin' out da deal. He live by dat. Mothafucka aine nevah mean nobody no fuckin' good, man." Daddy adamanatly and consistently said that about Murray when the spirits started to matriculate through his central nervous system.

And so, after Murray returned home from the Army, he simply abandoned Kayvass and their three childen and ran off to New York City. A year later, in 1954, Kayvass – a slight, hot-tempered, bronze-skinned woman – followed him, thus deserting her three young children to fend for themselves. The children were Herbert, six years old, who would become my father; Joelle, five; and Fichette, four.

I can still see Daddy on those Friday night benders, sitting in his recliner in our den, blowing Salem Regular smoke rings and talking about his biological parents, Kayvass and Murray Gadson. He would call Murray "that trifling somebitch," and Kayvass "dat ole irresponsible ass betch (bitch) who let Murray shit (fool) her into thinkin' he been gah take care her. Da nigga leave us so why da fuck Kayvass thought he been gah take care her I'll damn nevah know. Shit!" Kayvass and Murray were such a volatile mix that after she caught him in bed with her best friend, Kayvass would spend twenty-two months in a psychiatric hospital for riddling Murray's brand new rosewood and ivory 1961 Chevrolet Impala with bullets. Kayvass told Daddy that she would have "shot his black ass dead in dat bed" with her Saturday night special, but she wanted to make him suffer. So she murdered Murray's automobile. She replaced the new car scent with gun smoke.

Daddy always seemed to be contemplating whether he should reach back into the recesses of his all-too-vivid memory to bring the all-too-painful cerebral ghosts to the fore. And he would always, inevitably, ask me the question, or make the statement, I never could tell which, "How uh man can call hisself uh man an' he know he got chern out dey in da werl (world) he aine even know, an' dough wanna know, is beyond me. How uh man do dat?"

Sometimes Daddy would stare off into space and ask the question. Sometimes he would look directly into my eyes. When he did, tears would well up. I had a father, so I didn't know what to say.

I never knew Murray Gadson, but Daddy said his most conspicuous memories of him was his "beatin' da shit" out of Grandma Kayvass when they were all living with her mother in a three-room house. His fondest memory of Murray was the day that Murray, for reasons known only to Murray, unexpectedly gave him a silver dollar. Soon after that, he ran away to New York City.

The children were taken in by Kayvass's sister, Arthelle, and Arthelle's husband, LeMarion Titus Gadson, who was Murray's brother. And henceforth, the three orphans would call Arthelle "Mama" and LeMarion "Daddy." They raised the children into adulthood, although in those days, in poverty-stricken towns like Hollywood, raising children meant providing food, clothes and shelter – and not very much else. And beyond those basics, because times were so difficult, Arthelle and LeMarion couldn't offer much more that one may deem "positive."

They didn't know any better. From what I understand, their parents weren't the loving and nurturing kind either. Back then, people were just merely struggling and trying to scratch out a living; praying to make it, from one day to the next. Granddaddy and Grandma Arthelle couldn't teach what they didn't know.

LeMarion was a gargantuan, jet-black, tall and burly man. He worked on a crab boat and supervised the boat's crew. That was his legitimate job. His side job, which he liked to call his "hustle," was making, distributing and selling bootleg liquor between Bluffton and Hollywood. Bluffton was Granddaddy's hometown, and it was located about eight miles outside of the millionaires' paradise of Hilton Head. Both occupations earned him a lucrative income, and black and white folks alike referred to him as a "biggity nigga." He also had three families, two in Hollywood and one in Beaufort.

"Dey aine give uh shit 'bout me," Daddy would tell me on those Friday nights. "Mama always love me, but once she staht drinkin', kitty bar da damn dough (door), 'cause after dat first taste hit her stomach, she aine care neitha. Daddy only staht to git uh lil' bit uh feelin' fah me when he fine out I bin (been) smaht (smart). I already bin uh man when I bin uh chile, boy. Den I had tah turn roun' an' raise Fichette an' Joelle. We mighta been livin' in Mama an' Daddy house, but chu bess believe I did da raisin' uh dem two. Dem two was my chern, all da damn way.

"I run moonshine from here tah damn near Hilton Head an' back. Dat was da 'Three-H run.' See, I been da only somebitch out uh us chern had uh license; fifteen years ole an' I haulin' corn liquor cross da damn state. Dem five-gallon jugs now, dem big shits. Daddy had uh goddamn evahgreen '59 Pontiac Catalina, an' we used tah have dat somebitch load down wit' dat fuckin' shit. I use tah have fiah (fire) shootin' out da ass uh dat damn 'Lina. Shit! Dass 'cause da damn chassis been so weighted down, ya see. Dat some-bitch be so load down wit' da fuckin' liquor, the damn chassis used tah be scrapin' da highway. An' boy, when uh damn Pontiac Catalina have sparks shootin' out e (its) ass, dat shit look damn near like uh NASA liftoff. I run from Hollywood tah Hilton Head an' back tah Hollywood. I make all dat money fah Daddy ass. Dat somebitch aine nevah want me. He only wanna tah have somein' tah do wit' me when he fine out I been smaht. I always bin smaht boy. Always."

While Granddaddy (LeMarion) was a good provider and a fiscally responsible man, he was a notorious womanizer. Women flocked to him, and he made no secret of his three families.

I think that in order to cope with Granddaddy's infidelity, Grandma Arthelle drank to excess. That's opaque. My Grandma Arthelle was a fall-ing down drunk. Yet, she was enchanting. She had smooth, chocolate skin, the shape of a Coca-Cola bottle and the softest, silkiest black hair. She would get so drunk that men in Hollywood would load her in a wheel-barrow, roll her around from house to house and have sex with her. It is highly unlikely that she remembered these drunken escapades, but Daddy remembers them. He was teased mercilessly in school because of his moth-er's whoremongering.

"'Ey Herbert, you know yo' mama is a damn sloppy, drunk ass hoe?!" they would taunt him. "Dem fellas had jo' mama in dat wheelbarrow 'gen (again) yestaday!" Subsequently, Daddy learned how to fight early in life.

He knew the taunts were true. He clearly remembers the night a man they called Joota sneaked into his house while Granddaddy was gone and entered Grandma Arthelle and Granddaddy's bedroom. Joota, a peach-colored man with wild eyes and a reputation for being very well endowed, climbed into bed with her and pounded her drunken womanhood again and again. Daddy watched and listened from hiding. He could hear his mama screaming, in pain or ecstasy, or a combination of the two. When Joota finally finished satisfying himself, Daddy said, Joota walked right past him. He didn't even notice the little boy he had just scarred for life, squatting down alone in the dark and hiding behind the big chair in the family room.

As soon as he saw Joota take his final steps out of the side door of Granddaddy's house, he ran directly into Grandma Arthelle's room to see if she was all right. What he saw would be seared into his memory forever. He saw his mama lying in a bloody heap.

He loved Grandma Arthelle until the day she died, but never totally forgave her for that Joota episode. But in that moment, at the time, he did what any dutiful son would have done: he cleaned up his mama and held her in his arms. For the rest of Daddy's life, he secretly wanted to murder Lynton "Joota" Tallum for what Joota had done to his mama. But he also felt a seething hatred for Grandma Arthelle that he never wanted to feel for his mama. He never could reconcile the love and hate he felt for her.

Daddy said Grandma Arthelle allowed herself to be put in that "ole fuck up ass sitcha'ation (situation)."

"Whah normal man you know aine gah fuck if you put him alone in uh room wit' some ole, funky drunk pussy? Shitch'yeah, I blame Mama fah dat shit, but I still wanna buss Joota ass ovah dat shit. Dat was my fuckin' mama he did dat shit to. *My mama!* You hear me, boy?!"

I would always be too stunned to move or speak after Daddy's Friday night confessions. When he would ask me if I heard him, it would bring me back to my good senses. I would be sitting either on the couch or in my rocking chair, utterly shell shocked. These stories blew my mind. I could see Daddy in that La-Z-Boy going back to that night in his mind as he continued to blow smoke through his nose. I could visualize him in that room again with Grandma Arthelle. He was sitting there in the dark holding his mama's head in his nine-year-old arms, stroking her hair that nature softened because of the Edisto Indian blood that coursed through her veins.

It was in those darkened moments, in that bedroom in 1958, that the hardened and cynical man that he would grow to become gathered shape. The self-loathing and contempt for women that he would spend a lifetime cultivating took its form that very night. It was that night that alcohol took over Daddy's very being and consumed him the very same way it had engulfed Grandma Arthelle's soul, although it would be another six years before he took his first drink. That night, he would become who he is today: an alcoholic, philandering and, in some ways, very loyal and vigilant man.

"Dat nigga kill somethin' in me dat night dat I aine nevah been able to revive...dat little fella dat had uh heart fulla love, I aine nevah been able to wake him up afta that night...Lawd knows I tried boy, I tried."

I was so grief stricken that I could have melted into that couch.

"Bad thing is, Arthelle Gadson aine even 'memba da shit the next day Shay, but I got enough memories uh dat shit for the both uh us." He has replayed that event in his mind every day during the fifty years since it happened. I know he has. Herbert Gadson is a tortured and tormented soul. There is no question about that. In order to see exactly how this audacious and immutable tree of hate that is my Daddy took root, you have to first understand that this incident cultivated the fertile soil that took the seeds that Grandma Arthelle and Joota planted that night and created a devastating masterpiece: the boy who would be Mayor.

Daddy has been beating the odds all of his life. He flunked first grade because he would wail and holler like a banshee each morning because he didn't like going to school. As a result, Grandma Kayvass wouldn't make him. She didn't feel like hearing his screams because most of the time she was either hungover from a drinking binge or she was drunk. Despite this, he went on to graduate as the valedictorian of the class of 1967 of Baptist Hill High School. He was discarded like Alabama trash and left to his own devices to raise himself, yet he pulled himself up by the bootstraps and managed to raise a family of his own.

In 1983, he won a seat on the Hollywood Town Council as a write-in candidate. The fact that he could do this as a black Democrat, during the Reagan era, in a small Southern town, and in the staunchly Republican stronghold of South Carolina, boggles the mind even by 21st century standards. However, Daddy with all his achievements and accomplishments, has been struggling all of his adult life with a huge mountain that he just can't seem to get over. The mountain is his general mistrust of white people and his specific hatred of the socioeconomic power and societal bestowing of gravitas given to the notion of "the white man." I'm not sure if those feelings extended to white men individually. However, I do know that the event that molded and shaped his perspective on race relations in America was the Orangeburg Massacre.

The City of Orangeburg, South Carolina, is a six-mile stretch off of Interstate 26. An Indian trader named George Sterling founded it in 1704. Its namesake is the Prince of Orange, the son-in-law of England's King George the Second. Despite its royal ancestry, Orangeburg is a minuscule, rural and working class community. Of the thirteen thousand people who live there, I believe everyone knows everyone else. Orangeburg is just that tightly knit.

Surrounding Orangeburg are dirt roads and farmland with tobacco, radishes, corn and soybeans as far as the eye can see. Many of the people who work the land are fifth- and sixth-generation farmers who can trace their lineage back to either the farms' overseers or the slaves who served them in those very same fields.

Orangeburg, "The Garden City," is also a college town – a black college town. It is home to Claflin University, a small United Methodist college, and South Carolina State University, the largest historically black college or university (HBCU) in the state. The two schools are located next door to one another, separated only by a chainlink fence.

South Carolina State is the mecca of higher education for black people in the state. It is the best funded HBCU in South Carolina. In the 1960s, when

Daddy was a student there, State College, as it is widely called, and Claflin University were sources of underlying tension for a number of white residents in the town. The upwardly mobile black middle class in Orangeburg can be traced directly back to the education they received at State and Claflin, and that served as an unflagging and scintillating memorandum to white Orangeburg residents that black folks could achieve and climb the proverbial socio-economic ladder of success. Further, the fact that "nigger kids" from across the state converged on this town every year to educate themselves was another sore reminder to some white, "less progressive" Orangeburgands that one day their children might have to deal with these black kids on a level playing field – as far-fetched as such a theory might have seemed in the 1960s.

As desegregation of public facilities in the South began to take root, those adumbrations rose to the surface and this town became a powder keg. On February 8, 1968, that keg exploded with such fury that it rocked the state and reverberated throughout the nation. For on that day, South Carolina's state police opened fire on a student protest made up of two-hundred black students who were seeking to desegregate the All Star Bowling Lane, killing three of them and wounding twenty-eight others. Daddy was one of the twenty-eight who were wounded. The incident became known as the Orangeburg Massacre.

"By the national media ignoring what happened that night insomuch as they have failed to lend even a tenth of the historical credence to it (the Orangeburg Massacre) as they did Kent State, it only serves to reinforce the fact that young black lives in this country, especially young black male lives, are just not as important as those of their white counterparts," Daddy told a standing-room-only group of mostly white college students many years later.

Daddy was stone-cold sober that day in 1993. He was eloquent, and he held those College of Charleston ("C of C") students in the palm of his hand as he spoke. Most of the students were South Carolinians, but many came from across the country and had never heard of the Orangeburg Massacre. This Black History Month program was one that they would not soon forget. Daddy can't forget it. He won't forget.

"Not uh day go by that I don't think about dat night." Daddy relayed this message to me, for the first time that I could remember, when I was about nine years old. I'm sure he told me the story dozens of times before then, but on that Friday night he cut a swath of the bloody trousers he was wearing when he got shot, and gave it to me.

Daddy was drinking directly from a bottle of Crown Royal with that omnipresent Salem Regular cigarette dangling from his lips. As he threw the Harlequin green cigarette pack down next to his recliner, he grabbed the long wooden lever on the side of the La-Z-Boy, reared back in it and proceeded to tell me a story that stirred my soul.

"Da gubnah (governor) aine give uh fuck. Jess sen' (sent) in da state police tah kill us like dogs. Dey beat dat girl an' she was pregnant. Made her lose her baby. Dey lie an' say we shoot at dem. Shoot shit! How da fuck we shoot at dem an' aine not uh damn soul had a gun? Tell me dat?"

I was sitting on that couch, transfixed on my father. The pain from that night was still fresh on his face. His expression was a twisted and monstrous mass of disorientation and rage. I could see the dread etched on his face. He took a few drags from his cigarette and I watched the fire and brimstone stream from the dragon's nose and mouth. My father was more ferocious than a dragon. He held that white stick with that thundering inferno on the end of it between his middle and index finger. He continued. I was glad he did. I wanted to hear his story.

"See, dey was gone teach us uh lesson. Yeah, y'all niggas aine gah bowl ya (here). We protest dat damn bowlin' alley fo' (for) shree (three) fuckin' days before February 8. But when we staht dat bonfire on campus, dey know we wasn't takin' no mo' uh dey shit. Son, I sway (swear) on a stack uh King James Bibles, aine nobody had no damn gun dat night. Dey fire on us 'cause somebody threw a piece of uh damn wooden banister at them. Dey was tie'ud uh dealin' wit' us. Damn police fire into uh damn crowd!"

My daddy yanked the chair's lever so hard he almost broke it off. He pitched up in the recliner. I had my elbows on my knees as I sat on the green argyle couch, hands cupping my face. He had my full attention.

"Uh goddamn unarmed crowd, boy! We was jess chern, jess chern! We aine deserve dat shit. Dey kill dat girl baby an' all she was tryna do was help people get to da hospull (hospital)! Dey sprayed some shit in her face an' beat da livin' shit outta her. Damn police beat da fuck outta us. Damn state aine care. Damn media aine care 'cause we wasn't white. All da white media saw was a bunch uh niggas getting mowed down. We was da grass an' da state police was da lawn mower. See, dis shit happen long before dat Kent State shit. Not uh single fuckin' police gone nah jail. Da state police kill shree dat night. Dey shoot twenty-eight an' I bin one um. An' dey sen' Cleveland tah jail 'cause supposedly he bin from up North. Dat was da lie dey put out, ya see. The buzz words they had for Cleveland was he was a 'Northern agitator.' Dat was da horse shit dey put out to justify dey twenty-eight counts of attempted murder an' shree counts uh murder. Cleveland was SNCC- dass why dey blame him. Dey had to have a scape-goat. Man, Cleveland Sellers been right from roun' Orangeburg, boy!"

Now I don't know if before he told me the story I understood the full gravity of the situation, or even knew my daddy got shot that night on the campus of South Carolina State College. I've thought about it often since that day.

"Dey shoot us from behind. We was runnin' away from dey asses an dey fuckin' shot us. Dem somebitch shoot me in my fuckin' ass. I got da fuckin' bullet right cha." Daddy slapped his left hip. Hard.

He stood up, walked the four steps over to the couch and sat next to me. I was crying my eyes out.

"We aine been lookin' fah no trouble, Shay. We wanted to bowl. We din wanna die. Dey kill dem shree boys."

Daddy called their names, partly for effect, mostly in tribute. He held out his left hand and bent his left index, middle and ring finger with his right index finger as he named them: "Henry Smith. Samuel Hammond. Delano Middleton. Dey was the martyrs that night. Man, Shay, me an' Smitty [Henry Smith] used to hang out together sometimes, an' me an' Samuel had ROTC class together. I din know the high school boy Delano Middleton, but when I heard dem fellas was dead, all I could do was cry. I cried a long time that night. Shit, I cried a long time *since* dat night, boy. Delano Middleton was only a boy. He aine been but seventeen. He was only in high school. Dey aine had tah kill dem boys."

Daddy says it was cold that night. Freezing cold. He could smell the blood and he could hear the girls screaming as they were gunned down in a hail of bullets. He could hear the boys moaning in pain on the ground. The acrid smell of their blood in that blustering Siberian air has been trapped in his nostrils for four decades. But he knows he was blessed.

"Boy, Umma (I'm a) lucky somebitch. I know da Lawd was lookin' out for me dat night because dey coulda very easily kill my black ass. Um still here. Nobody had tah call my mama an' tell her some ole cracker redneck ass police done kill me. Samuel, Delano an' Smitty's mamas wasn't so bless an' I think 'bout dem fellas all da time."

His voice trailed off as if he was back on that campus, on that night, on the ground writhing in pain. "All the time."

Then he got up from the couch and walked back to his recliner. He sat down in the chair, wiped tears from his face and took another drink.

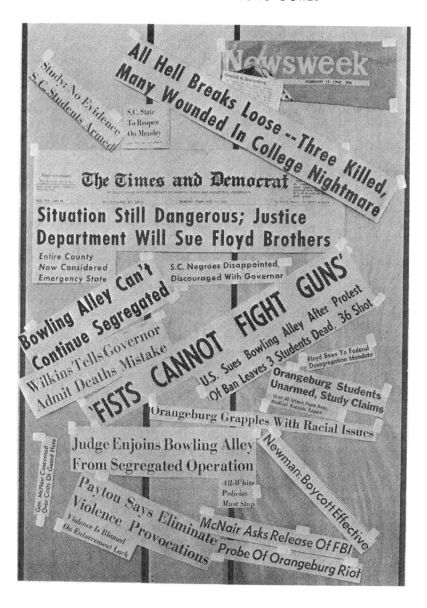

Collage of various newspaper headlines from across the country in the
wake of The Orangeburg Massacre from *The Bulldog*, (Volume XV),
the 1968 edition of the South Carolina State College yearbook.

In Memoriam

DELANO MIDDLETON
Wilkinson High School
Senior

"... verily I say unto you. Inasmuch as ye have done it unto
one of the least of these my brethren, ye have done it unto me."

—St. Matthew 25:40.

SAMUEL HAMMONDS
South Carolina State College
Freshman

HENRY SMITH
South Carolina State College
Sophomore

In 1968, The Bulldog was dedicated to the three young men who were mortally wounded in The Orangeburg Massacre.

lumbering State College freshman, hit the ground near the rear ranks, then got up to run, but dropped again as the shooting continued. Buckshot tore into his left hip as he lay there. Herbert Gadson, 19, a

The Orangeburg Massacre, written by Jack Bass and Jack Nelson, chronicles the events that precipitated The Massacre, the horrific tragedies from the night of February 8, 1968 and its aftermath. This excerpt from page 71 depicts how irrevocably life changed for a nineteen-year-old Herbert Gadson that frost-bound winter night.

CHAPTER 3

Caviar and Crack Smoke

Charleston, South Carolina, is arguably the most historic city in the nation. She played major roles in both the American Revolutionary and Civil wars, and many descendants of both those wars still live in Charleston, mostly south of Broad Street (called SOBs) or slightly north of Broad (SNOBs). It claims an impressive number of firsts, such as first public library, first opera performed, first building constructed solely as a theater, first municipal college and a host of others. She is a tourist mecca, drawing tens of thousands of visitors every year. Downtown focuses on the famous "Four Corners of Law," which got its name because City Hall (municipal law) occupies one corner, the County Building (state law) occupies another, a federal building (federal law) occupies a third and the huge, imposing, historic St. Michael's Episcopal Church (God's law) looms over them all on the fourth corner. It became a famous intersection after "Ripley's Believe It or Not" noticed that at some point every day the church's shadow falls on each of the other three.

Some of the best lawyers in South Carolina, called Broad Street Lawyers, ply their trade nearby. Just feet away from God's oldest house in the city, there are men and women in those old and venerable law firms who can help your cousin beat a murder charge, get your friend acquitted of cocaine distribution, or help you get a quickie divorce.

Hollywood, although just a mere fourteen miles south of Charleston, is a stark contrast. In Charleston, one of the tallest and most imposing landmarks is St. Michael's Church, with a steeple that rises more than one hundred ninety feet above street level. In Hollywood, our Piggly Wiggly grocery store serves as our landmark. It's one of the most visible buildings in town, if not *the* most visible. It is just as important and hallowed a monument to us as St. Michael's is to the lawyers, tourists, beggars and black women who make the striking sweetgrass baskets that are relics of slavery, and works of art, right in front of the chantry. White folks in Charleston may worship at St. Michael's, but we niggas in Hollywood pray at the Pig. Piggly Wiggly in Hollywood is a large brown warehouse-like structure with a faux brick front. Emblazoned on the building's front is a huge face of a bister-complected smiling hog with a butcher's cap perched on top of its head and cocked to its side.

Mr. Jacob Tanner, a deacon in his church whose shoeshine stand sits right under the pig's face, could shine your shoes as you walk out of the store with your groceries. He's the best at plying his trade.

He also could, and would, sell you any assortment of his illegal DVDs, three for fifteen dollars. He hid about a thousand DVDs, everything from *Titanic* to *Foxy Brown*, right behind his stand. He was a runty man with an awful disposition. He was nectarine colored, had huge flaring nostrils and lorded over and protected that stand and the illegal DVDs it contained. Just like the troll that he was, and true to the heritage of his bridge-patrolling brethren, he surveilled that stand with suspicion in his eyes for all who ventured to walk near it.

Deacon Tanner's stand separated Piggly Wiggly from New Dragon. New Dragon is in the storefront right next to Piggly Wiggly and it featured the best Chinese food in Hollywood or Charleston. Now you can't understand a word Diana Chu, the long-legged and fast talking Taiwanese siren, says when she's taking your order, but people in my town have long said New Dragon food was "good enough tah make you slap ya mama weave clean out she head."

Where Charleston is city, Hollywood is pure country. When Daddy became Mayor, he caused a controversy right off by trying to change the start of Town Council meetings from 8 p.m. to 7 p.m. The meetings always started at 8 because at Hollywood's inception many of the town's residents worked plowing fields and tending to crops. They couldn't attend them until the last light of the day disappeared. Daddy reasoned that while the fields are still a very prevalent part of the Hollywood landscape, the economy is no longer predicated on what is grown there. So, the meetings should begin earlier. When the Town Council balked, he took them to the woodshed in a closed door session.

"Man, who da hell gone stay in dese council meetings for two an' shree hours so by da time you look up, iss (it's) already 10:30, 11 at night? Dat was good fah Hollywood when Hollywood worked in da fields, but when I got in office, I told jall I was gone change dat shit. Shit, iss stone dark outside an' we still debatin' land ordinances. Man, shit no! People wanna go home afta uh certain time an' staht an' finish dey dinner an' get ready fah da next day. Da ole time jess aine make no damn sense no mo'! We got tah change da time!" After he spoke, Council voted unanimously, 7 to 0, to amend the time.

The blue bloods of Charleston own the businesses and black folks work in them. That's just Charleston. Charleston is pomp and circumstance, beauty, history and pretense. Charleston is diamond encrusted, radiant and princess cut. Charleston is caviar. Hollywood is country, poor and working poor people, where our character is shaped by our struggle. We are practical and accessible. We are tough and tin armored. We are sardines. The crime rate here is mostly related to the sale and distribution of illegal narcotics – more specifically, crack cocaine. Crack is the scourge of our community; just like every other community in the U.S. that has our demographic composition. Many of our brothers, sisters, cousins, nieces and nephews, to varying degrees, are using or selling crack. This is a culture that my brother is all too familiar with. Much like the Piggly Wiggly and the very dirt fields that no longer get planted or harvested around here, Reggie's soul is embedded into the very fiber of the Hollywood drug culture's being.

Reggie was not planned. When Mama was nineteen years old, unmarried, unsaved and a student at South Carolina State College, she got pregnant. Mama wasn't even close yet to establishing herself as the legend she became. She was just Linda Dingle, a statistic in waiting. Since Daddy didn't want a baby, and Mama was too terrified to tell Doozy, he didn't become unglued when he found out that Mama drank turpentine in a failed attempt to cause an abortion. (For a time, Daddy denied that the baby was his. Reggie in fact was Daddy's because Daddy is the first and last man Mama has ever had sex with. Daddy later admitted paternity.)

But even after Reggie was born, Mama knew she had to finish her education, so she applied for and subsequently won the Eleanor Roosevelt Scholarship. She became one of the first black students ever at the venerable College of Charleston. Baby in tow, and coming from a life of almost unbearable poverty, she eventually finished and became the first African-American woman ever to graduate from the school- beginning her march toward becoming a local icon.

Reggie, on the other hand, became a street nigga. He's a thief and a crack addict. He has been dealing with inadequacy issues all his life. He spit in the lunch tray of a Mexican child's plate when he was in the first grade because the little boy wouldn't give him his orange.

"Lazaro was my friend, but when dat lil' spic ass nigga aine give up that orange, I had to show his ass what time it was." That's how my brother described the incident. He almost lives by the motto, "I had to show his ass what time it was." Once during P.E. class, when he was in the eighth grade, his teacher would not let him use the bathroom. Reggie proceeded to walk up to her desk in the front of the room, pull out his penis and piss in the middle of the floor. The last day of school before Christmas break later that year, he took Daddy's Crown Royal and Smirnoff onto the campus. He found the liquor hidden in our garage behind the freezer. He and three of his friends got drunk for Christmas. They rang in the 1984 New Year on suspension from Skylar Middle School.

My brother has been to prison for everything from the arson of a crack house to grand larceny. He's been stabbed. He's been shot. He's shot at people. One of his two closest friends was Randolph "Outcha" Rivers, a ruggedly handsome man with skin the color of ginger with dark brown smoldering eyes. The girls loved Reggie and Outcha, both of whom were towering, august and lethal. Outcha got his nickname because he would constantly tell the girls, "Y'all gals betta undastan' who I is an' who y'all fuckin' wit' when y'all fuck wit' me 'cause I out cha. I *been* out cha. I out cha hustlin' tah git breaded up. Dass whah I do. *Sell crack. Car jack. Make stacks.* Aine no lil' boy scramblin' out cha. *Dis dat grown-man-real-life-live-dis-aine-Memorex-Hollywood-hustlin' out cha.* Every night I in uh goddamn movie out cha. I got Nino Brown nuts, nigga. Aine no rookies out cha. Susan Chewning [Charleston County Coroner] got all da rookie ass niggas on uh cole ass slab fin nah call dey mama an' tell 'em come identify da body- an' dass real cous' (cousin). Y'all kan' see me! *I da bad guy!* Y'all gals love da bad guy, right? Well, come fuck me an' tuck me in an' say good night tah da bad guy out cha." He said "out cha" so much, the name stuck.

At one point during the 1990s, Reggie and Outcha went on house-breaking spree. They robbed quite a few homes. While Reggie was in county jail one night, Outcha broke into a house alone but he never got out. The owner of the home put three .45-caliber slugs in his back as he was turning to walk out of the side door of the man's double wide trailer. Bill Sharpe said Outcha never heard or saw the man in the dark that fateful night. My brother said that when he saw on the news the blood dripping off of the broken television that Outcha dropped in the man's living room and the ambulance carrying his body out of the house, he cried like a baby.

AREA BRIEFS

Deputies uncover arson-for-hire scheme

Charleston County sheriff's detectives say they have uncovered an arson-for-hire scheme in which the arsonists were paid with cash and drugs.

Reginald Gadson, 24, of 6571 Highway 162, Hollywood is charged with third-degree arson, grand larceny, second-degree burglary and possession of a stolen motor vehicle. Gadson, a son of Hollywood mayor Herbert Gadson, was being held in Charleston County Jail on $130,900 bail set by Magistrate Jack Guedalia. The burglary and arson charges are unrelated.

Someone burned down the Corner Store at Storage and Mizzell roads in Hollywood. The building had been seized by the sheriff's office under drug forfeiture laws and sold at a sheriff's sale April 5. It was destroyed by fire April 22.

The former owner of the Corner Store, Edwin Youngblood, 51, of 2473 Highway 162, Yonge's Island, is accused in arrest warrants with paying two men to set the fire. Youngblood will surrender to authorities today, deputies said.

A third suspect is in a hospital and will not be arrested until he is released, deputies said.

I don't think a week has gone by since that night that Reggie hasn't talked about, or at least mentioned, his fallen comrade. And much like Daddy when he was drunk, when my brother was high, he loved talking about the shooting. He would talk about it incessantly. He talked about Outcha so much when he was high, I felt like I knew him far better than I actually did.

Also much like Daddy when he was blitzed, my brother, when he was high, kept me transfixed on every word he said. He and Daddy both knew that they had a captive audience in me. It was always the same rhetoric. I didn't care. I just liked to listen.

"Outcha was my nigga. I woulda been in dat house wit' him that night if I woulda been on da street. Dass da only house dat nigga evah been up in wit'out me. Uh fuckin' white girl (cocaine) possession charge saved my life. Aine no question I woulda been in dat house wit' my nigga dat night."

Reggie poured his heart out to me one summer night as I was driving him to another man's house so that he could defile his wife. He was smoking "boonk" (a cigarette made of marijuana sprinkled with crushed crack) and he told me that drugs and the life that comes along with them was destined to take him out.

"Shay, I jess dough give uh fuck no mo'. I know that Jesus is the refuge of my life, an' da strength get off dis shit [crack] rests with Him, but what chu 'posed tah do when ya get so weak dat cha kan' even find da strength tah get tah His strength? Huh? I been on da street too long tah stop doin' what Um doin' man. I done sold dope wit' da bess um. I was out cha hustlin' in da '80s back when hustlin' was hustlin'. I hustled wit' Ben Gilliam an' sold dope an' ran guns with Bessy, back when dey was the man. I did all dat wile (wild) shit man. But crack fuck me up, lil' brotha'. I stahted snortin' dat white girl in high school an' I aine nevah look back. But see Shay, I know da Lawd done been good tah me; so when I tell you I don't give uh fuck, I really don't.

"Da Lawd is my shepherd so I know if I got tah shoot uh nigga or uh nigga stab me uh (or) shoot me uh whahevah comin' tah me, I always know whah Mama said 'bout puttin' yo' truss in da Lawd. I know what it is tah smoke crack all night long den fall on yo' knees an' pray an' pray an' ax da Lawd not tah let cha fuckin' heart buss wide open. An' you *know* da lass hit done did you dirty. Da second time I got stabbed, it was two inches from my heart. Dat shit felt better dan when I thought I was 'bout to die 'cause my damn heart was 'bout tah buss ovah some bad shit. Man, I guess God maybe done jess allowed me tah not care no mo'– either God or da crack – man, I aine know."

My brother dropped out of high school three months before he was scheduled to graduate in 1988. He was teetering between the life of a carefree high school boy and full-fledged drug pusher. Reggie no longer had time to trifle himself with attending school every day. The thing that always amazed me about him though, was the fact that because he grew up in the house that he grew up in, with parents who were educated community leaders, the part of him that is scurrilous is often overshadowed by the part of him that is articulate and well rounded. My brother was blessed with many of the physical characteristics and personality traits that are typically inherent in successful people. His pecan-complection mirrors that of Mama's, he has dark brown eyes that sparkle and dance when he speaks, and an irresistible smile to boot. He can talk to anyone on a wide range of subjects and can read women to the point that he can make them feel as if they are the only ones on earth.

My brother loved women. He loved to enlighten me about sex. I learned early on that he was a ladies' man. He told me so and other niggas confirmed it. I learned rather quickly that no matter how far-fetched the story was, if it was concerning him and a woman, it was the gospel truth. Reggie was a liar and a thief, but when it came to women he was straight.

"Shay, one thing I know is women. I done fuck wit' mamas while da daughter I was messin' wit' was in the kitchen cookin' me dinna. I done fuck wit' cousins an' aunties. You know why I can do dat shit? 'Cause I understan' um. Da key tah dealin' wit' any woman is tah allow dem da space, within da true person dey are, tah be who dey are. You kan' change no woman. A woman is gonna adjust who she is fo' yo' sake or she ain't, but she aine gonna change dat person dat she truly is on da inside. See, unlike most niggas, I got sense enough to know dat. So, I govern myself accordingly. You be surprised what uh woman will do fah you when she know dat you comftahble enough wit' her tah not try an' change her."

Reggie started drinking when he was twelve years old. He started smoking marijuana when he was fifteen, and he did his first line of cocaine when he was sixteen. He said he and Daddy loved each other, but from the very start the relationship was strained because Reggie felt that Daddy took Mama away from him.

"Man, lemme tell you somein', God knows I love Daddy, but iss jess somein' 'bout dat nigga dat always made me feel like I wasn't good enough fah him. Maybe because he was da drunk and I was da addict, dat he thought he was betta dan me or somein'. Dass why we fight like animals. Dass why

I done buss dat nigga ass so many times ovah da years, I 'spose. I guess dass why he hate me, huh? I know Daddy love me, but dat nigga hate me an' I know dat shit. We too damn much alike."

Reggie also talked about death a lot.

"I seen da best friend I had in da whole world (Tyrone Cutler) get his head blown off right in front uh me. The coupla days before dat, we was snortin' dat girl like some fuckin' maniacs an' he just kept saying, 'Blue [Blue was Reggie's street name because as a child, Mama dressed him in blue all the time], dey gone rememba me my nigga. When I get off da scene, dey gone rememba who sold the most dope out dis bitch, who fucked the most hoes an' who got da most niggas hooked on dat hard white shit [crack]. You feel me, Blue? Dey gone rememba Tyrone Cutler in Hollywood fo'evah."

Reggie said that after he saw Tyrone's brains in his lap, he did more cocaine just to get that picture out of his mind.

"Dat nigga still got me shook 'cause dat was my nigga. We sold dope together. We snorted coke together. We fucked hoes together. We even did our first bid together; Tyrone an' Blue. After dat nigga got took off da shelf, dass when I got into da crack real heavy. I aine been da same since. Dat was uh fucked up year fah me. Tyrone an' Outcha man; both uh my niggas gone in '92. Shit, all I had left den was da crack."

If cocaine turned Reggie into an animal, crack made him a Leviathan on land. He has slept in horse stables, slept outside on the ground, robbed people and beaten people unmercifully. He philosophized about the fact that crack runs America's prisons, people no longer do.

"Jess 'bout every nigga lock up is in dat bitch in some way, shape uh form 'cause uh crack. You know dat, enny (isn't that right)?"

Like a docile child, I just nodded my head. He looked over at me and smiled that smile that had rendered a multitude of women helpless. Then he continued.

"Dat shit takin' niggas out an' it done took me out, but fah some reason, Um still here survivin' an' whether I get off uh (or) dough get off dis shit before I die, I still know my life meant somethin'. Crack aine touch my soul. My soul belong tah God. I dough even worry 'bout death 'cause I done seen it. When it come fah me, dat jess mean God ready tah make me uh street angel. Dass all.

"Umma be dat angel, Shay! But 'til den, I aine gah be worried 'bout shit. God'll make me concerned again, one day, I guess. He gone make me care again."

Then my brother just looked out in the distance as I drove my silver Isuzu Rodeo down Hwy 162 in Hollywood, on the way to this woman's house. It never occurred to me that I was being an accessory to adultery before the fact. He lowered the passenger side window matter of factly and blew the boonk smoke out. Everything on the highway that June night in the early 2000s slowed down for me as I realized I was getting a contact high.

"You think you'll ever get off dat shit, Reg?" The words escaped my mouth before I had a chance to think about what I was asking this addict, whom I loved so dearly, that was now getting me high as he drifted further away into the cosmos. Still looking out of the window, he responded:

"Lease Um still here; all dem niggas I ran wit' dead. Hollywood street legends. Last uh da real niggas. Hollywood Mohicans, my nigga. Bessy, Tyrone, Rodney an' all dem niggas dead an' dey kan' tell dey story. I kin tell my own story, dough (though). Thank God fah Jesus, 'cause Um still breathin'; might be exhalin' uh lil' crack smoke, but Um still breathin'."

Then he laughed and stared out of the window, riding on a cloud.

CHAPTER 4

Attempted Murder

The gun was a Remington Model 870. It weighed eight pounds and it had a twenty-one inch barrel. It was a 20 gauge and it was black and shiny. It could blow a tennis ball size hole into a deer- or a man. Reggie was always captivated by it. It belonged to Daddy, but Reggie knew its exact location. It was in Mama's and Daddy's closet, on the third shelf, on Daddy's side. It was right underneath the big husband pillow that had turned from Mikado yellow to jasmine from age and overuse. Daddy loved the gun and the pillow. Reggie loved the gun. Now, I wasn't there when it happened, but Reggie later told me he pulled that gun on Daddy with the express intention of "blowin' his fuckin' head off." He then followed up, "Daddy almost shit on hisself."

"Shay, when I saw dat nigga look at me wit' uh look I aine nevah seen before, and then at dat big ass gun, I knew he wasn't gone fuck wit' me no mo'." At least that's how Reggie ran it down to me. My brother said, "Daddy's dick an' his disrespect fah Mama house" almost got him killed. The only reason that he pulled that gun on Daddy, he said, was because Daddy was talking to "that woman" in Mama's house.

In Reggie's mind, it was quite reasonable, and warranted, for him to pull a gun on Daddy. In 1986, when this rifle incident happened, Daddy was a member of the Hollywood Town Council, and Reggie says Daddy didn't raise him to be "no damn punk, no matter who da nigga is starin' you in da face." Town councilmen weren't exempt from Daddy's decree, I guess.

And he was right. Reggie was going to protect Mama's honor if it was the last thing he did. As it would turn out, in Reggie's safeguarding Mama from adultery, Daddy's talking to "that woman" on the phone almost became the last thing Daddy did. And, as is the case with most wars, it was something almost incidental and seemingly insignificant that would prove to be the catalyst.

Reggie is deathly allergic to bee stings. When stung, he swells up like a balloon. A bee sting reduces my larger-than-life, bad-ass, crack-pushing, crack-addicted, kleptomaniacal and all-around nefarious hoodlum of a brother to tears. So on that June Thursday afternoon, when he called Mama from his job as fry cook on Kiawah Island and said that he had been stung, she rushed to pick him up. She took him to St. Francis Hospital's emergency room. Once there, a doctor said all Reggie needed was some Benadryl for the swelling. So, Mama brought Reggie home before she headed for the Piggly Wiggly to get his medicine.

When Reggie went inside our house, he told me later, "Dass when da bowshit (bullshit) started."

When he walked into the house, Daddy was drunk and sitting on the toilet with the door wide open. As Reggie promenaded through the kitchen and the den, then swung a hard right toward the bathroom, he walked past Daddy. Reggie's father's head was slumped and his arms were crossed as he clutched his stomach. He looked almost as sick as his son felt.

"'Ey Daddy, I git sting by uh bee at da job but da docdah say I gah be aw'right," Reggie said.

Daddy didn't respond, so Reggie just kept walking toward his room. Fifteen minutes later, the telephone rang. Reggie didn't make a move to pick it up. Daddy screamed at the top of his drunken lungs, "'Ey nigga, git da fuckin' phone!" You aine sick, aine uh goddamn thing wrong wit' cho ass! Pick up da damn phone! Bees sting people every day an' you ackin' like you damn near dead! Git cho ass up an' ansa da fuckin' phone!"

But as Daddy's misfortune would have it, Reggie got up at that precise moment to answer it because he wanted to shut Daddy's mouth. He wanted to show him that he wasn't the no-good scoundrel that both he and Daddy knew that the drugs had turned him into.

Daddy wasn't so intoxicated though, that he couldn't manage to drag himself off of the throne to run and get the phone. He was expecting an important call, and in that quick moment he'd totally forgotten that he'd just commanded Reggie to pick it up – which Reggie did, just in time to hear his father talking to a woman on the other end of the phone.

"You know I want chu to suck dis dick, right?" Daddy was saying.

Reggie didn't hear much after that. Fury took over. He said that it was one of those moments in life when time stands still and everything comes clearly in focus. In that moment he had an epiphany. He was going to kill Daddy.

Reggie took Daddy's gun out of the closet and sneaked it past him. He was lying across the bed he and Mama shared as he talked on her phone to some strange woman about some fellatio that was supposed to take place some-time in the very near future. Daddy didn't notice as his firstborn son walked down the hallway with a very large rifle hoisted over his right shoulder. Reggie marched outside as if he was on the warpath – which, in fact, he was.

Reggie deliberately locked himself out of the house and rang the door-bell. When Daddy stumbled to the door and opened it, Reggie cocked the rifle, aimed it at his father's head and pulled the trigger.

But instead of Daddy's head exploding like a dropped watermelon on concrete, the gun jammed. It only clicked. Reggie pulled the trigger again two more times before Daddy recovered from his stunned state of shock enough to slam the door in his face, lock it and run to his bedroom and lock that door too.

"I ran into dat house like dat crazy ass boy was da devil hisself standin' at my front door comin' tah take me tah hell wit' um", Daddy told me years later.

Reggie would say later that he was so high on cocaine that he didn't realize quite what he had done until he saw Daddy's "asshole an' elbows runnin' like a scared deer" back in the house toward his bedroom. Out of pure frustration because he had not gotten his man, he aimed the rifle skyward and pulled the trigger again. This time it fired.

He marched around the house, headed toward Daddy's bedroom window to finish what he had started. If necessary, he would climb into the house through that window and shoot Daddy dead.

As luck would have it, one of our cousins was passing by our house and noticed my brother was parading around our yard with a rifle. He pulled into our driveway, jumped out of his car and started questioning my brother about what he was doing. The intrusion caused enough of a delay to give Daddy the necessary time to call 9-1-1 and report he was being held hostage by his drug-addicted son. By the time Reggie could break away from our cousin and resume his attack, the police had Councilman Herbert Gadson's house surrounded and traffic on the highway in front of our house had come to a standstill.

Mama was in that traffic jam, and when she saw that the blue lights and the disturbance were in her yard, she started frantically blowing her horn. She let down all of the windows in her car and started screaming at the other drivers, "Dass my house! Lemme on pass! Dass my house! Whah all dem police doin' at my house! Lemme on pass!" The traffic on both sides of that two-lane highway pulled to the side of the road. The cars parted 162 like the waters of the Red Sea. And just like that, Moses had a clear drive home.

"Herbert, what in the world is goin' on?" By the time Mama pulled into our gap, it seemed to her that every citizen in Hollywood who was not stuck in traffic outside of our house was in our football field-sized yard. Upon investigation, what she found was a drunken husband, a son who was high as a kite, both of them in handcuffs and the police holding what looked to be Daddy's rifle.

The police department, along with Charleston County Fire and Rescue's two buses, had descended on our yard as well. Mama said it looked like the bowels of hell had opened up on her property.

"Ma'am, is this your home?" a portly, brunette police sergeant asked. Mama said that she didn't answer right away because at that point she wasn't sure if it was in fact her home or some horror movie set.

"Ahh, yes. My name is Linda Gadson. This is my home."

Then, before he could ask Mama another question, she lit into Daddy. He and Reggie were handcuffed and sitting side by side on the concrete at the end of the driveway in front of our garage.

"Herbert, what the hell happened?"

"Mama, I catch Daddy on da phone talkin' tah some lady asking her tah suck his dick. Um sorry Mama, but I wasn't gonna let him get away wit' dat."

"Fuck you, Reggie!" Daddy shouted. Then he turned to his wife.

"Linda, I wasn't talkin' tah no woman. Dis somebitch pull uh gun on me fo' no reason. I want his ass out my damn house! An' I want da mothafucka out da'night!"

Mama summarily took the jug by the handles. "Officer, my son is a drug addict and my husband is an alcoholic. I would like to deal with this matter as a family, but of course I understand that a gun was involved."

"Mrs. Gadson, you are exactly right. The gun takes this to an entirely different level."

"Man fuck you an' fuck uh level!" Daddy interjected. "Dis nigga try to kill me wit' my own fuckin' gun an' you talkin' 'bout uh level! I hate da fuckin' police! Kan' stan' y'all asses!"

"Herbert please!" Mama said. "Stop before you make things worse! Officer, my youngest son is at a Boy Scout meeting and I have to go and pick him up. Is there any possible way that nine-year-old does not have to see this?"

Now this entire time, Reggie and Daddy were sitting Indian-style on the ground, about a foot a part, and still handcuffed. They refused to look at each other. Daddy's navy blue housecoat was clinging for dear life to his listless body. Reggie was still dressed in his uniform – a charcoal pair of Dickies, a Splashed white oxford shirt and a Mountbatten pink apron. Because Kiawah was a world-renowned beach and resort, even the cooks were immaculately bedecked. Reggie would have made his bosses proud sitting there on the concrete, except for the fact that he'd just tried to murder his father.

"Mrs. Gadson," the sergeant said, "I'll tell you what. If you can assure us that you can calm these two down, we will clear these folks off of the premises and call this a wash."

"Officer, thank you. Thank you. God bless you. I will most assuredly handle it from here. God bless you officer. Hallelujah! Praise the Lord!"

"All right boys, let's move 'em out."

Just like that, the police dispersed the crowd from our yard. They took the manacles off of Reggie and Daddy and left Mama in charge of them. She then forced them to get into her car, a 1984 pewter Pontiac Bonneville. The shock and awe of the night's events rendered the three nearly oblivious to what was going on around them. As they drove through the horde of citizens in our yard and crept off into the night, they could hardly hear all the people, squad cars, fire trucks and police sirens as they followed my family off the premises. Such a surreal moment rendered the inside of the Bonneville as quiet as a church. The silence was so blaring they were deafened to the processional going on outside of their rolling tabernacle.

They picked me up from my Boy Scout meeting and the ten-minute ride back home was uneventful. In ten minutes, ten short minutes, by the time we got home, the police, the crowd and the fire engines were gone and both Reggie and Daddy were asleep. Herbert Gadson, two-term councilman, lay on the passenger seat, sleeping blissfully. They were both snoring loudly. Nobody breathed a word to me about what had happened.

CHAPTER 5

Hollywood Hog Nuts

We made history in Hollywood on June 6, 1989. We made Herbert Gadson, a thirty-nine-year-old town councilman, the first African-American ever to be elected our mayor. We dreamed the impossible dream, made him a write-in candidate, he won and the black people of Hollywood were jubilant.

This was *big*. Hollywood is in Charleston County, and in 1989 Charleston County, white people ran things. And this unamiable fact is no different than anywhere else in the good old U.S. of A. But because Charleston is stuck in an Antebellum time warp where, in Brittlebank Park, Civil War reenactors seemingly *only* fought the battles that the South *won*, (and that was completely indicative of the prevailing mindset of the city), black folks not only got the feeling that we were *behind* the eight ball, we knew that we were already *sunk* in the corner pocket. What we did that day defied conventional wisdom and thinking. In our own little corner of the county where the War Between the States commenced over slavery, the great-grandsons and daughters of those slaves elected one of their own to lead them. This kind of thing was not supposed to happen here. The black people in Hollywood had become empowered. The white people were mortified. This dynamic alone made council meetings events not to be missed.

A Hollywood Town Council meeting was something akin to a knock-down, drag-out heavyweight boxing brawl. When Daddy was in office, this was a sporting event, not a meeting. This was not the United States Senate to be sure. It was a World Cup Soccer Match between England and Scotland, only more combative. It was British Parliament, but our officials didn't represent lovely cities and hamlets like Stratford-upon-Avon and Maidstone. They screamed and yelled for hardscrabble and poverty-stricken areas like Church Hill and Peter's Field. The people on Church Hill didn't know who Churchill was. They'd never heard of him. We didn't have a House of Lords. We only had a House of Commons. This was Hollywood. We were all common.

This was small town American governance at its best. But moreover, what it was was a chance to vent. If my father was ever embroiled in a scandal, or if he proposed some controversial legislation, the members of this "direct democracy" would always let him know exactly how they felt. For as many detractors as Daddy had, council meetings were always a time for his supporters to have their say as well. And both sides said quite a bit.

First of all, our town hall wasn't your average government building. Hollywood Town Hall used to be the town bank. As soon as you pushed the rickety wooden doors open, the bent and disheveled venetian blinds that were once ivory, but had turned beige because of overuse and neglect, scratched and bled together. The invisible tellers, who had long since been deceased, stood next to the great oak council table that had replaced their teller stations. Instead of counting and watching money, these ghosts now stood by, every fourth Monday night of each month, and witnessed ordinary men tell extraordinary lies about my father. Daddy defended himself against them with half-truths and misrepresentations of his own.

Town Hall had Hooker's green tile floors with drab tapioca walls. Council meetings were held in a space that was the size of a small bank lobby, which is what it originally was. Its ambiance bored you to death because its intellectually gifted architects understood that too much excitement or too much hyperactivity in a banking institution is never good.

You always kind of got the feeling that you were, at any moment, going to be told to get on the floor and empty your pockets. Two steps into the bank and immediately to your left was the vault. When Town Hall was full of people, it always managed to give me the creeps because I could almost visualize a robbery. I guess that's why people felt so free to voice their opinions; if we were all going to die in a hold-up, we might as well get our two cents in before we got shot.

Daddy, because he had become as infamous as he was famous, had people who really loved him, and those who passionately hated him. He said that being Mayor wasn't necessarily about the letter of the law, but about the heart of the people.

"Man, shit, po' black people kan' always afford 'legal' because 'legal'costs too damn much," he would say. "My job is tah help people who kan' afford to live better dan what dey livin'. My job is to give dem da opportunity to at least try to pay somethin' every month on uh betta life."

Daddy helped people obtain mobile homes so they could escape living in housing that often was very similar to dwellings you see in Bangladesh. He brought water and sewer services to a town whose poorest people couldn't even afford wells. Some people were still hand-pumping water well into the 1980s. As much as my father was reviled in Hollywood, he was even more revered. So what if he made his share of enemies?

Effective people usually do.

One of Daddy's most strident opponents was Fritz Harvey, a white pig farmer and butcher in Hollywood.

Harvey remembered with fondness a time when black people had to run through town for fear of being lynched. Harvey was a short man. He was loud, angry, beer-bellied and uncouth, but extremely intelligent. He'd graduated from Texas A&M and he was, in Daddy's words, "da smahtest fuckin' redneck you evah wanna come across. Da somebitch smaht aw'right, but he aine smahta dan me." Harvey had dark hair and had red craters in his face, vestiges from an acne-ravaged youth.

Now Harvey was the kind of Southern gentleman who was flexible enough to understand that because times had changed, and because he was a business owner, he had to be cordial to black people if he wanted to survive. Oh sure, Harvey would call your old gray-headed grandmother "Miss" and "Ma'am". But, he would look at her black sons or grandsons with disdain and loathing. If you saw Harvey in Piggly Wiggly or in that frigid meat locker he called a butcher shop, he'd speak to the male African-American. He may have even smiled. But if you were black, especially a black man, you knew that Harvey, in his heart of hearts, wanted to completely objurgate you. The hate was so thick that when he looked into your eyes, it was as if he were trying pierce your soul and manhood.

Harvey was in the pork trade, a business that is predicated on the support of black people who have been loyal to the pig since our globe trot from Africa's west coast, which landed us on the beautiful shores of Charleston, and everywhere else for that matter. Harvey knew that he at least had to feign toleration of black people.

And, to our credit, we feigned toleration of Harvey because the man worked a pig like Picasso worked a canvas. The man was an artist. He was a virtuoso in the dismantling and reinvention of the sow from banal beast to sapid delicacy. If you've never eaten bacon, rice pudding, fried pork skins, hog's head cheese or souse meat from Fritz Harvey, I don't think you can fully appreciate pork. Pork chops, pig's feet and ribs were his specialty. So we, the righteous African-American residents of Hollywood, put up with Harvey because the man was a genius at making a pig serenade your taste buds.

But deep down, we knew Fritz Harvey's stomach turned at the sight of us black people. He especially hated Daddy. He execrated and reviled The Mayor of Hollywood all during the 1990s and he did so with an almost religious zeal. Harvey's fanaticism hadn't been seen since the Crusades. He chose Town Council meetings to do battle.

One night, just after Daddy called Council meeting to order, but before he could call for old business, Harvey fired off an especially strong verbal onslaught aimed at the Mayor.

4-B Sunday The News and Courier/The Evening Post, Charleston, S.C., July 2, 1989

Gadson takes office; missing records found

By JOHN HASSELL
Post-Courier Reporter

Hollywood's new mayor, Herbert Gadson, called the Post-Courier Saturday to report that important financial records were missing from Town Hall, but the records turned up shortly afterward.

Gadson took the oath of office as mayor Saturday morning. He said he then went to Town Hall to check over financial ledgers for the past year, but the books were nowhere to be found.

At 4:30 p.m., the records were returned to Town hall by the daughter of Peggy Dukes, the town's ex-clerk. Mrs. Dukes's resignation as clerk became effective at the end of the working day on Friday, but she said she took the records home with her to complete a year-end report for the town auditor. The new fiscal year began Saturday, and the report was a routine procedure.

"I brought home the books to finish up an end-of-the-year report that could not have been done before yesterday ... I think I did the right thing," Mrs. Dukes said.

Because the auditor's office does not open until Monday morning, she said it was perfectly reasonable to keep the records over the weekend. She could not return them to Town

Hall, she said, because she had already turned in her key.

But Gadson said "the records shouldn't have been taken out of there in the first place. If she had resigned, then what is she doing with the records?"

The records "should have gone to the auditor as of yesterday," he said.

At the swearing-in ceremony earlier, Gadson announced that he would create, with the blessing of the town council, a committee to put together a five- to 10-year master

plan for the town.

The group, to be called the Town Improvement Program, will represent "a cross-section of community members," and will "bring relevant concerns to council," he said. The body will have no policy-making or administrative power, but will serve in an advisory capacity.

"We hope that this group will take a close look at where we are now and make suggestions based on that as to where we should go in the next five to 10 to 15 years," Gadson said.

One of the major concerns that council and TIP will have to deal with is the drug problem, Gadson said. "We are putting the dope dealers on alert. We are not going to tolerate it any longer ... We're going to be hard-nosed about the drug thing, that's for sure."

Gadson also said he would continue a project started by former Mayor Leli Dickerson to bring sewer lines to densely populated parts of the town and the outlying rural areas.

Swearing in

George Tumbleston (left), chief magistrate of Charleston County, swears in Herbert Gadson as mayor of Holly-

wood while his wife, Linda, holds the Bible for him. Please see story, Page 4-B.

Staff Photo by Terrence Hardy

"You think Umma let chu git away wit' widening 162 an' takin' piece uh my land away tah do it? I dough care if you call um eminent domain uh whahevah, you aine gah do it. E too many people livin' out cha now anyways. If dey widen da road, Hollywood gah turn inta (into) Chowston (Charleston). Dass his goal: turn we inta Chowston. No Herbit; e aine goin' down like dat. No suh!"

Harvey, who spoke Gullah as naturally as any black person in Hollywood, would vociferate in Council meetings. He would go off the deep end. He loved an audience and on this particular Monday evening, there was an overflow crowd. People were even seated in folding chairs in the vault. Black people sat on one side of the bank and white people sat on the other;

Council meetings were always segregation's finest hour. We would have made Governor George Wallace whistle Dixie and dance a jig.

Harvey planned to put on a show that night and we all knew it. He was adorned in full hog slaughtering regalia: a butcher's cap, bloody snow white apron and latex gloves. He looked the part of the angry white butcher. And he was. But he wasn't so enraged that he didn't bring Daddy a gift. We all wondered, some of us clamorously, what the contents of the bloody Ziploc Freezer Bag were that he clutched tightly in his hands. It was plain to all that Harvey could hardly wait to end our suspense.

Almost as if Daddy expected the verbal barrage coming from the rickety wooden entrance of Town Hall, he looked over at Harvey, who was standing with his back pressed against the blinds, and smiled. We were all shocked. We all knew that the Mayor, who was always dressed to kill in Council meetings, perpetually came prepared to dual Harvey, in a fist fight if need be. Daddy had on a navy blue blazer with a powder blue sweater vest on underneath. He had on a crisp white oxford shirt with a perfectly matched navy blue necktie with powder blue polka dots. The crease in his cream-colored seersucker chinos was so sharp it appeared that you could cut your finger on it. We could almost see our reflections in his black wingtips as they patted pensively under the huge conference table.

As soon as Harvey stopped long enough to catch his breath, as every drop of blood in his body had rushed to his face he was so chafed, the Mayor saw his opening.

"Mr. Harvey, you sir are out of order. If you do not refrain from the outbursts, I'm going to be compelled to ask you to remove yourself from these proceedings. And if you don't leave willingly, one of these sheriff's deputies will be more than happy to help you discover how the other end of that door looks – you know, since you're already leaning on it and all. Highway 162 is going to be widened, whether you like it or not. Your land abuts the stretch of road that's needed to execute this. So you do the math, Mr. Harvey. Sir."

But before Harvey could respond, Ernest Mott, a longtime black resident of Hollywood, stood up and said, "Now Harvey, you know fah yo'self dis ya aine right. You might not 'gree wit' Herbit, but you dough have da right tah stand up in ya an' jess shout an' say what chu wanna say. Harvey, I bin knowin' you uh long time."

"Yeah, Erniss, but I…"

"No Harvey, you done had jo' turn tah speak. Now Umma say whah I gotta say. Harvey, I remheba I use tah have tah run fass as I could thu' Hollywood 'cause wasn't no tellin' what woulda happen to me if I didn't. I remheba when Hollywood aine been nuttin' but uh dirt road. Now look at us. We done come uh long way. We got paved roads, uh Piggly Wiggly, two convenience stores – yes, Lawd, we done come a long ways. But I see here da'night so clear dat some things dough nevah change. In (Isn't) dat right, Harvey?"

"What chu talkin' bout, Erniss?"

"You know 'xactly whah Um talkin' 'bout, Harvey."

Everyone in that bank lobby knew what Mr. Ernest was talking about. I was only sixteen years old, and even I knew. Harvey was in his late 50s, he was white and he longed to get that old Hollywood back that Mr. Ernest used to have to run through for fear of being lynched. Harvey yearned for the Hollywood of his youth where a black man was prohibited from ordering vanilla ice cream at Miss Fay Lynn's Creamery.

Fay Lynn Harkin was a blue-haired and leather-skinned white woman who owned an ice cream shop in Hollywood – if you could call it an ice cream shop. During the summers of Harvey's youth, she served chocolate, vanilla and strawberry ice cream that came from gallon containers she kept in a chest freezer on her porch. He remembered how as a boy he and his friends would play cops and robbers, shoot jacks and wrestle each other. When they got tired and needed refreshment, they would ride their bicycles down that long stretch of a dirt road that was Hollywood and Miss Fay Lynn would sell them an ice cream cone. It was two scoops for ten cents, any flavor they wanted.

Mr. Ernest also had lucid recollections of Miss Faye Lynn's ice cream. He recollected how, when he was in his twenties, he labored and toiled digging trenches for septic tanks during that same time. Each day, he and other black men would ride into town on the bed of the truck of the white man they worked for. Most days, that white man would stop at Miss Fay Lynn's for some vanilla ice cream. Mr. Ernest made the mistake one day of jumping off the bed of that sky-blue and white Ford truck and asking her for a scoop of vanilla. Hollywood summers routinely get well into the high 90s, and Mr. Ernest wanted some of that white ice cream that looked so good dripping off of his white boss's cone.

"How much fah some uh dat vanilla, Miss Fay Lynn?" Mr. Ernest shouted as he was dismounting the truck, and was about to walk onto her porch.

"Fah you nigger, e aine no price! I dough sell vanilla tah niggers! You hear me, boy? Fah vanilla from me, you got tah be white, boy! From da looks uh it, white missed you when you was in ya mammy's black belly. You welcome to da chocolate, but no vanilla fah you, boy! Not now, an' not nevah!"

Mr. Ernest's white boss interjected from the driver's seat of his truck: "You got uh nerve, Erniss, askin' white women fah vanilla ice cream. I thought you knew betta! Um vurry sahprised at chu, Erniss; vurry sahprised!"

Mr. Ernest was a shade over six feet tall. He was the color of vanilla bean, and he was a frame of bulging muscles. His jawline looked as if it were chiseled from granite and he had it clinched so tightly the muscles in his temples pulsated with unbridled fury. He wanted to rip his boss's head off for talking to him in such a way. He wanted to curse Miss Fay Lynn out. He wanted to tell her that he was a man, not a boy. He wanted to tell her *exactly* what she could do with her vanilla ice cream.

He thought better of it. It was 1956 in Hollywood. In Charleston County. If he had done any of those things, bloodhounds would have been on him by nightfall. Deranged and chemically impaired white men with shotguns, shells and Jack Daniels liter bottles would have wanted to know his whereabouts. Mr. Ernest contemplated all of this and he said, "Um sorry Miss Fay Lynn, my mistake ma'am."

"See, tah it dat it dough happen again," his boss retorted.

"Yes, suh," Mr. Ernest said.

He held his head high as he mounted the back of the truck and got into its bed. As that old Ford raced down the road, he hoped the other black men sitting in the bed with him would think that the water coming from his eyes was because of the wind hitting him in the face, but he knew better.

Oh yes, Mr. Ernest knew better than anyone else in that Council meeting room exactly what Harvey was talking about. He lived it in Hollywood all of his youth, and he was determined he wasn't going to relive it in his golden years. Harvey was younger than Mr. Ernest by about fifteen years, but there was no doubt that Mr. Ernest could have taken out the younger man in a fistfight. Harvey came to Council meetings to debate my father, but he had entered into a street fight with Daddy's staunchest supporter, Ernest Mott.

Daddy broke up what was starting to become a heated debate between Mr. Ernest and Harvey by banging his gavel and said, "Order! Order! I'll have order in this meeting!"

At this point Harvey and Mr. Ernest, who was a member of Wesley United Methodist Chuch and a leader in good standing in my church, were speaking very loudly at one another and would not stop.

"Harvey ev'rybaudy know dat dis issue 'bout widening 162 aine da real reason you got uh problem wit' Herbit. All uh us in here know, dough matta if we wanna admit it uh not, dat e too many people an' businesses movin' out cha fah dat road not tah widen. An' all uh us in ya know dat yo' land run dead center in da middle uh da prahjected (projected) path uh da widening. We all know dat. Harvey, YOU know dat. You need tah stop wastin' da people in dis town time in dese meetins' wit' cho foolishness. Why dough you jess come out an' say whah yo' problem wit' Herbit is?"

"Oh yeah, Erniss, whah my problem is?"

"Well Harvey, da way I see it, you done got so bitter an' set in yo' ways dat when you see a man like Herbit, a man dat you done seen grow up 'roun ya from a lil' boy, a lil' black boy, an' now he da Mayor – you got uh problem wit' dat. Well, Harvey lemme tell you: things aine gah be da same in Hollywood no mo'. We aine goin' back tah how Hollywood use tah be. I mighta had tah run thu' Hollywood, but I'll be doggone if my grandchern gah run thu' Hollywood! I'll walk slow as molasses thu' hell wit' gasoline draws (underwear) on fo' my grandbabies have tah run thu' Hollywood. Now you smoke on dat uh while, Harvey!"

Miss Peach Taylor got up and said, "Dass right Ernest, you tell um boy, Harvey need tah hear dat."

After the black folks in the crowd erupted with applause, Harvey started to respond to Mr. Ernest.

"Da only problem I got with dat fella dere sittin' at dat table like he God Almighty hisself is dat he is uh arrogant somebody. You might bully dem Council people sittin' up dere wit' chu, an' make um do whah you want dem tah do, but you aine gah bully me Herbit. No way!"

Jack Seaton, a licorice-skinned councilman sitting next to Daddy, was furious. He was a logger by trade, and he was a brawny, jheri-curled man. He stood a hair shorter than Daddy, but he stood much taller in the Mayor's eyes because he only spoke the truth. Jack Seaton played no games. What you saw with him is what you got, and he did not know the meaning of political posturing. Jack was fuming. As he sat to the left of my father at the big Council table, I could see the veins in his neck and forehead pulsating and throbbing in concert. Jack couldn't stand Harvey before tonight, and now he had reached his boiling point with the man. Jack was Daddy's enforcer. He took it as a personal affront to his manhood for anyone to even insinuate that my father's handling of the town or his decision making was less than competent. He was now seething at the notion that Harvey had any excogitation that he could get away with calling him a puppet. Jack's barrel chest was heaving through his burgundy Nautica collared shirt. Jack was impeccably dressed that night in a pair of Stil de grain yellow Polo knit slacks and a solid mauve bowtie. His burgundy penny loafers were buffed to a high gloss. Jack regularly gave Daddy a run for his money when it came to fashion and Council meeting chic. He wanted to show his mentor that along with the political lessons he'd learned from him, his fashion I.Q. had also increased exponentially by watching how the Mayor dressed.

When Daddy saw that Jack was about to explode all over the pig farmer, he gently placed his hand on his shoulder. I read Daddy's lips as he whispered, "Not chet (yet) Jack, not chet. Less see him step uh lil' deepa in da pile uh shit he makin' comin' from his mout'."

"Let me get um, Mayor," Jack responded. In the split second it took Jack to yell, "Timbeeer!", he'd jumped up out of his seat to confront Harvey.

"Who in da werl you think you are, Harvey? You think Um gone let you talk to da Mayor like dis?! Huh?! You betta be glad you standin' by dat dough (door), an' Um sittin' at dis table, dass whah you betta be glad uh! I aine nobody puppet an' da Mayor dough bully nobody up here! You jess mad 'cause you kan' outmaneuver da man. You in way ovah yo' head da'night, Harvey! Way ovah, bubba!"

Daddy was grinning from ear to ear during this entire exchange between Mr. Ernest and Harvey, and then Jack and Harvey, but he gently grabbed Jack by the right wrist and motioned for him to sit down, which Jack did. By this time, the room was buzzing. As I sat in the bank's vault I listened to the comments around me:

"Harvey gah mess right roun' an' git he ass cut da'night."

"He aine gah stop til' somebody git up an' knock da shit outta him."

"Whah Herbit need tah do is cut Jack loose an' let um buss Harvey ass."

"Harvey talkin' aw'right tah me. Da Mayor need tah at least let da man talk an' say whah e gotta say. Dis uh free country. Harvey 'titled tah his opinion."

"I know I aine no racist, but da Mayor need tah let da man talk."

The black people were bloviating in Daddy's defense. The white side of the room was speaking in muted tones, a little less audible, but audible nonetheless. Hollywood was sixty-five percent black and those black people were one hundred percent empowered because of Daddy. The white folks knew they were outnumbered in that room two to one by black people who were not afraid of going to jail for the simple assault of a white man.

The white people did not want to appear racist but each of them, almost to a man, wanted Harvey to continue to speak. They were not the Ku Klux Klan sheet-wearing, cross burning, arms-bearing crowd of a bygone era. These people were progressive. They were objective. But they wanted Harvey to continue to give this black Mayor hell – which he did.

"Jack, you an' Erniss kin insowt (insult) me all you wanna. I aine goin' nowhays an' I gah speak my piece. Umma man jess like he uh man." Then Harvey directed his angst against his original intended target.

"People dough have to take nuttin' off you. You da Mayor, you aine God!"

Then Mr. Ernest said what he had been implying since he started his stump against Fritz Harvey. He said what everyone else in that packed bank, both black and white, had known for years.

"No Harvey, da only problem you got wit' Herbit is dat he uh black man in charge uh dis town. But guess whah Harvey, dass da way e is! We aine goin' back! Herbit is da Mayor an' dass dat! You kin piss, shit uh go bline (blind)!" With his last unrelentingly brusque statement, we all understood that Mr. Ernest was unleashing over seven decades of frustration and degradation. He'd had it with Harvey.

Daddy, who had long stopped gaveling and was watching this train wreck along with the rest of us, finally hailed, "Order! I'll have order! Now if y'all don't stop with this sideshow, I'll have y'all put outta here now! I want order in this meeting!"

But inside of himself, Daddy wanted Mr. Ernest to continue. He wanted to let Harvey know what was in the Mayor of Hollywood's heart, even if the words were delivered by proxy through Leader Ernest Mott. But just to make his feigned indignation look legitimate, he almost broke the gavel trying to gain control of the council meeting as he once again started to slam the wooden hammer. But Harvey would not stop.

"Erniss, I done been in dis town all my life jess like you an' I git 'long with all da people in dis town, black and white, but I aine takin' no mo' off dat fella."

"Oh really?" Mr. Ernest interrupted. "Is dat right, Harvey? You git 'long wit' black an' white in dis town, 'ey? Well wonda why when you go in yo' sto' (store), you follah us foot tah foot? Wonda why seem like you short in yo' talkin' wit' all da black mens in dis town? Dass some kinda gettin' 'long, Harvey. I kin tell ya bubba: aine nobody in ya fool, ya know. We know, all uh us in ya know, dat yo' gettin' 'long wit' black people in dis town,'specially da black mens, is diff'rnt dan yo' gettin' 'long with da white. Lass I check, Harvey, if black folks stop buying dey swine products from you, you gah have uh whole yard fulla oink!" The entire room exploded in laughter.

"Now, Erniss, all I sayin…" but Mr. Ernest quickly cut him off again.

"Harvey, 'dat fella' you referrin' to is Mayor Herbit Gadson, not 'dat fella' but Mayor Gadson. Git it right, Harvey. Dass *my* Mayor and dass *yo'* Mayor."

"Whahevah you wanna call him, Erniss, I aine takin' no mo'off um, y'all hear me? I aine' takin' it! Do y'all hear me?!"

The majority of people in Council meeting that night were black, but both black and white knew he meant "y'all niggers." At this point, you could feel the tension mounting in the room, but before anyone could say anything, Mr. Ernest fired one last salvo at Harvey.

"Yeah, Harvey, you might so call 'git 'long wit' da black people in dis town, but Herbit da first black man to evah run Hollywood an' e killin' you. I know e killin' you, but I kin promise you Harvey, slave days are over an' it aine no way in hell we goin' back!"

The black people stood up in the meeting and roared wildly. Daddy said, "Order, order I said! I'll have all of you removed if you don't cease the noise and take your seats!"

The black people cheered even louder when he said that. Though it was booming, that was the most convictionless sentence that I had ever heard Daddy utter. He didn't want them to sit down. Herbert Gadson was thoroughly enjoying every minute of this. Harvey was forced to endure all of this and he was beginning to froth at the mouth.

Thirty seconds later the crowd was still roaring at Mr. Ernest's last comment. Harvey, who at this point was beyond livid, started beating on his chest amongst a sea of thunderously clapping and jubilant black people.

"Yeah, Erniss, he always talkin' 'bout he gah cut somebody nuts out, enny? Ev'rybaudy in ya know he like tah say dat. Y'all know e true! He love tah say dat! He always talkin' dat talk!"

That was true. Whenever Daddy got drunk he would tell anyone who would listen that he was going to cut his political enemies' nuts out. That was not a secret. Everyone in Hollywood knew that one of Daddy's mantras was that it was his fervent desire to "cut dey fuckin' nuts out."

"Umma equal opportunity nuts cutta. I dough give uh damn who dey is — nigga, cracker, man, woman or lil' chern. If dey call deyself risin' up 'gence me an' tryna stop me from helpin' my people, Um cuttin' dey fuckin' nuts out! Dass jess dat! I dare uh nigga tah try tah stop me! Shit, I dare uh *cracker* tah try tah stop me!"

Daddy always said that. He said it at home when he was drunk. He said it in casual conversation with the town's people when he was drunk. He had never said it in Town Council meeting however. When Harvey said it that night, the black people that were cheering just seconds earlier were stunned into silence. The white people who were mumbling and muttering as the black people cheered had turned into red-faced statues whose quiescence was so stark it was cacophonous.

Harvey had the complete attention of everyone in the bank. He grabbed a steel-folding chair and was now leaning on it for emphasis. Then he jumped on top of it. He leaped on it with such force that his sheer girth and unbridled anger made a deep dent in the seat.

"So you wanna cut people nuts out, Herbit?! Well, cut on dis den!"

Harvey climbed down off his chair and stormed over to the table where Daddy and the Council were sitting. He reached into his butcher's coat pocket, opened his sanguinary heavy duty plastic bag and poured hog testicles on the table.

"Now you cut dese ya, you bald-headed sucka!"

"Did Harvey just call the Mayor a 'bald-headed sucker'?"

"Man Harvey done gone too damn far!"

"Harvey is uh goddamn fool!"

"He gah get e ass cut in ya da'night!"

"You see dat man jess tho' some hog nuts at da Mayor?!"

"Da Mayor need tah whup e ass!"

"Turn Jack loose Mayor! Let Jack beat Harvey ass!"

"What was Harvey thinking?!"

"Harvey's lost his mind!"

The white and black people were both uttering these statements and both races had become moonstruck. Shock, rage, surprise and a deep sense of sadness permeated the bank lobby. We were definitely going to be on the news tomorrow. No question about it. We were on the news that very night as a matter of fact. There was a big article in the newspaper about the hog testicles the next day. No one was surprised who wasn't from Hollywood. We had an outlaw Mayor and his town was Dodge City. People were surprised however, that this time, Daddy wasn't to blame.

Daddy slammed his gavel down and yelled, "Harvey, I'll have order in the meeting! Leave here now before the police escorts you out!" Harvey had so infuriated my father that he broke the gavel into three clean pieces trying to wrestle back control of that meeting.

Now, by this time, everyone was up in arms. Black and white arms, ebony and ivory arms, were waving together. Chocolate and vanilla colored fingers wagged in Harvey's face.

Mrs. Julia Harris, a middle-aged white woman, a blonde who was almost as big as Harvey and who owned a business in the town, jumped up and said, "I dough know 'bout chall, but ev'rybaudy in ya know why Harvey kan' stan' Herbit an' e aine got nuttin' tah do wit' e land, neitha. Da Mayor uh good man who done done some wrong, but e done done a lot uh right. Harvey, you was wrong. You was dead wrong!" Miss Ruth Biddle and her husband, Mr. Paul, who were white, allowed their fury to transform their faces into erubescent seas of irascibility that would have made Pharaoh's heart soften. The couple jumped up and ran toward the venetian blinds that had certainly seen better days. But as Mr. Paul got to the door, he turned and addressed the gathering.

Hollywood road-widening fight takes on a new twist

BY ARLIE PORTER
Of The Post and Courier Staff

HOLLYWOOD—The residents of this rural community near Charleston are so bitterly divided over a proposed road project that it was hard to see how the uproar could get worse.

Then came the hog testicles.

"Well, I tell ya whah, y'all kin say whah y'all wanna say 'bout da Mayor, but Hollywood aine nevah been this far 'long befo'. We got sewer, businesses tryin' tah get out cha, an' Hollywood is da best place I know uh tah raise uh fam'ly. Far as da Mayor personal life go, da man wife aine got no problem wit' um so all uh us need tah leave da Mayor be." The crowd that had only moments before given Mr. Ernest a standing ovation, leaped to their feet again for Mr. Paul.

Daddy, this entire time, listened stolidly and did not say a word as that white man spoke and the crowd continued to holler. This was his night. He basked in the satisfaction of knowing that, at least for this meeting, and at this time, the Town of Hollywood was with him in full force. He tried to take his broken gavel to call the meeting to order, but the crowd in that place that night just wouldn't stop cheering. Mayor Gadson, at that point, did the only thing he could do given the circumstances. He said, "Meeting adjourned!" He then slammed the piece of the gavel that he could still get a grip on, and he and his Council walked out of the meeting hall into closed session. They all headed for the vault and the last councilman inside slammed the big steel door shut. The crowd never stopped cheering, and Daddy never stopped grinning.

CHAPTER 6

Assaulting Elected Officials

Daddy would always tell my brother and me that we were lucky to know him.

"I aine nevah had no fuckin' Daddy" was his familiar refrain. "Murray aine been shit an' LeMarion Gadson aine nevah take no time wit' me. When dey tho' Murray ass outta dat winda (window) in New York City in '64, I cun even cry at da nigga funeral. I barely even knew da nigga. I dough know how uh man could jess leave e chern tah fen' fah deyself like dat. I wonda if dat somebitch was thinkin' bout me, Joelle and Fichette when dem fellas tho' e lil' ass outta dat winda. How da hell you think you gah fight six niggas an' think you gah live to tell da story? Man, dass how I know fah uh fack Murray lil', short, runt ass been crazy. Dat somebitch was pass by crazy y'all. Dat goddamn Murray always had tah be uh bad ass. I wonda if he still thought he was uh bad ass when he hit da ground from eight stories up. Murray been bad now. Bad mothafucka. But I aine nevah even know um. Y'all lucky y'all even know ya daddy. I aine da bess, but lease y'all know who I is an' y'all know I bring my damn check home. Dass fah damn sho'."

So on that December day, when Daddy was going on his obloquy as the three of us sat in steel folding chairs under our pecan tree gorging ourselves, we postulated nothing of his diatribe because it was Christmastime and Daddy was on a continuous drunk from "Black Friday" (the day after Thanksgiving) until New Year's Day. As we got older, the "Black Friday" benchmark was moved up to at or around the first of November. He always wanted Reggie and me to know how lucky we were to have him as a father. Granted, he wasn't perfect by any stretch of the imagination, but he did keep a roof over our heads, food on our table and clothes on our backs. Because it was Christmastime, we were especially grateful for his presence.

Now, all of that withstanding, we also knew that it was only a matter of time before the police paid us our annual holiday visit. It never failed. Sometime between Thanksgiving Day and New Year's Day, Charleston County's finest were going to rap on our front door.

The year before, Mama and Daddy had a knock-down, drag-out shouting and shoving match because Mama found out that Daddy was cheating on her with one of her closest associates. When she confronted him, he grabbed her, and then Reggie and I grabbed him. When he got out of our grasp, he called the police claiming that Reggie and I had assaulted him for no reason. The police came to our house, listened to both sides of the situation and concluded that Daddy just needed some rest. That was that.

The year before that, the police brought the Mayor of Hollywood home because they caught him driving drunk. They brought him to the door, rang the bell and told Mama they noticed that he was swerving and driving at a snail's pace. The officers recognized him and knew that he was about a mile from his house, so they threw the blue lights on him and told him from the police car's loudspeaker that they were going to follow him the last one thousand feet to his front door. They told Mama to make sure that he stayed inside of the house and slept off his bender. That episode also ended without any further incident.

However, it is only so long that a series of unfortunate events will continue to end fortunately.

Mama, my sister, Telley, and I knew that a storm was brewing. We knew that the holidays brought out the worst aspects of Reggie and Daddy's relationship. We all knew that this could be the year that things between the Mayor and his eldest son ended in catastrophe. Something was bound to happen. When Reggie and Daddy were both sober, Mama had to make them speak to each other. If she wasn't around, they wouldn't. When Reggie was sober and Daddy was drunk, Daddy was jovial with him, but Reggie would only talk back to him out of obligation. When Daddy was sober and Reggie was high, Reggie would talk to him, and Daddy would forever find a way to leave the room because he just didn't know what say to Reggie if he had not been drinking.

Reggie deeply resented Daddy because, for the first four years of his life, Daddy wasn't around much. In fact, for all intents and purposes, he practically denied paternity of Reggie simply because, by his own admission, he "din want no damn chern." He knew in his heart that Reggie was his, but fatherhood was a chore he was just not willing to do. My brother was pissed off at him ever since. And it wasn't like Daddy hid his feelings from his children. If he got juiced enough, he would recite the statement to us verbatim, "I din want no damn chern. Ya mama want chall. Damn if I had want any chern." Then he would laugh his trademark Herbert Gadson cackle. We knew his true feelings.

Daddy despised Reggie because he felt that my brother squandered every opportunity that being the "Mayor's son" afforded him. He hated the fact that Reggie was a crackhead. He hated the fact that Reggie had been to prison four different times. Daddy also hated Reggie because he theorized that his drug abuse made him weak. He would tell Mama, Telley and me that all the time when he was lit.

"I can undastan' da drinkin, but I jess cun nevah undastan' dat crack shit. I dough know where Reggie git dat shit from," Daddy would say in explaining why he just couldn't wrap his mind around why Reggie chose crack in lieu of, let's say, Jim Beam, for example. Daddy didn't care for my brother because when he looked in Reggie eyes, my father saw a mirror image of himself that he wished he could bury. Oh yes, trouble was in the air on December 19, 1998. It was the day before my brother's thirtieth birthday, and God had already started to prepare Mama for it.

My brother had not had transportation of his own since the '80s. After the drugs and the prison stints started, the license revocations followed. Reggie walked or caught rides everywhere he went. Because he was well known in Hollywood, there were plenty of times that if I saw him on the side of the road on 162 and couldn't pick him up for some reason, by the time I got onto U.S. Highway 17 [the main thoroughfare that connects Hollywood and Charleston] he would already be standing on the shoulder of 17. This was a great feat for a man whose primary mode of transporation was two feet. Because he had no car, around the holidays I would become the resident taxi. When Reggie would come to Mama's house to visit and needed a ride back home, wherever home was for him at the time, I would do the honors. So naturally, when he said that he and his crackhead girlfriend needed a ride back to her house, about an hour and fifteen minutes away, I felt for my keys in my pocket. Daddy then invited himself along for the trip saying, "I gah take my damn son an' e gal home. Boy, less get on da fuckin' road."

Mama was at the stove cooking Hoppin' John, a Lowcountry favorite made of field peas and rice, and Reggie, Daddy and I were sitting in the den watching TV. Reggie and I had taken our positions on the green argyle couch, and Daddy was sitting in the La-Z-Boy. Reggie's girlfriend was in the kitchen with Mama, washing dishes. At Daddy's mention of his accompanying us on our road trip, you could hear a pin drop in that den and the kitchen as the one room led into the other. The three of us fell totally silent. We could all smell trouble in the air and it hung as thick as the pine scent coming from the Christmas tree in Mama's prayer room. Daddy broke our awkward silence.

"Wudda hell ev'rybaudy stannin' 'round lookin' like statues fah?"

Daddy said. "Shaytee, git cho ass up off uh dat damn couch an' less git da hell out cha. Shit."

The dye was cast. My daddy was going to ride with my crackhead brother and his crackhead girlfriend, both of whom were high as kites, on this hour-long sojourn that I was sure was going to last forever. Mama had been around Reggie and Daddy long enough to know trouble when she saw it about to happen.

"Herbert, dough get on dat road wit' Reggie. You drinkin' an' Reggie is high. I dough want no bloodshed on that road. Herbert, the new criminal domestic violence law in South Carolina says that in criminal domestic violence cases, they lock up both people. Herbert, dough be no fool on dat road. Aw'right now, Um tellin' you now. Dass da new law."

Then she told Reggie, "Son, dough let cho Daddy git chu into nuttin'. If he say anything tah you, ignore him."

Daddy cut her off : "Linda, please leave me da fuck alone; me and Reggie gah be fine. I gah take da boy to e gal house."

Reggie then interjected, "Mama, Um aw'right, me an' Daddy gone be fine."

And with those last words, they both jumped up from their respective posts in the den. Reggie motioned for Toffee to follow him as he and Daddy walked out of the house. Toffee, almost as if my brother had programmed her, wiped the suds off her hands and practically ran out of the door after Reggie. She forgot to turn the water off and left a half sink full of dishes for Mama to wash. I followed the three of them outside to my truck. As I walked past Mama standing at the stove, she had already started praying.

She followed me out of the door and said, "Shay, if dey staht fightin', turn right around an' come back home. Son I see trouble, so pray on dat highway an' O'wl be praying here."

So, with Mama's pep talk, I hopped into my truck, slammed my door and drove away. As we were pulling out of the yard, I saw my mama get on her knees on that cold December ground and start praying, as if she knew beyond any doubt that this was going to end up being a situation that we were going to regret. Looking back on it, I know she knew. God had already told her.

We pulled out of our gap and Daddy said to no one in particular, "You know whah? I hate dem damn crackheads. Make me sick. Dem fuckin' crackheads make me fuckin' sick."

This was an unmasked affront to my brother, but he said nothing in response.

"Shay, I wonda why your damn brotha refuse tah say why he keep smokin' dat shit."

My brother remained silent. I remained silent as well. Then Daddy turned to Reggie.

"I aine pickin' on you, son, but you need tah stop doin' what chu doin'. Reggie, please get off dat damn crack, son. Please!" He almost managed to sound sincere. Almost.

Then Daddy, as if he was about to give the soliloquy of a lifetime, said, "Reg, I thought fah sho' when we put you in Southern Pines (drug treatment facility) in '85, you was gone get cho shit straight. But you didn't. Son, why you jess keep on fuckin' up? You aine tie'ud uh seein' yo' life go up in crack smoke? You aine my damn son. Cun be. Gadsons is lushes. We dough fuck wit' dem drugs. I dough know whay you get dat shit from."

I continued to drive, knowing full well that Daddy was trying to illicit a response from Reggie. I also knew, as did Daddy, there were several other members of our extended family who were on crack, just like Reggie. I was dolorous that my father and brother's relationship had deteriorated to this point. I was trying to process why Daddy was trying to get Reggie to explode on this highway to hell, but I continued to say nothing. As Daddy was pontificating, Reggie, for his part, sat unflappable in the backseat. He remained just like the crack rocks that he smoked: hard, cold and voiceless.

My daddy, who basically had been drunk for that past month, was giving my brother advice on sobriety. I recoiled at the irony of the whole situation. I knew that because Daddy hadn't succeeded in getting Reggie to explode in a blind rage, he was going to say what I knew that he had been itching to say ever since we hopped into this chariot of impending doom. I was just waiting on him to say it. Daddy didn't disappoint me.

"An' Reg, you need tah try an' git dis damn crackhead ass betch uh yose (yours) off da fuckin' crack since you refuse tah do da shit for yo'self."

That did it. Reggie went ballistic. To this day, I still don't blame him because, really, how much verbal abuse can one man take? Crackhead or not, Reggie had feelings, and all of Daddy's comments deeply wounded him, despite the fact he was wasted.

So the volcano that is my brother when he is stoned, which is always bubbling just beneath the surface, suddenly erupted all over my father. Reggie, who was sitting behind Daddy in the back passenger seat, reached across the front passenger seat where Daddy was stooped, grabbed him around his neck and started to choke the life out of him.

Now my brother was the most kind and gentle hoodlum most people had ever met. He would steal food out of our green freezer in the garage and feed the other drug addicts in Hollywood. For every woman with children that he may have become involved with and subsequently started living with, and there were many, my brother treated that woman and her children like they were special. He was in a perpetual state of homelessness, but because of his smoldering good looks and charm there was always a woman ready and waiting to lodge and feed him. The same six-foot-three, two hundred fifteen-pound, caramel-colored frame that those women loved to the point of foolish obsession, was threatening to render him and me fatherless. As tender-hearted as Reggie was, I had heard many stories over the years of just how deadly lethal he could be if you made him mad. Reggie's psychotic episodes were the stuff of legend on the streets of Hollywood, and now he was attacking my father with an unbridled passion. Reggie reserved this special flavor of venom for adversaries who crossed him in the street. At this particular point, Daddy became just another nigga on the block to his eldest son.

"Mothafucka, Umma kill you! You's uh dead nigga! You uh dead mothafucka! You talk too fuckin' much! You dough know who da fuck you fuckin' wit', nigga! I done buss niggas' heads fah less dan da shit I done let chu get away wit' sayin' tah me, mothafucka! Dough chu fuckin' talk 'bout Toffee smokin' no fuckin' crack! Mothafuck you, Daddy!"

My brother was choking Daddy and spewing the hate-filled rhetoric that he had pent up inside of him all of his life. Daddy turned cardinal. Reggie squeezed some more, and then Daddy turned indigo. He just kept gurgling over and over again, "He killin' me! He killin' me! I kan' breathe! I kan' breathe! Shaytee, git dis crazy mothafucka off me!"

I don't know how I managed to keep my truck on the road because I had my right knee on the steering wheel trying to drive, simultaneously trying to uncoil my brother's arms, which were like two boa constrictors around Daddy's head and neck. All I could think to do was scream because I could see that Daddy was losing consciousness. Reggie's combination sleeper hold/rear naked choke was slowly causing the life to seep from Daddy's body.

"Reggie! You gah kill um! Stop! Stop! You killin' um!"

"No Shay! Fuck dis nigga! I want his drunk ass dead!"

For all of Reggie's bravado and tough talk, I knew he didn't want to go to prison. When he saw that Daddy was no longer fighting him, and that his head had now dropped to his stomach, Reggie let him go. Toffee was crying. I was still screaming. Daddy wasn't moving. I turned the truck around and headed back home.

As the sands of time would orchestrate it, though it seemed like we had already traveled the almost one hour it takes to get to Toffee's house, we had only traveled seven miles. Seven miles was all it took for father and son to turn my car into an ultimate fighting octagon. After Daddy composed himself, and resumed full respiratory function after being choked almost comatose, he talked shit to Reggie the entire trip back to our house.

"Yeah mothafucka, you wanna choke somebody? You wanna fuck wit' me? Huh nigga?! Reggie, yo' ass is goin' tah jail fo' yo' birthday bubba. You dough know who you done fuck wit' da'day 'cause yo' fuckin' ass is gonna hang fah dis shit. I hope you like prison nigga, 'cause dass way yo' black ass is headed. You mussy dough realize yo' daddy is da fuckin' Mayor, boy! Um da fuckin' Mayor uh Hollywood, nigga! You aine shit! I run dis fuckin' Hollywood show, nigga! Um da star uh dis here flick. Yo' ass aine nuttin' but uh damn extra. You bess believe yo' ass is goin' down fah dis shit!"

Now I don't know if Reggie believed he was going back to prison for a very long time for trying to kill our daddy, but he didn't say a word in the ten or so minutes it took for us to pull into our yard. When we pulled into the gap, we saw Mama still on the ground, still on her knees, still praying. I know she knew all the time.

As I drove down the graveled driveway, we could see Mama rocking back and forth on the ground. The closer my truck got to where she was kneeling on the concrete that was adjacent to our garage, as she heard the ground underneath her rumbling, I could see her modulating, "Praise You, God! Hallelujah!" Then she stood up and walked in front of my SUV looking at the four of us as we peered back at her through the windshield.

"What happened?" Mama said as Daddy staggered out of my car.

"Umma tell you whah happen, Linda. Yo' fuckin' son is goin' nah jail dis damn day right here. Yo' son tried tah kill me."

"Tried to kill you? How?"

"Da mothafucka choke me like uh fuckin' python snake! Dass how! Dis crackhead somebitch choke da shit outta me! You kin bail e ass out if ya wanna, but Um callin' da police an' his black ass, crackhead ass, is goin' nah jail da'night. You kin mock (mark) my fuckin' words."

Daddy stormed past Mama and ran into the house. She turned to my brother.

"Reggie, what happened?"

"Mama, I aine did nuttin' nah Daddy. He jess keep tellin' me 'bout me an' Toffee smoke crack an' I aine shit. Mama, all I did was grab um. He jess keep on messin' wit' me an' messin' wit' me. But when he staht in on Toffee, dass when I grab um. I cun take it no mo'."

Before Mama could respond to Reggie, we heard Daddy in the house on the phone. He had left the door open when he rocketed past us.

On the telephone with the 9-1-1 dispatcher, in his professional voice and most sober and precise diction, he said, "I would like to report a domestic disturbance at the Mayor of Hollywood's home... Yes, I am the Mayor... Well, my son and I were traveling down Highway 162, which is the road we live on, and all of a sudden he attacked me. He is on crack... Yes, he is here right now... Yes ma'am, it is a crying shame... No ma'am; no, we didn't act like that when we were growing up. That is the way young people do today; you are so correct... Yes ma'am. I am in excruciating pain, but I am fine. The address is... oh, you have the address... okay good... No, I don't need an ambulance... Yes ma'am, I am fine... Yes ma'am, he is still on the premises. His girlfriend is a witness and she also smokes crack. They smoke crack together... If the officer who is dispatched to my home searches my son, he will most assuredly find crack on him...Make a note of that on your computer: *SEARCH MAYOR OF HOLLYWOOD'S SON FOR CRACK COCAINE, INCLUDING BUT NOT LIMITED TO, A FULL BODY CAVITY SEARCH*...I feel confident the officer that comes here is going to have to search my son's asshole 'cause he's a slick ass somebitch...I know his ass and the mothafucka is not above putting crack up his asshole, nasty ass mothafucka...Yes ma'am, I do want an officer to take a report because I want him to go to prison. If I am not mistaken, isn't assaulting an elected official a felony? ...Oh, ok, well, I'll just ask the officer when he gets here... Yes ma'am, thank you... Merry Christmas to you as well, sweetheart. And Happy New Year, honey bunch."

Daddy came out of the house singing in a child's voice and taunting my brother saying, "Yo' black ass goin' nah jaaaaaaaiiiil! You gah spen' yo' birthday in jaaaaaaaiiiil! Ah huh. You wanna fuck wit' me, bubba? Yo' ass goin' nah jail dis night here. Da fuckin' police on da damn way here now. Aine nuttin' I kin do tah stop it. You cause dis shit on yo' own damn self. I dough know how Toffee gettin' home da'night 'cause yo' ass goin' nah jail. Son, do you know dat you assaulted an elected official? Do you realize dat? Da police jess tole me you lookin' at uh mandatory fifteen years in jail. Fifteen years, bubba! You aine twenty years ole no mo', Reg. Yo' ass is thirty an' nem young fellas in dat jailhouse gah eat chu alive 'cause yo' ass goin' nah jail!"

The entire time Daddy was singing his song, Mama was standing against the garage door praying.

When the police officer pulled up in his blue and white squad car, Daddy ran to meet him. I actually felt sorry for the officer. He looked to be barely into his twenties. He was a beanpole and he walked with a slouch. He tried to appear forceful and imperious, but his navy blue uniform wrapped around his lanky frame a couple of inches more than it was supposed to. Private Davey Blake still had pimples on his cotton-ball white face. I don't think he was more than a few shades darker than Sean Patrick

Flanery's character from the movie *Powder*. He was nervous because this was the Mayor of Hollywood's house and my father's loathing of the Charleston County Police Department was well documented. Daddy's title made him one of the few black men in Charleston County whose contempt could have negative repercussions for Charleston's finest.

Davey Blake was barely out of his car before Daddy started speaking to him in his haughty Mayor of Hollywood voice:

"Officer, my son assaulted me. He choked me for no reason and now I want him arrested. I am an elected official, a public official, and I want him to go to jail. He is a menace to this community and has been for a number of years. He and his girlfriend over there smoke crack. If you search them, you will definitely find crack on them right now. I'm sure the dispatcher has already alerted you to the fact that you are supposed to search my son for crack."

Daddy didn't have a clue as to whether they had crack on them at that moment, but he knew that mentioning that they did would bolster his case. Reggie stood there, by my truck, looking dejected. Toffee was crying. Mama stopped praying long enough to listen to the exchange between Daddy and the police officer. Davey Blake looked like a small kid in a shopping mall who turned around suddenly and when he looked up again, his mom was gone. This guy was totally out of his league dealing with Herbert Gadson, Mayor of Hollywood. Inasmuch as he looked dumbfounded and frightened, he was determined to make a good showing for himself.

"So, Mayor, you're sayin' that he attacked you for no reason?"

"Yes, that is exactly what I'm saying. He attacked me for no good reason. We were taking his girlfriend home; my other son was driving and that rogue attacked me."

Then Private Davey did what no one else, up to this point, had done. He asked me what happened.

I could sound just as articulate, but not nearly as pompous, as my father when I wanted to, especially when the police were involved. The Charleston County Police Department made me nervous, so when I spoke to Private Davey I was especially cautious with my tone and verbiage. I tried to come across firm and self-assured because I didn't want him to think that the cops scared me shitless, even if they did.

"Well officer, my father taunted my brother about being a crackhead and about the fact that my brother's girlfriend over there is a crackhead as well. I was driving and after awhile, my brother did choke my father."

"So you're saying your father provoked all of this by goading your brother with the insults?"

"Yes, I would say that's a fairly accurate statement officer."

Reggie was smiling. Daddy looked bewildered. No, Daddy looked like I just punched him in the gut. Hard. My mouth flew open in a guffaw. I couldn't believe it. This young white police officer was standing up to Daddy by simply asking me to recount my version of events. It became evident to me at that very moment that Private Davey Blake had more balls than brains. I had to admire him.

Ordinarily, Daddy would verbally browbeat any representative of the sheriff's office into submission. He would let them know, more than a few times throughout a conversation with any of them, whether it be for a speeding ticket or a DUI, that he was the Mayor of Hollywood. He would then tell them how unfortunate it would be for the esteemed department to be leveled with a police brutality suit from the Mayor of Hollywood, South Carolina. Daddy would sprinkle in the word "lawsuit" and add a dash of the word "brutality" throughout the verbal jousting with any local law enforcer. I use the culinary terminologies "sprinkle" and "dash" because the Mayor of Hollywood was accustomed to making mincemeat out of any representative of the Charleston County sheriff. Next to drinking, politics and women, and not necessarily in that order, my father's passion was backing down local police.

This cop, however, was tougher than I gave him credit for. He looked my father square in the face, eyeball to eyeball, and said, "Mayor, based on what your son is saying, it looks like you started it."

"So mothafuckin' what?! How da fuck kin Shaytee tell you what da fuck happened when his ass was 'sposed tah be drivin'?! Huh?! Riddle me dat,

Batman! If you take his word for it, den lock his ass up fah bein' uh nosey somebitch an' not payin' attention to an' obeyin' da laws uh da fuckin' open highway! Who gives uh shit what da fuck he say?! I sure as shit don't! *FUCK HIM!* I didn't lie, Barney Fife! Reggie did attack me! *Ferociously*, I may add! He assaulted me and I want his black ass locked up! Now, what da fuck is you not understandin' about dis sitcha'ation, Columbo?! Damn, I hate the fuckin' police! 'Cause uh dis same type bowshit y'all always pullin'!"

"Well Mayor, it's not that simple. See, you instigated the situation and the law states that in criminal domestic violence cases like this, you are just as culpable as your son."

"So Baretta, what are you saying? Are you saying that he is not going to jail for assaulting an elected official?"

The cop then said to Reggie, "Sir, what is your side of the story?"

"Officer, I did choke him, but he kept messin' wit' me about some crack an' callin' my girlfriend uh crackhead, so I defended myself. I was just tryin' tah make him shut up."

"So you choked him to shut him up?"

"Yes sir, I did."

Daddy then shouted, "Okay, officer, you heard him! He choked me! Lock him up! Take his ass off of my property and to the damn jail!"

"Well Mayor, it's not that simple."

"*Whatdafuckyoumeanit'snotthatsimpleBarnabyJones?!* He choked me! Are you saying that you are not going to arrest a man that has admitted to assaulting an elected official?!"

Daddy was foaming-at-the-mouth angry, and I could *almost* see the Crown Royal flavored spittle forming on his taste buds. Davey Blake was inscrutable. I could *definitely* see the new vertebrae forming his once nonexistent spine. This guy was good.

"Mayor, this is the situation: Yes, your son did assault you and I am going to arrest him. But the charge will be criminal domestic violence, not assault of an elected official. Quite honestly, Mayor, assaulting an elected official isn't even a charge that exists on the books."

"You really think I give uh good goddamn if it exist or doesn't exist, Horatio Caine?! Get this man off of my property and take his ass to jail. Just take him to jail, Wyatt Earp! Book da mothafucka, Danno! Shit!"

Daddy was so incensed that he couldn't see straight. I noticed that he'd gotten that familiar maniacal look in eyes. He'd gotten so close to Davey Blake as he was trying to explain to him why he should take his son to jail, I'm sure that Davey could smell his breath. Daddy got so close to Blake, in fact, I could have sworn that he was about to live out one of his adult fantasies. He often told us or anyone else who would listen for that matter, that it was his dream to "walk up to one uh dem somebitch an' slap fiah (fire) out dey ass." He said that it was his fervent desire "to ketch (catch) one uh dey ass in da mall, or in Piggly Wiggly, or Krispy Kreme, walk up to one um an' say, "Good day officer, mighty fine weather we havin'," and before the cop could say, 'Sure is, ain't it?', haul off an' box da shit outta dey ass!" He would always laugh after he said it, but he said it often enough that I knew he'd contemplated it almost as often as he blinked.

To his credit, Private Blake didn't flinch. He was so close to Daddy, I knew that he could smell the Crown Royal emanating from his pores. Simultaneously, the cop slapped the cuffs on my brother and read him his Miranda Rights. He told Reggie to spread his legs and he then patted him down from chest to ankle, assiduously but quickly. I could see Reggie prattling along with the ghost of Joseph Miranda, because he had heard the apparition's speech so many times before, he knew the manifesto by heart. Blake then blurted out, with the deliberate intonation and thinly veiled sarcasm of Judge Judy, "No crack here, Mayor!"

The sheer acrimony in Daddy's eyes snatched Blake's tongue out of its orifice and hogtied him with it like one of Harvey's sows. However, the heart, nerve and sinew of Daddy's body respected his badge, just enough, to let the comment ride. Reluctantly. Daddy's malevolent body and genius brain compromised with one another by the shaking of his head and an audible lament of "fuckin' cracker." The two words were a letter signed in blood from his soul and bullet riddled hip, sent from one public official to another. It was postmarked Orangeburg and dated the night of the Massacre. The Mayor intended to sucker the cop into a police brutality fueled frenzy. The good constable, lumbar region now fully constituted, didn't take the bait. Luckily.

Then Private Blake turned back to Daddy and did exactly what Mama had said he would do.

"Mayor, put your hands behind your back. I'm placing you under arrest."

Daddy was stunned. Reggie was smiling wider than a six-year-old on Christmas morning who'd awakened from slumber, ran into the living room, looked under the tree and saw exactly what he'd requested from jolly old Saint Nick. Mama was blathering at Daddy in slow motion, "I told you so! I told you not to call the police!"

Daddy said, "Officer, what's going on here?!"

"Well, under the new criminal domestic violence statute of the state of South Carolina, whenever a criminal domestic violence charge is leveled, both parties are to be arrested if it is found that both parties have established culpability in the incident."

As the cop put the handcuffs on Daddy, he murmured, "I can't believe this shit. I aine did nuttin'. I aine did nuttin'!"

Reggie and Daddy sat in the back of the police car doing what they had done since this holiday season started. They argued. Reggie was wasted with handcuffs around his wrists, arms behind his back in the vinyl navy blue interiored Crown Victoria. Daddy was sloshed, sitting in the same position on the back passenger side of the car. The windows were up so we couldn't hear what they were saying, but they were definitely arguing. They were on their way to jail, and we could see that they didn't calm down until the cop jumped back into the squad car.

Then the Mayor of Hollywood, the Mayor's son and one of Charleston County's finest left our driveway. Mama, Toffee and I followed them with our eyes until they became a small dot in the distance. Reginald Everette Dingle Gadson, a career criminal, twenty-nine years old and a lifelong resident of Hollywood, along with his father, Herbert Gadson, Mayor of Hollywood, were headed to jail. They were going to be together to celebrate my brother's birthday. They were going to be locked up for the holidays.

"All I kin say is thank ya Jesus," Mama said as she, Toffee and I walked back into the house. "Hallelujah, God! Somethin' had tah happen 'cause dey could not continue on like that. I knew this thing had tah come to a head. Um jess glad dey didn't kill each other."

Toffee said, "So wuss gonna happen now, Mama Linda?"

"I don't know, baby. I guess they will call us from the jail later, but Shaytee will take you home. I will let chu know what happens when I hear from them."

Toffee was short, toffee colored (hence her nickname) and kind of oblong in shape. I would later learn that she acquired the nickname because as a child, her skin was so clean and pure in color that the Crunch 'n Munch that she used to love to eat, and her skin, were exactly the same hue. Because the popcorn confection was covered in toffee, which gave it its color, an older cousin of hers started calling her toffee. The name stuck. I imagined that, as a child, she must have been beautiful. It was undeniable that the crack had mercilessly ravaged what used to be an obviously flawless light brown complexion. You could still see the remnants of that once pristine skin. She must have had such promise as a child. How did she come to such a pass? My heart grieved for her.

I looked at her as she sat on the passenger side of my truck as we drove out of our gap. The football shaped crackhead had her head bowed into her enormous breasts and she was blubbering as she sat there in a folded heap.

"What chu think gone happen to Reggie an' Daddy Herbert, Shaytee?"

"Only God knows, Toffee. All we can do is pray."

We rode the rest of the hour-long journey to her house with Hip Hop & R&B drowning out the silence.

After I came back home, no sooner than I walked in the house, the phone rang. Mama said, "Hello... Shay, pick up on da otha phone. Iss them."

The robotic sounding recording on the other end of the phone said, "This a collect call from the Charleston County Detention Center, do you accept the charges?"

"Yes."

Reggie, with all deliberate speed, started talking where the recording left off.

"Hi, Mama; iss me."

"Boy, are you all right?"

"Mama, you know me, Um fine. Daddy back dey cryin' like uh baby dough. I tole da guard tah put him in uh cell by hisself. But Um okay; you know I do two weeks in here standin' on my head. Dis home tah me. So Mama, when you comin' tah git us?"

"There should be uh hearing tomorrow so we will see about uh bond then."

"Okay, Mama, Umma tell da guard tah keep checkin' on Daddy so nobody dough fuck wit' him da'night. I dough wanna have tah kill one uh dese niggas in ya fah fuckin' wit' my daddy. Um sorry for cursin', Mama."

"Iss okay son, I'll be praying."

"Aw'right, Mama, I love you."

"I love you too, son."

Harve Jacobs was a mixed and quite rare breed. He was equal parts pit bull, bulldog and bloodhound. He was a wiry, chisel-faced, balding and high cheek-boned truth seeker. His eyes could peer right through the lies embedded in a man's soul until he uncovered the truth. He was all newsman. He was the longtime crime reporter for Channel Five local news. If Harve ruminated that one of his interview subjects was being untruthful, he bore in. He growled, clinched his teeth and tore the flesh off the lie. He got to the bone of the truth. He did not accept a differing version of the truth, or even the truth itself for that matter, if an answer did not jive with logic, or conventional wisdom, or the facts of a particular case. Harve Jacobs was a damn good reporter. And on this day, he had the Mayor of Hollywood in his crosshairs.

When my older sister, Telley, who was morbidly obese and had a personality just as large to match, Mama and I pulled up to the Charleston County Detention Center on December 21, 1998, a throng of media types, led by Harve Jacobs, accosted us. This was one day after Reggie's thirtieth birthday, and almost as a special present to my brother, Harve showed up to wish him an awful birthday. Our local paper, The Post and Courier, Channel 2 and Channel 4 News also were well represented in the media circus. Each camera crew had already set up under the county jail's big top as they waited for the extravaganza to begin.

The three of us were there on cue to commence the show. Our nondescript and prosaic unmarked vehicle was surrounded as soon as we crossed the threshold of the Detention Center, which also housed The Charleston County Courthouse. Someone who worked at the jail tipped off the media as soon as Daddy was booked and processed. We figured as much so we decided to drive my aunt's forest green Buick LaSabre, which was the most vanilla vehicle on the road. Harve and the rest of the reporters apparently had a pretty reliable source at the jail. They sniffed us out forthwith. Somehow they knew that we would be driving the most regular car into the most irregular of situations.

As we pulled into the parking space of the dull, drab, ecru-colored, rhombus-shaped block building that allegedly housed some of the most dangerous criminals in Charleston County, the real criminals were outside of our car about to hijack any semblance of privacy we figured we had on that day. Mama looked at Telley and me, bowed her head and began to pray aloud:

"Father God, in the name of Jesus, I ask You to protect us just as You protected Daniel from the lions because these media vultures are not bigger than You. It doesn't matter what media outlets are represented on the outside of these four doors. Father God, I will continue to praise You from the White House to the outhouse! Lord, show my children and the rest of the world today, no matter what happens, even in Hollywood, you can still say Halleluhah! I ask that You fix this situation today and that Your will in our lives be done. Hallelujah! Praise You, God! In the name of Jesus, Amen."

Telley and I, in unison said, "Amen."

"All right kids, let's go."

As soon as our car doors slammed, Harve was on us.

"Mrs. Gadson, who's to blame for both the Mayor and your son being incarcerated? Was your son high at the time of the incident? Was the Mayor drinking when this happened?"

As we walked through the Red Sea of reporters, they politely parted and let us into the building. As Mama "no commented" her way through the line, Telley leaned over and whispered to me, "Thank God no one at seminary will be able to see this. This is so embarrassing. Um so glad I go to school in Atlanta. What da hell were they thinkin'?"

I was beginning my third year at The College of Charleston at the time. I had a not so sneaking suspicion everyone at school would see it on television – and they did. I think that day was the only time I ever seriously wanted to go to seminary at Emory to become a preacher like Telley. Atlanta sounded like the best place in the world. At that moment I guess anywhere other than Charleston would have sounded like paradise to me.

We walked toward the cinderblock courthouse doors as Harve followed us until he couldn't tag along anymore. His questions came rapid fire at us as the warm breath from his wide mouth and flaring nostrils made the steam billowing from his face in that icy cold look like a meteor trail. That human blowtorch was the disc jockey that provided the soundtrack for our stroll through perdition that blistering cold December day. We ignored him as much as we could, and did not answer any questions.

Telley was wearing an olive Lane Bryant pantsuit with her chartreuse Dooney and Burke clutch to accentuate the look. Mama had on a mauve blouse and wine slacks. My blue Levi's jeans and apricot polo shirt clung tightly to my scrawny frame as I shivered and hugged myself because of the cold. The flashing camera bulbs made all of our outfits seem iridescent as those obnoxious lights bounced off them. Those refulgent lights illuminated our nightmare.

A few minutes after we were seated in the courtroom, Daddy and Reggie were brought in. Both were locked in wrist and ankle shackles that made them walk in a shuffle. Daddy wore a Civil War Confederate grey jailhouse jumpsuit. Reggie was clad in county jail orange.

Judge Jack Guedalia was almost seventy-five years old and he was the chief magistrate for Charleston County. He was a silver-haired and leather faced white man who lived, breathed and slept South Carolina jurisprudence. He had a steely constitution, but he was as fair-minded and even-tempered a judge as there was. You couldn't pull the wool over Judge Guedalia's eyes, he wouldn't allow you to gild the lily in his courtroom and you couldn't smear shit on his face and attempt to tell him it was Noxzema, either. To their credit, the two thugs standing in front of him didn't even try. He didn't throw the book at Reggie and Daddy. He just kind of opened it a little, tore out the first few pages, wadded them up and gently lobbed them in their general direction.

Judge Guedalia gave Reggie and Daddy personal recognizance bonds and let them out with just slaps on their wrists. He knew Reggie personally from their past run-ins, and he knew Daddy from being the Mayor. Judge Guedalia scolded them – and good.

"You two know better than this. Reggie, aren't you getting a little long in the tooth for this tomfoolery? And Mayor, you know you have no right to be here; no right whatsoever. Against my better judgment, I'm going to let you two go home. I'm going to release you guys to the custody of Mrs.Gadson because it's clear to me that you all can't be responsible for yourselves. What kind of example are you setting here, Mayor? You're far too smart a man to be in this courtroom. And Reggie, I thought you were turning a corner. Now I'm going to give you two a break today. Don't make me sorry that I did. Are we clear here, gentlemen?"

Daddy and Reggie both nodded in unison and said, "Yes sir."

Judge Guedalia slammed his gavel down and bellowed, "Next case!"

Reggie and Daddy, both with their shoulders erect and heads held high despite the shackles, and trying to exude as much confidence as they could muster for our benefit, arrogantly walked out of the courtroom, knowing full well that they'd both just dodged the same bullet. Mama, Telley and I looked knowingly at one another, fully aware that this experience hadn't taught either one of them a thing.

After they were released, Daddy came home and sopped up some more rotgut. He cursed the day and damned the hour that Reggie was conceived. That evening, after he had gotten sufficiently buzzed and the phone calls finally stopped, Daddy's tongue loosened again.

"Shay, that night I got cho Mama pregnant, I shoulda put cho fuckin' bubba in uh goddamn napkin. I shoulda nevah put his crazy ass up in yo' Mama. Every time I think about whah dat mothafucka did tah me it make my stomach turn like smellin' ten miles uh beat up donkey dick. I kan' stand dat somebitch. Yo' bubba is uh no good, low down somebitch. I had tah spend da night in jail 'cause uh his crackhead ass."

I tried reasoning with Daddy. "Reggie an' you were headed tah jail long before dat night. Da both of y'all need tah stop an' think befo' y'all do certain things. It aine Reggie fault by hisself, Daddy."

Daddy cut me off. "Man, fuck you, Shaytee! You kin kiss my ass an' go straight to hell wit' dat ole bowshit!"

I shrugged my shoulders, stretched out and lay down from my seated position on the couch. Daddy took off his glasses and soon was sleeping soundly on his recliner. Reggie went out, smoked some crack and kissed the sky for his birthday. It was just another Yule-tide season in Hollywood. 'Twas another Merry Christmas at the Mayor's house. God bless us every-one.

☆　　☆　　☆

CHAPTER 7

Preachers Need Love, Too

For my sister to have grown up in the perfect storm that was the Mayor's house, she turned out superlatively. She is quite simply the consummate daughter. Her flaws are non-existent. Her pain however, is persistent. I think that anytime a female child has as a father a man who is powerful, an alcoholic and is as sexually charged a human being as Telley Gadson's father was, it has a profound impact. The way that Daddy treated Mama devastated my sister. Telley's situation differs from that of the classic case study of your average daughter in her station. The unexceptional daughter would lash out at her father with bad behavior and sexual promiscuity. In my sister's case, that didn't happen. The hell in our house pushed her to the polar opposite end of that spectrum of the "average daughter." The Reverend Telley Lynnette Gadson has never been average a day in her life.

Telley has always been fat. She has been big ever since I can remember. Telley was a capacious baby, she was rotund as a small child, she was a roly-poly teenager and she was commodious as an adult. Telley was as short as Mama and she weighed three hundred seventy pounds. She is the color of cocoa with the face of an angel. That may be part of why she decided to become a United Methodist pastor. Her cherubic face and Daddy's failing grace prepared her well to serve the Lord.

She has always been a nurturer and a mother hen. Telley's always been smart, too. She was a part of the first graduating class of Buist Academy for Advanced Studies in 1988. Buist was located In downtown Charleston. It was started because the city fathers deemed it necessary to place all of the academically gifted and talented elementary aged children in Charleston County in one centralized location. The conventional wisdom was that these students, who were the best and brightest in the area, would be better suited in an environment where every other child they were competing against would be just as smart or smarter. Thus, greatness would be the rule, not the exception, as it might have been in their former grossly inadequate elementary schools. If you're considered smart and elementary aged in Charleston, and you don't go to Buist, you may be astute, but you most assuredly are not gifted and talented. Not in 1988 Charleston.

Telley went to Buist from C.C. Blaney Elementary School. Blaney is a modest, provincial school in Hollywood. Its curriculum wasn't as strong as maybe some of the weaker predominately white elementary schools in Charleston, but Telley went to Buist and not only competed with the best and brightest, she excelled.

Nothing could have prepared Telley for high school, even a high school where lesser-talented kids weren't allowed. High school is another world. Even if you go to high school where there are no special groups, no nerds, no athletes, no cheerleaders, no popular kids and no morons, it's still high school. Even if all the kids are adroit and *au fait* and their primary concern is education, it's still a brutal melange of hormones, the fight for acceptance and the need to fit in.

Telley's high school, Academic Magnet, was created specifically for the first graduating class of Buist so that they would have somewhere to go instead of being forced to assimilate back into the mediocrity of a subpar academic community. The school, later renamed The Academic Magnet

High School of Charleston, is one of the top-rated magnet high schools in the nation, according to US News and World Report. Today, it stands on a spacious collegiate-looking campus with lush greenery in North Charleston. Back during the 1988-89 school year however, it was a pilot program housed on the campus of Burke High School. Like Buist, Burke is located downtown. Burke was full of athletes, cheerleaders, popular kids, bright kids and miscreants. It was a predominately African-American high school and those kids, to a person, did not want these nerds and geeks invading their space. They let Telley know exactly that on her first day of school. Telley was too young, too fat and too gifted.

The very first day that my voluminous sister walked into Burke's cafeteria, a hush fell over the packed lunchroom. Then it happened. In concert, two hundred fifty kids at the second lunch period at 12:15 p.m. on August 29, 1988, had a simultaneous convulsion scrutinizing and laughing at Telley.

"Damn, dat bitch big! PHAHAHAHAHA!"

"Da last place dat fat ass girl need tah be is in dis damn lunchroom. Tell ya dat shit."

"I hope dat big bitch dough try tah eat me. She look like she hungry dan uh maufucka, too! WHOAHOAHAHAHAHAHA!"

Those kids were merciless. My sister heard it all that day, but tried to show it didn't bother her. She took her lunch tray and sat down at a table by herself, all alone. Although people were laughing at her and pointing at her and making pig noises, she knew they would love her once these Burke kids got to know her. After all, the kids in Academic Magnet loved her. The black kids, the white kids, the Asian kids and the Latino kids, they all adored her. My sister just ate her food and smiled right along with them. She didn't cry until she got on the bus at the end of the day to go home.

As Telley drank her tears on the long ride home, she told herself she would make these Burke kids know her and love her, even if it took four years to do it.

But her immediate present did not appear so optimistic.

"Aine nobody gah evah want me 'cause da blood uh Jesus is upon me an' da weight of da werl is all ovah me," she she would cry to Mama. "Um sixteen, Um saved an' Um fat. Aine nobody gah want me, Mama."

"Baby, it's somebody out dere, plenny uh somebodies out dere fah you. You beautiful and ya smart. Plenny uh young men would jump at da chance to be your friend. All you got tah do is trust God. Tell, you have tah trust dat He is protecting your virtue for the right young man."

"Aine no right young man fah me, Mama. All I got is church an' school. Aine no prom fah me 'cause it aine no right young man fah me."

Telley and Mama would have these conversations in the prayer room almost daily. They kneeled at the prayer stool praying, crying and talking to one another and to God, desperately trying to figure out why my sister had to suffer for being ponderous. They petitioned God for a prom date for her. Telley would yammer and yowl. Almost daily, Mama prayed the same prayer as she held Telley close to her:

"Father God, in the name of Jesus, You see the suffering of Your children and You always answer with wisdom. Your servant, Telley Gadson, has been faithful to You. You can deliver the right and perfect prom date. We know You will, Jesus. We pray this prayer in Your name and consider it done. Hallelujah, Father! Amen."

Two years had passed since the debacle in the Burke lunchroom and Telley did make good on her vow. The Academic Magnet kids, all of them, to a person, admired her. Burke kids knew who she was because there were courses like ROTC and P.E. that they and the "maggots" took together. "Maggot" was the term the Burke kids used to describe these uber intelligent kids who had overtaken their school.

That didn't matter to Telley. The Burke kids had learned that the "smart, fat girl" was kind-hearted. Telley had showed them that all right, but now it was three weeks before prom and Telley didn't have a date, nor did it seem possible she would find one. No amount of encouragement from a loving mother and reassurance from a benevolent God was going to change that.

I think that at some point I've had crushes on just about all of my sister's friends. Raven. Darci. Nichole. Kendra. Connie. Demetrial. I was in love with all of them. Each girl was pretty, ranging in hue from banana yellow to blackberry. Some of them were slender and graceful. Others were voluptuous with young, heaving and fully developed breasts and ripe orb shaped behinds at the tender age of sixteen. In my prepubescent mind, I was in a loving and committed relationship with each young lady. They all had prom dates, every last one of them. Three weeks before prom is an anxious time for a girl. She has to make certain that she has chosen the right dress, the right guy, whether to have sex with the guy and at what restaurant they were going to be dining. These are extremely important decisions that must be made. From a sixteen-year-old girl's vantage point however, I probably did not list these quandaries in order of significance. All of Telley's friends were buzzing about the prom. Telley said that they would be in class talking about the prom and who was taking them to the prom and what kind of great time the prom was going to be. The only thing that my sister could do was laugh with them. She would laugh and wonder. The entire time she was dying inside.

Telley spent a lot of time in church, partly to fill the void of an inactive social life. Subsequently, Mama and I would be alone in the house together at night quite a bit. This gave me the opportunity to hear Mama in the prayer room praying to God for a date for her only daughter. Mama's prayer when she was alone was far different than when she and Telley would pray and petition Jesus together. She told the Lord that she knew and understood that disappointment was a part of life, but that Telley didn't deserve a letdown of this magnitude.

"God please, please Jesus, do for Telley what only You can do Lord. I can't make a prom date for Telley, but You can Lord. You can do it. All I got is You, Lord, an' all Telley got is me. I've been an overweight teenage girl, Father. I know the pain and the agony. The only person I could talk to then was You, God. Now, I cry out for my daughter. God, please fix this situation as only You can. I can't do anymore for Telley, God. I know You can, though. I know You will. In Jesus' matchless and mighty name I pray. Hallelujah, Jesus! Praise You, God! Amen."

Now the Lord always answers Mama's prayers. Always. The prom was no different. As luck would have it, there was a guy at Burke who did not have a prom date, and two weeks before the big shindig, he was still looking for one. In less than fourteen days, he and Telley's friends arranged for the two to go to the big bash together.

The guy was long-limbed and tomato colored. He was big-boned as well. None of that mattered. On prom night, Mama and Daddy paid for the entire soirée. They were glad to do it. My parents sprang for Telley's dress and the young man's tuxedo. They bought dinner for them at an expensive restaurant.

Telley picked him up in her car, but they barely spoke on the way to and from the prom. They never danced together. The entire night, he kept looking at his watch and the clock on the wall of the Burke gymnasium to see if it was his imagination, or was time moving as slowly on the wall as it was on his left wrist. Telley was back at home in her bed fast asleep by 11:30 that night.

But she couldn't have cared less. My sister went to the prom and she has the picture to prove that she did not go alone. For many years now, it has sat in our den, diligently collecting dust.

I was fourteen years old when Telley left home to go to college. For all intents and purposes, she is my second mother. When Mama put Reggie out of the house in 1989, this time for good, it was just Telley and me. The day we packed up her stuff and whisked her away to school in August of 1992, I cried like a toddler. My sister, my best friend and my surrogate mother, was leaving me. Forever. And if it wasn't for forever, it certainly did seem that way to me. I boohooed when Daddy and I were loading her clothes on the back of his 1989 midnight blue GMC Sierra pickup truck. The truck had cranberry stripes going all along its borders. I hated that truck. That truck took my Telley away from me.

I was still bawling as Mama, Daddy, Telley and I squeezed into the one seater as we left home. I cried from Hollywood to Columbia, home of the

University of South Carolina. The trip was about one hundred thirty-five miles and one hundred thirty-five million tears.

But once there, Ambrose Shepherd made all of us feel a little better about leaving Telley in that brick and mortar wilderness alone. Ambrose, or A.B. as we would all soon know him, was a student ambassador at USC. It was A.B.'s job to help the new students move into the dorms on moving day and help their parents get acclimated to the fact that their babies were going to have to be left at this big new place for the next four, five or six years.

When we pulled up to Baker Hall, a five-story maroon brick monstrosity, a young man ran up to the truck. As soon as the truck came to a rolling stop, he started unloading Telley's belongings from the back of it. It wasn't until he made one and a half trips up the five flights of stairs with two armfuls of Telley's worldly possessions that he found time enough to introduce himself.

"How's everyone? My name is Ambrose. Ambrose Shepherd. Most people call me A.B. So good to meet you all!"

We all then introduced ourselves to him and shook his hand. It was impossible not to like him. He had a mouth full of perfect teeth that were so white he could have been in a Crest commercial. He was Hershey Bar brown and about an inch or two shorter than Telley. He was wearing extra short khaki pants, a black polo shirt with vertical garnet stripes with USC emblazoned in garnet on the left pocket and Docksides that were nearly new. He was also muscular. I figured that was probably from years of moving heavy refrigerators, TVs, microwaves and computers up and down flights of stairs. Most of all, A.B. was a genuinely nice person. And motivated. He told us he was from a small town in South Carolina's Upstate, that he was a biology major and he planned to attend medical school at Duke.

As we attempted to say our heart-wrenching and tear-filled goodbyes to Telley, Daddy told A.B. to look after his only daughter for the rest of the day. The combination of A.B.'s career aspirations and the fact that he looked more like he was headed out sailing the Pee Dee River, as opposed to carrying the luggage of a bunch of scared freshman, really impressed Daddy.

"You look afta my daughter 'til she git tah know her way 'round ya, A.B."

I thought that was quite suppositious of Daddy, considering the fact that I was certain that Telley was going to navigate her way through this maze of statues, grotesquely huge buildings and twenty-five thousand kids in no time. It never occurred to me that Telley might have wanted this character to help her get to know her way around. What the hell did I know?

A.B. then did something Daddy did not do in his haste to find his daughter a protector. He asked Telley if it was it okay if he showed her around.

"Is that something that you would like, Tell? I'll make sure that you learn how to get to and from where you need to go for the next couple of days."

He had started to call my Telley "Tell", as if he'd known her for years. I was seething inside. He didn't know her like that! I figured Telley was going to let him have it. And good!

"I don't wanna have you go out your way or anything. I'll be okay."

"I'll be okay?!" Was that all she was going to tell this presumptuous asshole?! I suddenly hated him!

"Tell, didn't you hear da boy say dat he would show you around?" Daddy interjected. *"Let da boy show you whay tah go."*

Daddy had lost it and I wanted to punch him. We didn't know this guy from a can of paint and my father was telling him to look after my wonderful sister? Indisputably, Daddy had lost every bit of his good sense. That much was crystal clear!

First, this A.B. asshole calls Telley "Tell" and Daddy didn't say anything. Now, Daddy's urging Telley to let this person we don't know act as her campus tour guide?! I was furious! Nobody else was. On that hot August day, as we stood in the shadow of that huge dorm on the campus of the University of South Carolina, everyone, except yours truly, was cool. They were cool because the winds of change were blowing through for Telley and everyone, minus me of course, could see and feel it. I was hot because it was blazing out there and I was incensed at this guy for trying to take Telley from me.

"I promise, Tell, after you get to where you're going, I'll make myself scarce," he was saying.

But not only was this clown calling Telley "Tell", this pretentious jerk was calling Mama "Mama Gadson" and Daddy "Papa G". I detested him. But, at the same time, it was impossible not to like him. We all did.

"Well, okay A.B.," Telley told him. "But as soon as I get to where I am going, I'll make sure that you can be free to go and help other students. Deal?"

"That's a deal, Tell."

Up until that day that we met A.B., Telley had never had any male gentlemen callers. She never knew what it was like to be loved by a man. She never knew what it was like to be held by a man. She had never been kissed. Our man Ambrose Shepherd, pre-med at USC, was going to change all of that.

Telley and A.B. were inseparable, almost from the day that A.B. moved her in. A.B. loved Telley and Telley was in love with A.B.. Now they were never officially "together" at The University of South Carolina in Columbia, but as far as the Gadson family of Hollywood was concerned, they were in a stable and exclusive relationship. If you were to have asked any of the black students at USC at the time if A.B. and Telley were an item, they would have told you yes. They went out to dinner together. They went to the movies together. They even went to church together. As an unwritten rule, in the African-American community, if a young man and a young lady go to church together, they are not just friends, they are courting. They are dating and they are a couple. In the black community, it's just as simple as that. Over the course of two years, Telley's first two and A.B.'s last two of six and a half at USC, she helped him raise his GPA from a 1.3 to a 3.4.

What Mr. Pre-Med failed to mention to my parents that day was that while he made a great presentation of himself for parents and unsuspecting freshman girls on moving day with his jocular wit and disarming charm, he loved the cannabis sativa. He loved it so much in fact, that clearly the Mary Jane made him forget why he came to school. It seems as though the Maui wowie made Ambrose Shepherd, for three entire semesters before Telley arrived on campus, willfully and wantonly neglect to achieve any grade higher than a C-minus. Telley would change the direction of his whole academic career.

Ambrose Shepherd, one year after Telley met him, had his academic probation rescinded by the the school. Telley, even as a freshman, was driven and focused. She let A.B. know clearly that if they were going to be friends, he was going to have to get some actuation as well. He did in fact. In the fall of 1992, A.B. achieved a 3.98 grade point average. Telley would not let him fail. She taught him how to study. She taught him how to take more effective and clear notes in class. She taught him better test-taking preparation. Most of all, Telley encouraged him to be better than he fathomed he could ever be. He had been smoking weed since he was thirteen years old. The future minister implored the future doctor to quit smoking. He did, and as a result he was no longer lethargic. In the spring of 1993, A.B. achieved a perfect 4.0 GPA. He'd logged eighteen hours of biology classes and made an A in all of them. The following spring, Ambrose Carter Shepherd, a former reefer smoker on the verge of being kicked out of college, after six and a half years graduated with a degree in biology from The University of South Carolina. He even managed to get accepted into the medical school at The University of North Carolina.

While Telley was helping A.B. to rehab his grades, he pushed her to rehab her body. They joined a gym near campus and for two years, A.B. pushed Telley to her physical limits. He made her walk; she enjoyed walking so much, she started jogging. He made her do so many push-ups, she decided to try sit-ups. They lifted weights and then more weights. On A.B.'s graduation day in May of 1993, Telley was five dress sizes smaller and sixty pounds lighter than the day she walked onto campus. A.B. made my sister feel special and beautiful. Telley made A.B. feel as though he could achieve anything. One of Telley's best friends from high school, Malloy Early, would even join them at the gym sometimes. Malloy loved the fact that ever since they had entered college together, Telley had found happiness with A.B.. Malloy relished being with the two of them. They were all one big family.

Now the first time that A.B. came to Hollywood, Daddy gave him the spare key to Telley's 1989 taupe Mazda 626. As Daddy handed A.B. the shiny fat black key, he told him to "take care of my Telley." Daddy then dropped the key into A.B.'s flat palm. A.B. made sure that the oil was changed in that car. He kept it washed. He even made sure that it was kept waxed to a high gloss. He always kept it full of gas. If Telley had choir practice or a sorority meeting, A.B. went and got her car, picked her up from her dorm and dropped her off at the meeting. He waited outside in the car for her meetings to end, drove her back to her dorm and then parked the car. He was totally devoted to my sister and he didn't even want sex from her. The only thing that he wanted was for Telley to be her best. They would hold hands and A.B. would kiss her on top of her forehead at her hairline. That was it. Their relationship wasn't sexual and A.B. valued the fact that Telley was a virgin. He never wanted to deflower her. He never even attempted to. A.B. just wasn't that kind of guy. As her immediate family, we were glad about it because Telley had someone in her life who loved her and she didn't have to trade sex for that love. We didn't find out the real reason why until years later.

Malloy Early was simply gorgeous. And Malloy was well aware of it. Whenever Malloy walked into a room, all eyes were transfixed on Malloy. Malloy always kind of sucked the air out of any room. Malloy was one of my sister's best friends. Telley was the kind, affable and accommodating one. Malloy loved anyone who loved Malloy, which is why Malloy loved my sister. Physically, they were complete opposites. Malloy was spectacular, tall and sinuous. And Malloy never walked; Malloy glided. Malloy's lithe build was well suited for a Paris or Milan catwalk.

And you know those people who constantly refer to themselves in the third person? That was Malloy. Malloy would always say, "Tell, dey hate Malloy chile 'cause Malloy too much for dey life, hauney (honey). I overwhelm dey life. Umma hurricane dey jess aine ready fah. Da werl aine ready fah Malloy Early. Dey kan' do nuttin' wit' me, neitha."

Malloy was the color of nutmeg and, just like nutmeg, Malloy was an acquired taste. Some people liked Malloy. Most folks didn't. It always struck me as odd that Malloy and A.B. hit it off as well as they did. Telley loved it because most times a girl's friend may not get along with her boyfriend, but A.B. and Malloy were almost as close as Telley and A.B.. Telley loved the fact that the three, when they were together, were like one mind, one soul and one big laugh. Malloy was the life of the party, and A.B. was Telley's life.

After A.B. graduated, he still made regular trips to Columbia to see my sister. He would leave Chapel Hill on Friday and make the four-hour trip down to Columbia. On Friday night, he and Telley would go to the movies and dinner, just like old times. Then A.B. would take her back to campus while he went to his hotel room. Alone. They would hang out Saturday and then on Sunday go to church. A.B. would leave Columbia after church on Sunday following a hearty brunch with Telley. That was his routine two weekends a month for a couple of years. The only other person who knew his schedule on those weekends was Malloy and the guilt in knowing had taken a toll.

It was one of those moments in life that you don't ever expect. No one expects to get hit by a ton of bricks, but those slabs fell on my sister one day and she's been carrying the burden ever since. Telley and Malloy were riding to the Burger King near campus when her friend hung a millstone around her neck that she would carry for life.

"Hey Tell Tell, you evah wonda why A.B. aine nevah kiss you?"

"Yeah, he does."

"I mean like uh real kiss, Tell Tell."

"'Cause he knows Umma virgin."

"Telley, I love you."

"I love you too, Malloy."

"I want chu tah listen tah me an' understand dat I have struggled wit' how I was gonna tell you whah Um 'bout tah tell you for two years."

When she looked over at Malloy in her passenger seat, staring out of the window in tears, she knew that what was going to be said was serious because Malloy Early didn't cry.

"Telley, I know why A.B. aine nevah kissed you."

Telley wanted to vomit and she nearly lost control of her car. Malloy hadn't yet gotten to the point, but tension hung in the air like humidity on a summer day in Charleston.

"Telley, I aine nevah had uh girlfriend – you know dat. In high school, dey teased me 'cause I din ack like uh man. I din talk like one. I din walk like one. I guess dass why we hit it off. You was da nice fat girl an' I was da boy dat was too damn soft tah be on da football team, or da basketball team, or any team. Da same way dey teased you, dey teased me. I went to da prom only 'cause I din want people to think dat I was gay. I din even know I was gay. Da whole night I was jess hopin' that that girl would ax me tah take her home. Somein' changed in me dat night. I knew for certain, that night, that I was nevah gonna have a girlfriend or a wife. I jess figured dat I was gonna be single forever because I wasn't gay. I cun be gay."

"Malloy, you know I love you no matter what. Gay or not, you know I love you an' you know you always got uh friend in A.B.."

Malloy cut her off.

"When I got to USC, Telley, as big as da school was, I knew it was my chance tah staht my life ovah. I jess wanted tah staht ovah…"

Telley knew what Malloy was going to say. She was just trying to brace herself and keep her car on the road.

"Telley, A.B. was da first male friend dat I evah had. He was jess like you. He din judge me. He din ridicule me. He was jess good people. You know; we was jess friends, jess like y'all were."

"Malloy, what da hell you mean, 'jess like y'all were?!'"

"Telley, I din mean for it to happen. A.B. an' me was in da dorm one night just playin' aroun' wrestlin' an' one thing led to another an' we kissed; then we made love. Um sorry, Telley. I begged him tah tell you, but even afta two years of us messin' aroun', he still said dat he wun gay. I cun take it no mo'. I love you like uh sistah. I had tah tell you."

Telley was too numb to speak. She was too hurt to respond. She said Malloy kept speaking and every once in awhile she heard, "Tell Tell" or "Please say something." She said that the trees were just mammoth green and brown monsters on the side of Bush River Road, taunting her. They leaned in on her car and just hovered there imploring her to drive into one of them. Between her tears and Malloy's endless litany that Telley could not make out because her ears were so hot, and at this point everything Malloy said sounded like one big fat Greek lie, she doesn't know how she made it back to campus. She said that she doesn't know how Malloy made it to his dorm because she doesn't remember driving him there.

Over the course of the next few days, the tears in my sister's eyes turned into blood. Her initial shock and confusion became rage and mental proactivity. Hell hath no fury, right? To the layman she appeared fine. She went to her classes and her choir practices. She continued her obligations as a Resident Assistant in Baker Hall. She settled roommate disputes and made sure the maintenance people tended to any plumbing or electrical problems any of the girls in her dorm had.

That was on the surface. In her heart and mind, she'd already hatched a plan. She and a car load of her Tau Eta Tau sisters were going to drive the two hundred thirty miles to Chapel Hill, clad in fuchsia and mint, their official sorority colors and thrash A.B.'s ass black and blue. These girls may have been sagacious, demure, pretty and sophisticated, the virtual paragons of African-American womanhood, but Telley's sorors loved her dearly and they would go to war against anyone who would dare hurt her. It would be nothing for them to get baseball bats, bricks and pure cane sugar for gas tanks to deal with the medical school student and his car.

A.B. made a huge mistake. Ordinarily, in times like these, Telley prayed. This time, she wanted to make A.B. fall to his knees. She didn't want to calm down. She did not want to be rational. But the more Telley thought about it, she knew what she had to do.

After a few days, which seemed like years, she finally mustered the strength to make the call. Every muscle in her index finger ached with disillusionment as she dialed his number in her dorm room on her Mickey Mouse phone with the extra large pushbuttons. Telley loved Mickey Mouse. On any other day, that loveable rat would have made her feel oh so much better. She remembered thinking that she'd had that phone ever since freshman year at Academic Magnet. She laughed and cried as she waited for A.B. to pick up. She had a tendency to hold on to every thing that was comfortable and familiar. That fact is what made the lump in her throat so huge and this impending conversation so excruciating. As soon as he answered the phone, she began:

"Malloy told me what happened between y'all. I forgive you, but I hate chu!" She could hardly believe she had made the call or had said those words.

It took an aeon before he responded. "Telley, I'm not gay. Malloy – I …I don't love him. I know I'm not gay. It just seemed like that boy put some kinda spell on me, Telley. I don't love him. I'm not gay."

He kept saying that, over and over. He was trying to convince himself.

"I used to pray for you to kiss me, A.B.. I asked God was I so fat and ugly that the man who I loved and was in love with was just that unat- tracted to me that he couldn't stand to kiss me? I cried myself to sleep many nights."

"Telley, I love you. Please!"

"God forgives me all the time, A.B. I have to forgive you, but I cannot talk to you again. You hurt me too bad – too bad…."

Telley gently placed the phone back onto Mickey's ears. She and A.B. haven't spoken since.

CHAPTER 8

An Inglorious Sunday

Wesley United Methodist Church in Hollywood is what we in the black community call a "whosoever will, let him come" church. Wesley is a 6,500-square-foot, candy-apple red-brick edifice with thirteen wood-stained, ten- foot-long pews on each side of the middle aisle. The stained glass windows have pictures of John the Baptist baptizing Jesus in the Jordan River, Jonah in the belly of the great fish and Paul and Silas making their prison break.

Our congregation runs the gamut from professionals, politicians, drug addicts, alcoholics, prostitutes, whoremongers and other flawed individuals. They all attend my church. But what makes Wesley so different is that the atmosphere there is so open that, at any given time, you may find members of any of these groups openly confessing to any of a number of character maladies. One woman got up in church one Sunday and said, with a mixture of the liberation that can only come with being surrounded by a church full of black folk, and vindication, that she was "tie'ud."

"Church, good mahnin'. I done cry all night an' I done been sad fah too many years. Church, I tie'ud uh bein' run outta my house at all hours uh da night. I tie'ud uh bein' scayed all da time. I tie'ud uh lyin' nah my family. I tie'ud uh lyin' nah my church an' I tie'ud uh lyin' nah my own self. Church, I only been uh memba here uh short time, but Reverend Goodwin always say lyin' aine nuttin' but da devil's rhetoric an' tah continue tah tell da same lie ovah an' ovah only give da devil authority tah have dominion ovah ya life. Well, church, I come dis mahnin' tah silence da devil an' let him know dat he aine gah speak inta my life no mo'! It gah end right cha dis mahnin'!"

Now as Sister Freeman was testifying, the church was as hushed as the inside of a closed casket. No one knew what she was going to say or where she was coming from. But because in the three or four years that she was a member of Wesley, very few people had witnessed her speak above a whisper, and because she was growing louder and more authoritative with each word, at this point in her harangue, the congregation started responding to her. People shouted, "Tell it!," "Yeah girl, tell yo' story!," and "Jesus see what chu done been thu', gal!" The entire church was bobbing their heads in agreement. She had yet to tell us exactly what she was alluding to in her speech, yet most people suspected what she was going to say. Brother Ronald Freeman, husband of Sister Miranda Freeman, was known, at least in some circles, as a physically abusive husband. From the way that peoples' heads were ricocheting back and forth from the base of their necks to their throats, I think I may have been the only one in the church who didn't know that Brother Freeman was a wife beater. Everybody else was just waiting on Sister Freeman to say it. Subsequently, we were content to let her continue.

"Church, I kan' hole dis no longa; da Lawd done freed me dis mahnin' an' I takin' my freedom! Um takin' it!"

Reverend Goodwin was used to characters in our church taking moments of personal privilege because he was a character himself. He wore a jheri curled afro that was dyed sooty black, although his eyebrows, beard and goatee were bone white. He stood about six-foot-four and was quite frankly a bovine, apple juice colored man with a high tenor speaking voice that, as he grew more excited in his sermons, began to boom with just a tinge of baritone. And when he really got wound up, his mouth would grow frothy like a root beer float. White saliva would fly out his mouth when he got totally carried away in his Sunday messages.

Reverend Livingston Goodwin had grown accustomed to this type of atmosphere at Wesley. One Sunday, as we were waiting on church services to begin, Patricia Murphy and Donna Wright started fighting because Patricia, who was sitting only one seat behind Donna, overheard Donna talking to her sister.

"Yeah, she know 'bout me an' I gah keep on ridin' (having sex with) Elgin. She dough know whah tah do wit' um, so Umma satisfy um 'til we git tie'ud uh messin' 'roun."

Now judging by the way Patricia grabbed Donna and snatched her out of her seat, I think she had long suspected that her husband, Elgin, was having an affair with Sister Donna Wright.

I'm not saying that I condone Brother Elgin Murphy having sex with a woman who wasn't his wife. I was only twelve at the time. But even I realized that just about every man in Wesley had impure musings about Donna. She was what we in the black community called "thick". She had double D breasts and she had a grotesquely large, but shapely behind. She was a redbone, too – an inclusive and all-encompassing term that means that Donna's skin hue could have ranged in color from ruby to copper. Donna was closer to the ruby red side of the red bone spectrum. She always looked like she was waiting for a man to proposition her. I guess that's because most men in Wesley always looked as though they wanted to proposition her.

Donna was tantalizing and full of lust, but Patricia was a woman on a mission. She'd had five children by Elgin and because of that, I suppose, her body had turned on her. She always looked tired and you could see the lines in her face on Sunday morning. Her breasts pointed downward as if they were in constant prayer. I guess having five children suckle at your breasts, along with wearing ill-fitting bras, will create that optical effect. Patricia was not obese, but she was kind of awkwardly shaped. Her coconut skin tone was impeccable. She was angry with Elgin for cheating on her. She was choleric because each of those five children played a role in her body's physical erosion. Donna didn't stand a chance.

Patricia was choking Donna, yelling, "You think you could jess keep screwin' him an' I wasn't gone fine out, huh slut?! Did ju?!"

Patricia grabbed Donna by her hair and dragged her across two pews, banging her head as she went. Donna's body was flailing in one direction, her head in another. Then Patricia slammed her down on the hardwood floor aisle. She grabbed Donna's head, which by this time had developed a huge gash by the left temple and began to pummel her skull into the floor. People were screaming at Patricia to stop the assault.

"Stop dat gal before she kill uh (her)."

"Enough is enough!"

"Ahh Lawd, somebody get dat chile off uh her fo' e kill um."

"Patricia, think 'bout cha chern man!"

"Dat gal aine worse (worth) it."

Sister Rhodes, who was an emaciated-looking, chestnut-colored woman of nearly 75 years – and Donna's mama – ran up to the fight from her spot in the choir line in the back of the church. She jumped on Patricia's back to get her off Donna, but Patricia threw Sister Rhodes off and began to pummel her as well.

Livingston Goodwin just stood there at the podium, discombobulated and shell-shocked, where he was still waiting to welcome the choir into the church. He was frozen in that pulpit, looking utterly stupefied. When Brother Salisbury, Brother Crandall, Brother Reid and Brother Cyrus, who were the ushers on duty, had finally gotten the situation under control and had grabbed both women kicking and screaming out of the church, Reverend Goodwin – once we as a congregation lamented our "Lawd hammercy on us's", "Please help us Lawd's", and "Do Jesus's" – simply said once we all got quiet, "The Lord is in His Holy Temple, let all the earth keep silent before Him; we will now receive the choir."

We were so moved as a congregation with the spirit that had just flowed through our church, we just continued on with the services as if nothing had happened.

And now, some thirteen years later, it was Sister Miranda Freeman's turn to vent.

"Y'all, I aine nobaudy punchin' bag an' I rafruse (refuse) tah get beat up on anymo'!"

Reverend Goodwin arose from his seat as if to say, "Ok, you've said enough," but Sister Freeman continued.

"You know church, sometimes you think you done marrid uh good man, but den he turn out tah be uh monsta. Church, I din know I was gone have tah go thu' all dis jess tah say I got a husbin. My kids dough deserve dis no mo' church, an' I aine goin' thu' it no mo'! Y'all dough know whah iss like tah have uh man tell you he love you, den in da same breath turn 'roun an' choke you 'cause you whoa let him jump on top uh you. Y'all dough know whah I been thu' church; I been thu' pure-dee hell."

The church erupted in a hail of signifying and clapping. Someone shouted, "Gal, sho' I know whah you been thu'! You think you da only one?!" Then someone else exclaimed, "Gal, aine gah be dat way always!" Then another: "Gal, get out dey fo' you have tah kill um!" "Gal, get cho chern an' get outta dey!"

Her opus probably would have been a bit less uncomfortable if Brother Freeman wasn't sitting right next to his wife and stepchildren. But when Sister Freeman broke down and started crying, partly because she must have felt like she had just removed a cancerous tumor from her soul, and partly because she knew that Brother Freeman was first embarrassed, then indignant, then livid, that's when ole Livingston Goodwin saw his opening.

"Sister Freeman, Gawd is watchin' you an' He loves you! He knows what chu goin' thu'! Hole on, chile! Hole on to Gawd's unchangin' han' an' everything gah be aw'right! Just let Gawd work for you, chile! Please let Him work fah you!"

The Freemans, as a family, didn't come to church much after that Sunday. I heard that Ronald and Miranda Freeman divorced not even six months later. Brother Freeman still continued attending church regularly. He sang in the young adult choir and participated in other ways. Nobody asked about Sister Freeman anymore. And Brother Freeman never mentioned her again.

CHAPTER 9

Rape!

Right around the time that Daddy was charged with rape, people's true feelings about him came to light. They didn't hold back much about how they felt about us, either.

Mama got up in church one Sunday and asked for prayers for us, and that's when people started muttering. Sister Chastine, who was the biggest busybody of them all, started expatiating just under her breath while Mama was making the appeal for the church to pray for us.

"They finally got um, 'ey? O'wl be doggone if I pray fah any Herbit Gadson. He shoulda keep e han' to eself."

Then the choir members starting weighing in. "Oh man, Herbit," "Not again" and "Dag! Um so tie'ud uh da Mayor messin' up, man," spilled harmoniously from their lips. I turned around to look at the back door to gauge what the mood was in the rear of the church, to this day, as God is my witness, I know I saw Sister Albertha spout, "Good fah his black ass."

Sister Albertha wasn't alone in her sentiment because when I looked in the choir loft, I saw Sister Grimes whisper something to another woman.

They both burst into wide, toothy grins and muted laughter while Mama was asking for prayers for us.

"Church, please pray for us because this hasn't been easy, but God has prepared my family for a time such as this. He knows that if we say that we are Christians, we have to be ready for the times that will try us because truly church, there were times that tried Christ. Hallelujah! Praise You, God!"

Another one of the busybodies in our church, Sister Mary German, said that when Mama made that comment about Christ being tried, Judy Lee Smalls said, loud enough for her [Sister German] to hear sitting two rows back that, "Yeah, Christ maybe been tried, but Christ wasn't no whorin' behind drunk. Herbit need tah try an' get hisself some help 'cause I get da feelin' he goin' down for dis ya. Mmm hmm, the Gadsons aine gah be able tah get his ass outta dis. Herbit gah fry fah dis ya."

All of these words were uttered before Livingston Goodwin got a chance to get a good froth going in his sermon. Mama, Daddy, Telley and I, and even Reggie, knew that Daddy was in serious trouble after that Sunday in church. The Hollywood court of public opinion had tried him and found the defendant guilty. Daddy was going to need a miracle.

"I said 'no comment' then, I'm saying 'no comment' now," Daddy told the media when they asked about the crime of attempted criminal sexual conduct that he was accused of. That was the official malfeasance according to the South Carolina criminal code. In Hollywood, Charleston and the surrounding areas, however, that charge translated into rape. As the news cameras flashed in his face as he left the courthouse that day on February 26, 1991, he appeared to be his normal, confident and nattily dressed self. He had on a button-down light yellow Geoffrey Beene shirt, khaki slacks and brown Sebagos. He was the picture of self-assurance. He had no reason to fear anything. He was the Mayor of Hollywood.

But Daddy was scared to death. "No comment" may have been his official words to the news media that day, but a few days prior, after the state of South Carolina *very publicly* filed the rape charge, his unofficial and "off the record" words to Telley and me were far different.

"Kids, I am being framed for a crime I did not commit. Charleston has a huge problem wit' me 'cause Umma black man runnin' uh town. Yo' Daddy love y'all. I aine no rapist."

As Daddy spoke with us, he was sitting in the La-Z-Boy, as sober as he could be that night. Telley was sitting on one end of the green argyle couch; I was sitting on the other. We were both transfixed on him.

"Daddy, you goin' nah jail?" Telley fired the question at him as if she was shooting it out of one of those cannons on The Battery downtown.

"No, Tell, I'm not goin' nah jail. Daddy gone fight dis, 'cause yo' daddy is completely innocent. I din rape nobody."

I interrupted: "Daddy, the kids teasin' me at school 'cause dey say you rape dat girl an' you goin' nah jail fo' forty years. Dey keep messin' wit' me, talkin' 'bout 'Fuck yo' daddy, Shaytee. Yeah he rape dat bitch. Y'all maufuckas gah be broke 'cause e gah take uh million dahliz fah y'all tah git e ass outta all da trouble he in. Fuck yo' rapin' ass daddy, nigga!'"

Daddy was completely aghast at the vitriol that spewed forth from my lips. The only thing that he could do is look off into the distance and painfully shake his head. He grabbed a cigarette from the Salem Regular pack that perpetually rested on the arm of his recliner. He pulled out the elephant tusk colored lighter that was always lodged in between the plastic and the pack. The cigarette trembled as he placed it to his lips. When he popped the lighter and the bowels of hell opened up at the end of it, he quickly put the flame to the end of the dynamite stick for comfort. He nervously and furiously shook his right leg and crossed it over the left at the knees. He blew the billow of smoke skyward. Daddy then took his right thumb and index finger and started gently, but deliberately, pulling at his right eyelashes. He always did that when he was too mad or too sad to speak. Children can be so cruel.

Sixth, seventh and eighth graders can be downright pernicious. I was in the eighth grade at Timothy D. Skylar Middle School. The school was named for a racist white local area Superindent of Education who sought to "keep good niggers good by givin' um a foundation for dey life so dey will always know dey place." He was actually quoted as saying that. Timothy

Dilligard Skylar would be rolling over in his grave in hell if he knew that his "good niggers" had renamed his school "Timmy Sky High" because of the proliferation of great marijuana smokers we had on campus between the ages of eleven and fifteen. The fourteen- and fifteen- year olds renamed the school "Sky High" because that was the closest to high school that their chemically altered brains were going to allow them to get, save for social promotion. But both the overaged kids and kids in their proper grades thought that my father was a rapist. They obviously hypothesized that I was confused about the facts of the case because they felt it was their duty to bring me up to speed on the issue of my father's guilt.

Timmy Sky was ground zero for the persecution of the Mayor of Hollywood's youngest child. Telley went to Academic Magnet downtown. She was far enough removed from the oppression I had to endure in Hollywood. Charleston was buzzing about the incident, but Hollywood was roaring about it. The kids roared so loudly that I nearly lost my hearing. And my sanity.

Daddy blew smoke and shook his leg for what seemed like a fortnight before he could manage a response.

"Shay, listen. Dem kids is kids, an' kids gonna say mean things. But you gotta believe Daddy. I din rape no girl. She want money. She want the notoriety dat comes wit' uh story like dis. Yo' daddy aine touch nobody."

"Daddy, why dey sayin' you rape her den?" Was the entire world lying on him?

"All I did was pick dis girl up an' give her a ride to work. Some ole kinda way, she sayin' I rape her. Daddy love y'all too much to do uh thing like dat. You believe Daddy, right? Right?"

I desperately wanted to. "I believe you, Daddy."

"Daddy love you, boy."

"I love you too, Daddy."

My father loved me so much that on that February day in 1991 that he raped – or did not rape – that girl, he constructed for me my very own twenty-nine thousand-square-foot prison on the campus of Timmy Sky High Middle School. I was serving my sentence there for a crime I did not commit. It was a blessing in disguise, I suppose, because out of the two hundred thirty-five kids there, I was the only inmate. Sky High Middle served free breakfast and lunch, for those who qualified, in the prison mess hall, or the school cafeteria. I don't know which name is more apropos because I only went in there once after Daddy decided to, or not to, "rape" that girl and ruin my life.

The kids talked about Daddy so fiercely that I couldn't bring myself to go back into the cafeteria the day after I got murdered by the school's one hundred thirty-five-person hit squad. The seventh and eighth graders ate lunch together. Since I was still in the dark about whether Daddy did it, some of those in the lynch mob lifted up their torches so they could see the look on my battered and bruised face; first to bring the light of the truth to me, and second so the others could have enough light to know exactly where to aim their guns. It was the Orangeburg Massacre all over again. They were the state police and I was Daddy. Then, they started shooting. The big difference between Herbert Gadson then, and this reincarnation of him twenty-three years later, was that I didn't have anywhere to run.

Some of the kids told me, most times with insidious blasé, "Ey Shaytee, you do know yo' daddy gah get fuck in e ass when he go tah prison, right? I mean, you do *know* dat, enny?"

"Yeah nigga, ya daddy gah come outta prison with no teet' (teeth) 'cause dem boy gah knock all e teet' out so he kin suck dey dick betta."

"Man fuck uh Mayor an' fuck you, wit' cha big ass head."

I carried my rectangular, yellow compartmentalized lunch tray to my seat on the far end of the cafeteria to eat by myself. I took my perp walk from the lunch line walking past several groups of kids who were asking me why my daddy couldn't "jess keep e dick up in yo mama pussy instead uh fuckin' uh young ass gal." The lunchroom/prison mess hall was also the school auditorium. It had a big stage complete with a velvet navy blue curtain with "TDS", Sky High Middle's namesake's initials embossed in Navajo white, emblazoned on it. The beige cement blocks that lined its walls were closing in on me as I walked the Green Mile to my seat. Not even John Coffey could have helped me.

I couldn't breathe. I felt as if I was walking to my execution and that seat on the far end of the huge lunchroom/mess hall that I was approaching was my electric chair. I felt like taking that yellow lunch tray and bashing one of those shit talking kids upside their heads with it. I was then going to jam the pizza and red jello in their mouths and tell them to suck on that since my daddy was going to have to suck dicks in prison.

Next, I was going to stomp one of the poor bastards to death with my Hush Puppies as I yelled, "Fuck you and fuck all uh y'all!" The last thing I planned to do was run up on that stage, up the three side steps, and across the navy blue and Navajo official school colored tiled floors and scream, "Fah each one uh y'all shit talkin' maufuckas who decided to fuck wit' me, I got a message fah y'all asses: 'If ya aine one uh da ones talkin' shit about my daddy, keep eatin' ya lunch an' close ya ears. But if you are one uh those maufuckas, dis fah you: INSTEAD UH FUCKIN' WIT' ME, Y'ALL DUMB ASS MAUFUCKAS NEED TAH BE LEARNIN' HOW TAH READ- FUCKIN' ILLITERATE ASS BASTIDS! I FUCKIN' HATE DIS RAHTODDED (RETARDED) ASS SCHOOL! I DIN WANNA COME TO DIS BITCH NO WAY! I HATE ALL Y'ALL MAU-FUCKAS WHO TALKIN' SHIT! QUIT FUCKIN' WIT' MAAAAY!'"

I didn't, of course. On the long walk home to my seat that day, I learned that there are about a billion block-shaped lines in your average prison mess hall/school cafeteria linoleum floor pattern. I know that because I counted each block. I was looking down at the floor because I didn't want the kids to see the monsoon that was materializing in my eyes.

Hollywood mayor charged in assault on young woman

FEB 2 6 1991

By RHESA VERSOLA
Of the Post-Courier staff

Hollywood Mayor Herbert Gadson turned himself in to authorities Monday after he was accused of trying to sexually assault a young woman.

Gadson is charged with assault with intent to commit criminal sexual conduct, according to court records. He was released after posting a $35,000 bond set by Magistrate Jack I. Guedalia.

"We're all human," said Linda Gadson, the mayor's wife. "We're not tried in the press. We're tried in the courtroom. He is innocent and these are just allegations."

A 20-year-old woman told Charleston County Sheriff's deputies that she accepted a ride to work Saturday from a man she recognized. The woman told investigators she was driven to a secluded area and then fondled, deputies said.

Afterward, the man told the woman he would drive her to a motel, according to court records. The woman told investigators she jumped out of the car when the man stopped at a traffic light at Main Road and U.S. Highway 17, a deputy said.

Gadson was a three-term town councilman before he was elected mayor of Hollywood in 1989. He holds bachelor's and master's degrees from the University of South Carolina.

The navy blue and Navajo big square blocks all started to look the same to me. I started thinking to myself that they may start to get angry with me because I couldn't distinguish the blue from the white anymore.

It disturbed me as I walked because those blocks became my only friends that day. I gave them all names as I walked to my seat. The only drawback was because my eyes had flooded as badly as downtown Charleston when it rains, I couldn't tell them apart. The blocks stuck with me that day. They held me upright. They encouraged me not to faint and fall on them because then the mean kids would have won. They also told me that smashing my head on top of them as I hit the ground might have killed me. So I just kept walking to my seat. The tears streamed down my face. The water just kind of turned my friends on the floor from distinct blue and white to meaningless shades of tear clear.

The good thing about my time in lock-up was that I never had to stay there overnight. Each day at 3:15 pm, they allowed me to leave. I had home visitation until 8:20 the next morning. Mama would drive me down to the prison/school again the next day so that the verbal shanking could commence.

Daddy left two hundred thirty-four children to be my wardens after the "rape" happened, or didn't happen. They were nice enough to let me go from cell to cell and change classes with them when the bell for each new period rang. Sky High Middle School/Prison had no bars. It had no wire fencing. It was a psychological and emotional jail that those kids constructed for me. I allowed myself to enter and leave it as they deemed fit.

The correctional officers, who pretended to be teachers, didn't know, couldn't see or couldn't hear the mean kids flog me for the crime of rape. I was the rapist. I was taunted, teased and cut by sharpened pink tongues because the man they were looking for wasn't in the police line-up. Since I looked just like him, I guess I was going to have to go down for rape. It didn't matter that I was a virgin. It was the worst case of mistaken identity in the history of Hollywood.

For the rest of the school term, I had to hear that the Town of Hollywood had "uh ole rapin' ass Mayor." And that wasn't even my biggest problem. Victor Crable, along with the other mean kids, since I arrived at Sky High Middle, took a perverse pleasure in letting me know just how huge my head was. They also took some joy out of telling me that my circular-framed, coffee-colored glasses were "too fuckin' big fo' yo' big ass head an' long ass face."

Before I came to Sky High, I attended a predominately white Christian school where I spent sixth and seventh grades. I loved that school and the people there loved me. I was a star on the junior varsity basketball team. But while Mama and Daddy agreed the school was great, it wasn't reality. They said that I was going to have to live in the real world with real problems one day and the cocoon of a milk-white private school wasn't going to prepare me for living on this planet as a black man. Having to leave Evangel Christian School devastated me. Knowing that I was going to Sky High Middle for eighth grade demoralized me.

I don't know if the white kids, and the smattering of black kids who went to Evangel Christian School, or E.C.S. as we called it, realized that my head was big or not. Maybe they just didn't want to tell me. Either way, Victor, who was a curly haired, molasses-skinned mountain of a boy at Sky High, decided that he was going to personally monitor the growth of my head each day.

"I know yo' mama pussy buss oh'em (open) when she had ju tryna push dat big ass head out; I know dat shit. Good thing you been yo' mama lass chile 'cause if you had uh lil' bubba uh (or) sistah, yo' mama woulda had to have uh C-Section. An' why dem glasses so fuckin' big? Goddamn boy, you bline? I know you aine fuckin' uh damn thing Shaytee, 'cause aine no girl fuckin' you wit' dat big ass head an' dem zifuckin'focal glasses. *And* yo' daddy done rape dat bitch? You jess all da way fucked up, boy!"

I think I heard him recite that exact same homily at least three times a day from the end of February to June 2, 1991. The only reason that I didn't hear him call me everything but a child of God on June 3rd was because June 2nd was the last day of school. I heard it in P.E., English and Algebra. I heard it every day and everywhere. It wouldn't surprise me at all if Victor practiced his speech for me when he went home at night. He must have, because he knew it far too well. Each day and each time he would start shanking me, some of the children would laugh like hyenas at the bloodletting. You would have deduced that every day was the first day they had seen this baby lion cub get his flesh torn off his bones by Victor the Head Hyena.

What Daddy failed to mention to my sister and me was that he was drunk when he did, or did not, "rape" that girl. He drove a twenty-year-old girl to a secluded area and fondled her. Allegedly. After he did that, he told this woman that he was going to drive her to a motel. The girl got scared on the way to the motel. She then jumped out of Daddy's car at a traffic light. Allegedly. While his official words to the media were quotidian, and his unofficial words to Telley and me heartfelt, he was downright unconvincing when Mama deposed him.

"Linda, I din rape dat betch!"

"Herbert, how you know whah you did? Nigga, you was drunk! Drunk Herbert! Da gal say you did it!"

Now Telley and I may have been in our beds with our eyes closed, but we were far from asleep. We heard everything that was going on in the den.

"Linda, you think I rape dat betch, don't chu? Um tellin' you dis gal lyin' her ass off!"

"Herbert, you uh no good ass nigga an' yo' dick do all yo' thinkin' fah you! You aine think 'bout me or dese kids. You was drinkin', an' you did it an' yo' ass goin' nah jail! Wudda hell wrong wit' chu, man?!"

"Aine uh damn thing wrong wit' me 'cept I got uh wife who believe any damn thing anybody tell her! I dough give uh fuck about wudda werl say Linda. All I care 'bout is whah you an' dese chern say! Dass all I care 'bout."

"Yeah, you care wudda werl say aw'right. Herbert, you done mess up. You done mess up real bad!"

Jesus Christ himself couldn't have told me after that night that Daddy wasn't going to jail. Mama basically said so herself. I started preparing myself from that night on for the reality that awaited me. I was going to be a statistic: another black boy with a black daddy in prison.

The charge of attempted rape in the state of South Carolina carries a thirty-five thousand dollar fine and a four-decade-long prison sentence. More than anything else, Daddy needed a good lawyer. Mama and Daddy also found out during this period that because they had done so much good for Hollywood and the surrounding communities, Daddy had stored up enough good will that someone came up with the idea for a legal defense fund. One of Daddy's trusted advisers, Leon Youngblood, told him this the day after the Mayor of Hollywood got arrested for attempted criminal sexual conduct.

"Herbit, I dough know if you did it or if you din do it. All I know is dat you shun have tah fry fah dis. We got tah raise some money."

Leon Youngblood was a mechanic by trade. He looked the part as well. He was a cigar-chewing, broad-chested, deliberate man. He was the color of the motor oil that he put in the car engines that he fixed. He was as tough as a fan belt. Most importantly, he had the ear and respect of a ton of people in my town. He was a power broker, and when he talked people didn't just listen, they listened for instructions. He could fix any type of machine you took to his garage. I wasn't sure if he could fix the Mayor of Hollywood's life that had corroded in front of our very eyes like a car battery. Daddy was going to soon find out. We all were.

Mr. Leon assembled a team of folks who were friends of the Gadson family and the movers and shakers of Hollywood. Their purpose was to save Daddy from getting recalled by the governor of South Carolina, and to keep him out of prison. In short, Mr. Leon and his wife, Miss Bernice, James and Jackie Heyward, Chrissy Smith, Aunt Sissy and Uncle Benjamin, and a few others, were to raise money to save Daddy.

They, along with Mama and Daddy, met at our house every Sunday after church for three months and came up with every conceivable idea that you could think of to try and scrape up some cash. They received donations from some of the wealthiest people in the greater Charleston area. They sold crab, fish and fried chicken dinners. They had yard sales. They even gave money to the cause out of their own pockets. But after all was said and done, Team Save Herbert from Going to Jail was still fifteen thousand dollars short. The trial was fast approaching.

Mama was, and is, a beloved, almost cult-like figure in Hollywood. Because of this, she developed close relationships with quite a few very wealthy white folks. As a matter of fact, one of her best friends in the world was a white woman who happened to be a multimillionaire. She was a tow-haired, mazarine-eyed, delicate and porcelain-skinned woman, and exactly like Mama she loved Jesus Christ with all of her mind, soul and might. Anne Hennessee and Mama were as close as sisters. For all intents and purposes, Mama and Anne were sisters. One day, after they had finished praying together, Anne nonchalantly asked Mama, "Linda, how much do you all need for Herbert's legal defense?"

"Anne, we need fifteen thousand dollars. The trial is less than a month away and I trust God."

"Linda, what are you all going to do?"

"We gone pray for a miracle."

"Linda, I love you and regardless of whether Herbert did this or not, the fact is he cannot and should not hang for this." Anne then reached into her pocketbook, pulled out her checkbook, ripped a check from it and started scribbling away.

Anne handed her the check, kissed her softly on the cheek and started hugging her. With tears in her white sister's eyes, Mama said Anne uttered these words: "God's gonna make a way for you, Linda. He always will." Anne then got up and walked out of our house.

Mama, as was her Sunday ritual, conducted a symphony of culinary harmonies. The hand blender mixed the pancake batter. The big sterling silver spoon clanged against the side of the cast iron pot as she stirred the butter into the Quaker grits and the sizzle and pop of the bacon, sausage patties, sausage links and salmon all synchronized in concert. This was always music to my ears as I stood by the refrigerator, or walked back and forth from the den into the kitchen. I could hardly wait for Mama to place the bacon in the silver aluminum pan on the side of the pea green stove top. As I waited for the ten or twelve pieces of paper towels inside of the metal pan to absorb my bacon grease, as if on cue, with all the phlegmatism she could muster, Mama blurted out over the brunch concert, "Herbert, I know for a fact that you are not going to jail!"

Daddy ran past me. I'd heard the click-clack of the recliner, signaling that he had pulled the recliner from a lying to a seated position; almost in unison, I'd heard him clear his throat. He sprinted from the den to the kitchen so quickly, his Sunday after church uniform of a white V-neck t-shirt and white briefs, covered by his trusted navy blue flannel robe, was upon me in the kitchen before I could blink.

"Gal, whah you say?!"

"See Herbert, the Lord wants you to humble yourself to Him. He wants to save your life. You are King David, Herbert Gadson; Hollywood is your Israel. The Lord wants you to repent. Salvation is free Herbert, if you want it. Legal defenses, however, are not."

Mama handed the check from Anne over to Daddy. He screamed.

The kitchen and the den were basically the same room, but we never ate together. We loved each other so much we couldn't stomach one another long enough to eat at the circular maple wood table just off the side of the kitchen. Our kitchen was the most underused and overused room in the house. We never ate in the there because we could not stand to be on top of each other at a dinner table, talking about our day, what we did and who we did it with. We, as a family, valued our personal space. Quite frankly, what we wanted to do most at meal time was watch television. And we did not want to watch television together like a real family, either. When Daddy suggested that Sunday that we sit down as a family for breakfast, my mouth dropped.

Normally, we would take our food out of the kitchen and into our bedrooms. Daddy would eat in the den in his La-Z-Boy. On Sundays, he loved doing this while watching padded Eagles, Bengals, Colts and Falcons with helmets destroy each other in a friendly game of football on CBS. He would sit in his recliner, shaking his right leg as it crossed the left leg at the ankles. Then, he would clear his throat. Ad nauseum. His robe would move a million miles a minute as his leg shook. My sister ate in her room. Reggie ate at the homes of various women, at friends' houses, at the Charleston County Detention Center, Lieber State Prison, or MacDougall Correctional Institution. I ate in my room. Mama cooked, washed dishes and ate in the kitchen. This was fine dining on Sunday in our house.

Daddy summoned all of us to the kitchen table. By this time, he had tucked "The Check" in his navy blue pocket on the side of his robe.

"We gah eat tagetha 'cause da Lawd done deliver dis family. I gah fight like I aine nevah fight before. I done – we done – now got da tools tah fight wit'. Da Lawd done ansa! Praise da Lawd! Thank ya, Jesis! Lawd, I know you aine been gah let me fall!"

I don't think I'd ever seen Daddy that happy before or since. I'd definitely never seen him praise the Lord like that before or after that morning. I could see him taking in the mundane sights and sounds of our kitchen. The Nilla Wafers, Honey Maid Graham Crackers and Oreos that Mama kept on that counter, the humming of the big white refrigerator and the maple wood cabinets, all seemed to reassure him. He knew that at least he had a fighting chance against all the years in prison. He'd been fighting all of his life so he didn't mind one more brawl.

As good fortune for Daddy would have it, when the word spread that the "Save Herbert from Going to Jail" defense fund was starting to make a dent in the legal fees and Daddy was hiring one of the best criminal defense attorneys in the "Holy City", the word got around to Daddy's accuser that she was going to be grilled ruthlessly if she testified on her own behalf. It was discovered that the young lady had a less than stellar past which was going to cast doubt as to the validity of her current claim. Mere days before trial was set to begin, the state dropped the charges because she refused to cooperate. Daddy's accuser didn't even appear at the bond hearing. We didn't know the rationale behind the decision at the time, but we would later uncover that Granddaddy arranged to have a duffel bag delivered to the young lady. The bag contained thirteen thousand dollars. It was ransom for the freedom, restoration of normal life and political career of his only son. The Hollywood grapevine ejaculated that the reason Daddy was so adamant in his denial of the rape was because he and the young lady had more than a few sexual liaisons prior to the day of the incident. Some people said you could actually classify it as full bore affair. When Daddy wouldn't get up off the money she requested for a Honda Accord, she vowed to make him pay for it. One way or the other. Reggie was actually the one that brokered the deal. My brother and she had sex sporadically when they were in high school. He was still extremely cordial with her and he called her one day. He asked if there was a dollar figure that would make this situation "go away." When she named her price, Reggie got Granddaddy on the horn. LeMarion Gadson played the "fixer" like he always did. Granddaddy never admitted to Daddy the truth about how he got him out of forty years in prison. When the details of the Hollywood (California) style "arrangement" emerged years later, Daddy asked Granddaddy if it was true. LeMarion lied to the Mayor of Hollywood, South Carolina, and said he had no idea what he was talking about. As it turned out, Daddy didn't even need that check that Anne had written for fifteen thousand dollars that day in Mama's prayer room.

Aside from the den, the living room was the largest room in our house. It was two hundred sixty square feet. It had wall-to-wall brown shag carpeting. The walls were cornsilk in color. Despite its' humdrum motif and color scheme, it was a raucous den of iniquity. The TV and record player were in there. We watched early eighties TV shows in there that were rife with violence. We listened to Prince and Michael Jackson sing their hearts out on that record player in there. We even had dance contests in there. By the time Mama had the one-eyed monster and the Apollo Theater moved out of the living room after her Great Awakening, there were permanent indentures left in the floor from their once mighty presence. Those impressions remaining in the floor, in the far right corner of the room never to be vacuumed away, were a constant reminder to Linda Gadson of the sin she had to stamp out daily. Mama would have even made John F. Whitley shout, "*Amen!*"

About three months or so after Mama accepted Jesus Christ as her Lord and personal savior in 1986, and after she exorcised the demon spirits of the nightclub and the TV out of our living room, she turned it into the prayer room. She started praying without ceasing in there as soon as she got saved. But the living room didn't get smitten on its Damascus Road, change its name from Saul to Paul and go out into Hollywood and then all the world and preach the gospel – until Mama got her prayer stool.

Mama's prayer stool was a solid mahogany wood masterpiece with a red velvet pillow on top of it. It was sent direct from heaven, via this affluent white couple on Kiawah, just for her. The thick wooden stool curled at its edges. When we prayed, kneeling beside it with our elbows embedded in the red velvet and our fingers interlocked a la *The Praying Hands*, we could always feel the presence of God around us. We used it every day, and the velvet pillow on top of it eventually started sliding off because the adhesive holding the pillow to the wood had long since given away. Mama said it was caused by "years of prayers and tears".

Mama called Mr. Matthews and asked him if he could restore the three-foot-long and one-foot-tall work of art back to its former glory. Mr. Matthews was a pot-bellied, salt and pepper and wavy-haired russet-colored man, who did everything slowly and purposefully. He said that was the hallmark of a "master wood worker." It took him, in his words, "two tejess an' reff (tedious and rough) weeks," but that worn and tattered mahogany wood shined when he was done. The red velvet pillow looked like new. The living room's metamorphosis was complete. Much like the Apostle Paul, the living room that once thought, acted and spoke like a child had put away the childish things. The room had matured. It was now officially the prayer room. Herbert Gadson didn't like the new digs. He didn't like them one bit.

"Turn my house into uh goddamn church. Sick uh dis shit! 'Nuff uh (enough of) one thing is uh damn 'nuff, now!" It seemed like every time Daddy went down the hallway and had to decide whether he was going to turn to the right, in the direction of the prayer room to get to the kitchen, or turn to the left and detour through the den, he started talking to himself. He evangelized loudly under his breath about the fact that his house was no longer "my house." Daddy reasoned that slowly but surely his home had become a place of worship. He was absolutely correct. The sad part about it, for him, was that the church had invaded his home and he had no choice but to confront it. Much like the St. Louis Arch is the "Gateway to the West," our kitchen was the "Gateway to the Gadsons." So each day, Daddy was left with a decision to make. If he wanted to leave or enter his home, or didn't want to starve to death, he had to decide whether or not he wanted to go through the den, or go to church. Daddy always took the den less traveled.

Our house had indeed become a cathedral of praise. Every day at 4 a.m. we would hear Mama praying, singing and praising the Lord – loudly. When she woke up, the entire house had to rise, shine and give God the glory. The prayer room was the one place in all of Hollywood that unsaved wretches and saved saints alike could come get food vouchers, marriage counseling, applications for home repairs and light bills paid. Most of them almost always left confessing or reaffirming Jesus as their Lord and Savior. Mama had cornered the market in Hollywood on improving the lives of people. She showed them that if they lifted their eyes to the hills, as instructed in Psalm 121, they would indeed receive their help.

"Herbert, this is what happens when you trust God for everything you need. He'll give you anything you ask for," Mama told Daddy that as they stood in the kitchen while she cooked on that Sunday afternoon after the Friday evening when Anne wrote her the check. That's how we referred to it in our house. "The Check," much like any significant event in history, only needed to have the "The" placed in front of it to signify its importance and to brandish it into lore. There were many sicknesses after "The Plague" in Europe during the medieval times. There were many before it, but only one is known as "The Black Death." "The Crash" of 1929 of the stock market preceded the 1987 crash, but only one caused "The Great Depression." There had been many checks written and received in the history of the Gadson family. Checks for the mortgage were written each month. Mama and Daddy got paychecks every two weeks. There were also my checks for school lunch for the week that were written every week from the early to the late '80s.

There was the occasional bounced check in which Mama would always have to go to the bank and personally meet with the bank president to rectify. She would pray for him, and then tell him that if he didn't offer sufficient recourse for the situation, her Lord thy God in heaven would smite him tout de suite. Right there on the spot. Mama would then tell that white man that he was required to correct the obvious bank oversight and that he was required to do it by law – God's law. She would tell him that she was a tither and that she had no money to pay the returned check fee. She would then tell the now rose-colored white man that she rendered unto Caesar that which was Caesar's, and on that day, and at that time, she intended to render no more. She would reiterate for the man the fact that she had no intention of paying the returned check fee because she did not have the money. Then as the fuchsia tinged white man looked across the desk at my mother, first with a face that was incredulous, then befuddled, Mama would laugh her patented "Linda Gadson chuckle". That chuckle was a mixture of confidence and more fearlessness than you could shake a stick at. It lasted about five seconds. "HA HA HA HA HA HA." It demoralized; then it disarmed. After the chuckle, Mama would look the powerful colored white man sitting across the table from her dead in his eyes, who at this point was bewildered and say, "I'm not worried about that check because I trust God." The confused, florid white man would then laugh, then proceed to laugh uproariously.

Later, when Mama would go into a bank, after she created a healing oil, she would pour it all over the bank lobby. She would then pour oil in the bank president's swank office. Then she would apply oil to him. My mama has never been refused a loan or a refinance. She helped put two kids through undergraduate schools and the one through seminary. She has also never paid a returned check fee because the bank president would always classify them as a "bank error".

Much like The Crash of 1929 caused The Great Depression in America, The Check of 1991 caused "The Great Resurrection" in the Gadson Family.

Mama has said on many occasions, when times get tough for her, Anne's words still echo in her spirit as clearly today as they did when she first uttered them.

"God's gonna make a way for you, Linda. He always will."

The Evening Post, Charleston

Mayor Gadson Re-Elected In Hollywood

By SCHUYLER KROPF
Of the Post-Courier staff

Hollywood Mayor Herbert Gadson was re-elected to a second term Tuesday, beating challenger Harold J. Dukes by 155 votes.

Unofficial returns show Gadson collected 369 votes to Dukes' 214.

In the race for Town Council, incumbent MacKenneth Rivers was defeated by newcomer Charlie Porter III. Rivers was the only incumbent not to be returned to office out of four seats up for election.

Other winners on council include incumbents Moses Middleton, 489 votes; Willie Robertson, 402 votes; and Jackie Seward, 372 votes.

Tuesday's losers included Rivers, with 218 votes, and former mayor Lela W. Dickerson with 219 votes.

The results will be certified at Town Hall at noon Thursday, said Josephine B. Youngblood, chairman of Hollywood's Election Commission.

After the election, Gadson said he was pleased with the results. He said his support soared in the days after a sexual assault charge against him was dropped.

"We felt confident we could win with the allegations there," he said. "But since the allegations were dropped, the cloud was totally lifted."

The charge, filed by a 20-year-old woman, was dropped when she declined to cooperate with prosecutors.

Dukes said he saw no reason to protest the results. "It was a good race. I was a little disappointed, but that's the name of the game," he said.

Hollywood, a rural town in southern Charleston County, has an estimated 1,000 registered voters.

CHAPTER 10

Crown Royal Communion

At some point in our lives, Reggie, Telley and I have all come to fisticuffs with the Mayor, simply because Daddy was being Daddy. The difference between the three of us was that Reggie and I would beat and batter him out of his drunken stupor and wouldn't care where he fell because he wounded us emotionally. Telley would beat the hell out of him, then clean him up and pray for him despite his wounding her emotionally.

Reggie and I were Daddy's sons, to be certain, but Telley was exclusively Linda Gadson's daughter. Telley often says, "How can I preach the word of God if I let hate build in my heart for Daddy? Worse yet, how could I ever preach again if that hate were to consume me?" But that was Telley for you. She took my mother's teachings of "forgiveness at all costs, even at the risk of your own comfort," to heart. She not only applied it to Daddy but, in a strange way, because she was able to absolve him for all the havoc he wreaked, he became almost a demigod to her.

She knew Daddy was reprobate, but she begged Mama not to divorce him. For far too many years, Mama listened to her. As Daddy's only daughter, Telley in her cerebrum, was in the business of reconstructing what he represented to others. Almost without fail, whenever there was a "Daddy driven" crisis in our lives, Telley would be the first to say, "Dass my daddy and Umma protect my daddy. He aine perfect, but Umma do my best tah take care uh him." She felt that way because that is exactly how Mama would have felt if she were Telley. If any daughter was ever an extension of her mother, Telley was that daughter of Linda Dingle Gadson. Herbert Gadson prepared her extensively for the mission of bringing souls to Christ, because for more than twenty years Telley watched Mama try to bring Daddy's soul to Him.

Before Daddy left home for good in 2002, never to return, he had taken an extended leave of absence from 6571 Hwy 162 in Hollywood a few years beforehand. The woman he had been seeing decided that since Daddy had paid for the new roof on her house, it was only logical that he stay with her full time to enjoy it. Mama had to pass the woman's house every day on her way to work. Sometimes she would see Daddy's car in the yard, sometimes she wouldn't. But eventually, as was Daddy's usual pattern with outside woman, he eventually grew tired of the routine. He wanted to return home. Mama said the only way that she could allow him to come back was if he sought treatment for his alcohol problem. Telley, within a week's time, had secured Daddy a spot in a rehabilitation center in North Carolina, had his mail forwarded there and had him packed and ready to go. On the day that Daddy was slated to leave, he called the house and said, "'Ey, Tell, I dough think Umma be able to go."

"Why not, Daddy?"

"'Cause Mary said she need me here to help her out with her bills."

"Do you wanna go, Daddy?"

"Yeah, Tell, I wanna to go, but Mary gah be in a bad sitcha'ation if I leave."

Daddy's concubine heard his end of the conversation and made the mistake of her life by snatching the phone out of his hands.

"Look Telley, yo' daddy uh grown man an' he can make his ownt decision. He aine goin' tah no rehab. He gah stay right cha whay he belong; wit' me! Y'all kan' stop him from stayin' ya. He uh grown man an' he my man. Yo' Daddy gah be here long as he like an' it aine uh thing nobody kin do 'bout it! Now!"

That's when the Reverend Telley Gadson, a highly respected minister in good standing with the South Carolina Annual Conference of the United Methodist Church, and an elder to boot, went apeshit:

"Look, woman, I don't know you and you damn sho' don't know me. Now I traveled over one hundred miles today to come home to make sure my daddy get the help he need. My daddy need help and he gonna get it today if I have to come to your house, run through you an' get him outta dey. I don't repeat myself so da first time you see me will be the last time you see my daddy you no good, enabling, adulterous slut. Good bye, you trifling bitch!"

Telley arrived at Mary's house later on that evening with the police, Uncle Butch, Uncle William and Uncle Benjamin. She politely got out of her car, walked up to the door and rang the bell with all of the congeniality of the Girl Scouts. Mary came to the door and said, "Herbit, you better leave fo' iss trouble out cha." Not once did she even look at Telley – she was that petrified.

Daddy came out of the house with everything he brought with him except for that roof he had put on. Telley, as she was leaving with Daddy in tow, looked at Mary and said, "If you say one word to me, I'll lay you out on dis front porch; you undastan' me?! An' I want my daddy car keys, too. You won't be drivin' dat baby no mo', Miss Daisy!"

Mary, speaking almost in a whisper because she obviously was afraid that my sister was going to knock her teeth down her throat, said, "Herbit say I coulda keep da car." Then, without further word, she reached into her bra and handed Telley the key.

As Daddy and Telley were walking down the yellow cinderblock steps of Mary's front porch, Telley got to the bottom of the third step, turned around, looked up at Daddy's mistress and said, "Mary, you have a blessed evening here."

My family was so diverse that I have to chuckle to keep the tears at bay. Two people who are polar opposites get married. One is a do-gooder who finds Jesus, and the other is a drunkard and a calculating politician to his core. It shouldn't be surprising then, that any children born from this union would face the possibility of becoming mentally and emotionally unstable.

Mama and Daddy, in their many attempts to help Reggie deal with his burgeoning drug problem in the '80s, took him to see a child psychiatrist. He lamented that we all had our roles to play in Reggie's lot. Mama was the nurturer and unwitting enabler. Telley was the superstar child. I was the unassuming baby bird. Reggie was the scapegoat. And Daddy? Well, the expert asserted that Reggie's problems were a direct result of the fact that he grew up in an addicted home. The tell-tale heart, the root of all of our problems, all traced back to the contents of that purple and gold draw-string bag made of felt: Crown Royal.

Long before I actally tasted those contents, that omnipresent purple and gold bag was as much a part of my life as hot dogs and apple pie are a part of Americana. And just like the felt fabric of that bag and the embroidered C-R-O-W-N-R-O-Y-A-L that was lovingly stitched onto it, the effects of the liquor inside of it are etched into my very consciousness.

The first time I saw that damned bag, I was instantly entranced by it. That Friday night remains as transpicuous to me as Neil Armstrong's moonwalk was to the 180 million Americans who witnessed it. I was Buzz Aldrin. I saw the whole episode live and living color just a few feet away. I was in kindergarten, and we'd had May Day festivities earlier that day at school. Daddy came home from work drunk; this was the weekend's clarion call that it had indeed descended upon us. He was the Community School Director for St. Johns High School, a small rural school, located on Johns Island, just a hop, skip and a jump from Kiawah. He coordinated the after-school programs for St. Johns and the other schools in that district. Daddy loved his job, not necessarily because he loved children, but because of its autonomy. He pretty much set his own hours and he loved Friday nights because, as Daddy always said, "Friday evenin' mean I aine gotta look in no damn unruly ass chern face 'gen 'til Monday, so I gah git tank up (drunk) on mothafuckin' Friday evenin'."

I never knew, specifically, what he drank until that point. I just knew that he came home on Friday nights reeking of what I ratiocinated was beer. He sat in his recliner and kept turning that bag up to his head. I think that Daddy, either because of the respect that he had for us or out of fear of what Mama would say, never let us see the actual Crown Royal bottle. He would just drink from the purple and gold bag. In my five-year-old reasoning, I figured that since Daddy was a "big boy" and he drank from that ornate bag, one day I was going to get a bag like that as well. I rationalized that someday, I was also going to be a "big boy". I was going to be just like Daddy.

I believe that it was about a year later when I first uttered the words, "Um nevah gone drink as long as I live." I know that my timing is correct because it was the first argument I remember Mama and Daddy having about another woman.

"Herbert, da slut called da house last night, din she? Dass why you got up outta da bed an' went in the kitchen – ain't dat right, Herbert? Nigga, you should know every close eye aine sleep. I heard da whole damn conversation. Herbert, you uh dirty ass nigga! I picked up da phone in our room when I got up an' went to da bathroom. Do you really think Umma let you bring some tramp in my house?! How many times you done screw da bitch, Herbert?! Just from what I heard, I figured it could'na been too long 'cause when she axed 'bout payin' her rent, you said no. I know you an' you dough staht payin' bills 'til at least three months in, ain't dat right?!"

It was Christmas time. A fire was roaring in the fireplace. Carla Thomas's sultry voice had commandeered the record player in the living room. Her timeless holiday classic, *Gee Whiz, It's Christmas,* wafted through the air like one of Mama Clay's fresh baked Christmas hams. She glazed them with pineapples and honey and they were always at the ready on Mama's stove. All was right with the world. Reggie was outside chopping wood, and Telley and I were in the kitchen where she was helping me with fractions. When Telley and I heard the commotion we ran to the living room and saw Daddy on the floor where Mama had pushed him into the Christmas tree. He was picking pine needles out of his afro, and she was standing over him. But most alarming was that Daddy's "drunk glasses" were on the floor across the room from him. That alone signaled cause for serious concern, because my father was never – *never!* – bereft of his glasses if he was awake. He is so nearsighted that without the aid of contact lenses or eyeglasses, he is nearly blind. He wore contact lenses whenever he left the house and wanted to look as though he was a man of the people, and he wore gold wire-rimmed glasses with the Ben Franklin lenses whenever he left the house and wanted to look austere, perspicacious and well read. Those were the sober glasses. He wore his drunk glasses – large, hard, black plastic-frames with huge lenses – when he got glazed, or even started drinking, because he knew that his gross motor skills and dexterity would be compromised. Those glasses were so big and durable that regardless of how drunk he was, he knew he would never lose them or have them fall off his face. The only time that my father didn't have on the drunk glasses, the sober glasses, or the contact lenses was when he was in deep slumber. The fact that Daddy was semiconscious, breathing and didn't have on one of the three at the moment was unbelievable. The fact that they were off his face, and the reason why was because Mama had pushed him down, was cause for widespread panic.

"See, I din put my han' on you Linda. You had no damn right tah hit me. I tie'ud uh yo' shit, Linda! You always think I got some damn woman!"

Telley stood in front of me because she instinctively knew something that, at six years old, I had yet to realize. Whenever Daddy's voice went down about two octaves, he was about to get violent. Daddy, whose normal speaking voice was deeper than that of the average man's, sounded like a growling bear when he was drunk and about to lash out.

Daddy roared, "You think you can put cho fuckin' han' on me, woman?! I done tell you, I aine screwin' nobody, but you got tah have da lass word, enny?! Big, bad, Linda Gad!"

"Herbert, I aine no dog! You uh disrespectful ole evil ass nigga! I hate chu!"

"I hate cho ass, too! Now, how 'bout dat?! An' you aine gah damn put cho fuckin' han' on me no fuckin' mo' afta dis day here! Dass fah damn sho'!"

During all this, Daddy crawled from one end of the room to the other, put his drunk glasses back on, stood up and got close enough to Mama to grab her if he wanted.

"Linda, you know what cho problem is?! You dough leave well enough alone! Leave me da fuck alone, woman! You wanna hear Um fuckin' da betch?! Huh?! Yes! I fucked da betch; Um tie'ud uh dis shit! I aine no damn chile! I'n (I ain't) got tah listen tah you uh (or) no damn body else."

"Herbert, Um yo' wife! If you don't respect me, at least respect your children!"

"Betch, dough bring my kids inta dis shit!"

With that, Daddy made his move. He lunged forward, grabbed Mama and started to twist her arm around her back. I started crying. Then I started screaming, "Daddy, stop! Get off uh Mama! Leave my mama alone! Telley, please stop um fo' he pull Mama arm off!"

Telley ran up to Daddy and hit him in his face, which knocked off his drunk glass again; but he didn't care. I don't even think he noticed because he was just that plastered. The most important thing to him was that he was making Mama feel pain.

"Dass right, talk dat shit now Linda!"

Then Daddy twisted her arm some more. Reggie, who had just come into the house, sneaked up behind Daddy, who had his back to the door and never heard him enter. My brother had been chopping wood for the better part of the day and had on logging boots. He proceeded to put his size thirteen left boot into Daddy's back. Daddy never had a chance. He fell to the ground and gave Mama her arm back. As he fell to the floor, Reggie jumped on him.

"Mothafucka, if you evah touch my mama again, you uh dead mothafucka!" he screamed, at the same time beating Daddy about his head and face. Daddy was on the ground writhing in pain as Reggie beat him to a bloody pulp.

"Son, please stop; dough hit me no mo'!"

"Fuck you, Daddy! You wanna hit my mama?! My mama, nigga?! Umma kill yo'ass!"

Then he beat him more. Mama realized that he was about to kill Daddy and intervened.

"That's enough, son." Mama told Reggie those three words and it was enough to calm the beast, at least for that day and for that time. It was almost as if a spell had been cast on him and her words were the antidote. Reggie let go of Daddy seemingly seconds before he was to bring about his untimely death. He got up off of Daddy, took his knee out of the man's chest and said, "Um sorry, Mama."

"That's all right, son."

Reggie said to Daddy as he walked back out of the door, "Don't chu evah put cho fuckin' hands on my mama again! Nevah again in yo' life, nigga!"

Daddy lay on the floor coughing, crying and trying to catch his breath. He just kept saying over and over again, "Dat nigga try tah kill me. Y'all see dat shit, enny? Da somebitch try tah kill e own daddy!"

Daddy was covered in pine needles with a face full of cuts and bruises with blood dripping from his mouth. Mama was rubbing her arm and extending it back and forth trying to regain the feeling in it. She was whispering, "God, I thank You," repeatedly as she did it. Telley grabbed me, picked me up and said, "Come on, Shay." I lifted my head up off my sister's shoulder and said, "Um nevah gone drink as long as I live."

Telley said, "I know Shay. I know."

"OOW-WOO! OOW-WOO! OOW-WOO! WOO, 'rillas! Y'all da 'rillas now, fellas! Y'all enjoy y'allselves- y'all boys earned it!"

On February 15, 1997, with that infamous and legendary howl, I became a member of Zeta Rho Xi Fraternity, Inc., at The College of Charleston. After fourteen months of pledging, we had finally done it. The Guerrilla Dingoes, or G Dingoes as they were referred to, were the baddest men on the planet, bar none, and they had finally accepted us into the fold. They were clad in royal blue and sterling silver and exuded the type of unmitigated and unabashed masculinity that college-aged girls adored. And they were fiercely loyal to each other. Like my father had done in the spring of 1968 at South Carolina State College, I'd become a G Dingo. It was the fulfillment of a dream. I was going to make my father proud of me.

I was pledged by some of the most physically imposing young men in all of creation. Most of the brothers, or the 'rillas as they called each other, were the size of your average NFL lineman. They had beaten me with four-inch thick wooden paddles that were fashioned out of the trunks of trees. They had ridiculed me and slapped me on the back of my neck as I stood motionless with my head bowed, chin touching my chest and arms hanging in front of me. The first time I got "necked," as the aforementioned practice was referred to, the 'rilla who did it took three telephone books and stacked them on top of a coffee table that already stood three feet off of the ground. First, he soaked his hands with hot water. When they decided to use water in the donnybrook, the 'rillas then dubbed it, "aquaneck." Unbeknowst to me, because minutes earlier he had ordered me to bow my head and keep it bowed, he'd spent that entire time letting the water run from the faucet over his hands. He wanted to achieve the desired effect. He then ran over to the coffee table and hopped on it. With almost superhuman agility and quickness, he balanced himself on the telephone books. The 'rilla jumped from about five feet in the air and slapped me on the back of my neck. He succeeded in achieving the desired effect. I did, in fact, see stars.

He went on to repeat the action three more times. I'm pretty sure I went unconscious on my feet. Armahn Hamilton, or Arm an' Hammer as he was known, partly because of his name and partly because his arms were so muscular that they looked like the famed logo on the baking soda box, had hit me so hard I couldn't feel my legs. Armahn was all of six-foot-six and he weighed nearly three hundred pounds. He'd transferred to the College of Charleston from a school up North after he'd gotten hurt playing football. He was a Psychology major with a 3.98 grade point average- on a 4 point scale. Arm an' Hammer was a gentle giant and he was one of the sweetest people in the world. He'd laugh so hard sometimes that his peanut butter colored flesh would turn titian. Course, I didn't find out that Arm an' Hammer was a great guy until after I crossed the burning sands of Zeta. That night, to me, he was a sadistic son of a bitch and I wanted to kill him. I was certain that he'd paralyzed me. I'd continued standing, but I still couldn't feel my legs. I was five-foot-seven and weighed about one hundred twenty-five pounds. I was the color of a brown paper bag and just as tough, or at least I thought so. Actually, I wasn't tough at all. I was a mama's boy and I was horrified. I was as tough as a brown paper bag all right. A wet one. There was no way I was going to make it through the pledge process the G Dingoes had in store.

All of the horror stories you hear about the fraternity initiation process, I've lived them. I don't call it hazing because I knew full well what I was getting into when I decided to pledge Zeta Rho Xi. My father had his own war stories. I'd heard them on those Friday nights of my youth as he promulgated from the La-Z-Boy about how I was going to become a G Dingo when I went to college. I constantly heard his voice in my spirit when I was pledging.

"Yeah, dem boys whip my ass, boy. Box me in my damn chest and back, fuck me up wit' dat wood (paddle) an' tell me everything in da fuckin' werl tah make me think I'n been shit. But, dat was tah make me uh betta man. See, you got tah be uh man fo' dem boys tah even fuck wit' chu. You kan' be no damn G Dingo an' be no pussy, boy. Dey do all dat shit tah see if you gah fight uh if you gah quit. See, I fight dey ass! I fight 'til I earn my damn fraternity lettas. An' you gah fight, too. You hear me, boy?! You gah be uh G Dingo. You gah have tah persevere. Zeta Rho Xi is yo' damn legacy, son."

Both The Mayor and I chose to take the beatings. I was going to prove to myself that I had what it took to be a Zeta. I wanted those black Government Issue brogan boots that the G Dingoes spray-painted sterling silver- they were accentuated by the royal blue shoe strings, and that dog collar, that were the 'rillas calling cards. They would walk around campus howling when they saw each other and nobody said anything about it. The black kids marveled at them, and the white kids were intimidated by them. I wanted that power and I was prepared to sacrifice life and limb to get it. If it meant I had to die in one of those pledge sessions, so be it. Who cares if they tore the shirt off of my back? Literally.

They made us run up and down the length of the football field in Johnson Hagood Stadium, the football home of The Citadel, the Military College of South Carolina, under the cloak of night, until we vomited. They made us squat balanced on the balls of our feet with our arms stretched straight out, parallel to each other and perpendicular to the floor, until *they* got tired of seeing us in that position. This was called the "airchair." They would make us remain in the airchair until first, our arms started to wobble. Our legs would follow. Then, our entire bodies would start to shake because we'd be in that position for so long. Eventually when it looked like we'd fall over, and most times we did because our joints would began to lock up on us making our entire bodies go numb, the 'rillas would at that point give us a choice so that we could alleviate our suffering. We could either get necked or get wood. I always chose the wood because I hated getting necked just that much. They made us eat dog food. Their rationale was simple: How could we in good conscience, call ourselves G Dingoes, if we had not known the joys of the partaking of K-9 cuisine? I preferred Alpo Prime Cuts with Beef in Gravy because of its hearty and robust texture and flavor. It tasted like Filet Mignon to the palate after you've gotten the shit kicked out of you and you were famished after a thorough flogging. You had only the option of eating it or getting trounced for not eating it. We did it all in the name of brotherhood. We didn't really think anything of it because this was not only pledging, it was tradition. It was expected.

Kristian Watson, my dean of pledges, was tall and golden brown. He could also become as mean as a rattlesnake when necessary. Because Kristian had the requisite college student's apartment – small square footage, thin walls and nosey neighbors – he would always turn up the stereo so as to drown out the sounds of the crashing of the wood as it walloped our asses. He would play *Shadowboxing* by The Gza featuring Method Man, original members of the seminal hip hop group The Wu-Tang Clan, in continuous loop. I had nightmares about that song at least three times a week the entire duration of our pledge process. While he administered the bulk of the beatings, it was his job to make sure that the other 'rillas didn't kill one or all of us during one of our sessions, or sets, for muddling fraternal knowledge or history that we were charged with knowing. And we had to know it like the back of our hands. I can still recite it like it was the ABCs:

- *"Greetings, Big Brothers of Zeta Rho Xi Fraternity, Incorporated! Zeta Rho Xi was founded in Virginia Beach, Virginia, on the campus of Dred Scott University on November 7, 1911! Three undergraduate students, Brockington Homer Henry, Grenadine Ethan Davis, Dawson Elias Shivers and their faculty advisor and Chairman of the Department of Zoology at Dred Scott, Allambee Alarico Goolagong, built this illustrious fraternity on the bedrock characteristics of fortitude, wisdom, stoicism and integrity! Zeta Rho Xi Fraternity, Incorporated, or the G Dingoes as they are most commonly known, are identified by their fraternal colors of royal blue and sterling silver! The members of Zeta Rho Xi are nicknamed "G Dingoes" as a way of paying homage to founder Dr. Allambee Goolagong, a world-renowned zoologist who was of African-American, Colombian and Aboriginal ancestry! Colombian Guerrilla Warfare is the most effective way to crush your opponent so thoroughly and completely, that when it is applied correctly, it is the equivalent of strategically and militaristically ripping his heart from his chest cavity; this will cripple his will to fight! This particular art of war is centuries old! It has stood the test of time! The ONLY way to subdue an opponent who is bigger and better armed than you is to take his strengths and turn them into weaknesses! If he is bigger, he is slower, thus you are faster! If he is better armed, use stealth to take his weapons and eliminate him with them! The Australian Dingo is the most rapacious species of dog inhabiting planet earth! It has supreme dominion over the Outback! Dingoes have made life for both shepherds, and sheep, a nightmarish existence! To the Dingo, "quit" is a concept that is unknown. It is resolute! It is unwavering! It is unequivocal in its pursuits! If I look deep within myself, I will find that the spirit of the Dingo permeates my soul! If I look even further, it will become abundantly clear to me and all who look upon me, that I am the quintessential guerrilla warrior – capable, effective and resourceful! I repeat, GREETINGS BIG BROTHERS!"*

Now, if we didn't spit out that greeting loudly and with enthusiasm, each time we were in a set, the 'rillas would try to kill us. And most times, if we misspoke in any way whatsoever, my line brothers and I did indeed wish death upon ourselves. It took us about a day of pledging before we realized that even when we enunciated our greetings and anything else we were required to know perfectly, the 'rillas were still going to get us. It became very lucid to us, very quickly, that when we were wrong we were wrong and when we were right we were wrong. That's just the way it was.

"Y'all maufuckas got tah have stoicism, goddamn, if y'all wanna survive. Shit, y'all got tah know dis shit like yo' lives depended on it goddamn, 'cause it does." Every now and then, I can still hear Kristian's voice ringing in my ear.

Kristian would always tell us that we could get murdered in a set if he didn't protect us. He was right. He was the only one that could protect us from getting killed. As the dean of pledges, he was our surrogate father and we loved him just like that. He had to feel good about not letting the dogs maul us. The only way to make him feel good was to make him look good in front of the 'rillas.

We would have a set at Kristian's, and when we arrived there it was always a room full of two-legged dingoes awaiting us. If we'd done well that night, the 'rillas would have kudos for him. "'Rilla, you doin' good wit' dese boys." "Dass good shit, 'rilla." "'Rilla, dey gone be good in da dingo pack." Conversely, if we didn't know what we were supposed to know, they would let Kristian have it. "Fuck you, 'rilla! Dese boys aine shit!" "Da fuck you get dese mothafuckas from?!" "Kristian, dese boys aine shit! Dey gone put on dem lettas an' get fucked up 'cause dey don't know shit!"

Then Kristian would have to collide. Whomever the 'rilla happened to be that was talking the loudest about how awful a job we did that night, Kristian would make an example out of him for disparaging us too badly. Whatever we did was a direct reflection on how well he was preparing us. Kristian had a short fuse even for a G Dingo, and G Dingoes had notoriously low levels of tolerance and patience, so if a 'rilla talked too recklessly about us, he knew that Kristian was going to take him to task for it.

Colliding is what we did amongst each other to settle disputes. It was wrestling, only this wasn't the WWE. This was far more violent. This was war with real blood, and sometimes broken bones. A collision could start because of the most mundane and seemingly insignificant things. One could start because a 'rilla didn't like the way another 'rilla answered a question. It could start if a 'rilla wanted the fraternity shirt that you had on. Or, a collision could start just because a 'rilla felt like colliding. Sometimes, we collided with each other within the chapter just to keep our techniques sharp. But believe you me, Kristian would collide with any 'rilla and toss him clean out of his silver boots for incessantly implying that we were not going to make good G Dingoes. I saw him do it. Kristian's response to the 'rillas would mostly be the same though: "Umma get dese boys right, they just fuckin' up, 'rillas. Dass all." And much like a real father would do when he didn't want to let someone know that they had just cut him to the bone by speaking ill of one of his sons, Kristian would play the 'rillas comments off. But inside of himself he would be ebullient. He would stare us down from across the room. Kristian's glare was worse than any of the beatings. We would rather get beaten senseless than to disappoint him.

In Zeta Rho Xi, if you went to another school as what we termed a "visiting 'rilla", and you didn't know what you were supposed to know as a Zeta, or you could not prove that you were ready to wear the letters, the 'rillas at that school would rip the shirt off of your back and then collide with you. This was standard operating procedure. The chapter at C of C, which included members from The Citadel where fraternaties are not allowed, was notorious for sending visiting 'rillas home shirt-less, battered and bruised if they came on campus ill-prepared. Going to another school and having your manhood taken away from you in such a way would reflect poorly on your entire chapter. You and your chapter would be deemed "Garfield" because Garfield is a euphemism for feline. We are G Dingoes. We are tenacious and fierce. So if you are not tena-cious and fierce, you are not an authentic G Dingo. If you are not a G Dingo, you are Garfield. You see, we used the word Garfield as an adjec-tive, not a noun. The term Garfield in our world was tantamount with pussy. We were "raucous ass G Dingoes" that existed and perished on the strength of our dicks, our individual reputations and the reputations of the chapters we represented. Period. If you were not raucous, meaning you did not get on the road and visit 'rillas at other colleges, did not have sex with a host of women and weren't willing to help another brother, no matter what, you were a Garfield ass 'rilla. If you're Garfield, you might as well crawl into a hole and die. Those were the rules. That was the life we chose.

We were not all about testing each other. The Zetas community service work is legendary. We were an integral part of the Civil Rights Movement, and today we're involved in everything from youth mentoring programs to HIV/AIDS prevention and awareness campaigns. Our brotherhood extends from all across the United States to Europe and Africa. I was proud that these guys chose me to be part of this family. You had to be callous and tough to endure what we did.

It was I, Kevin Summers, my friend since our first day of our first semester at the College of Charleston, Micheal Dross, Stewart Markell and Craig Olivent – all from The Citadel, who were chosen by the 'rillas for the spring of 1996 pledge class. The Citadel may have been only six miles from C of C, but we were worlds apart. They had curfews, and the freshman, or plebes, had to run to and from their classes and there weren't any women there. None of that mattered. These were my line brothers, my L.B.'s, and they went to war with me every day from January 4, 1996, to February 15, 1997, against the brothers of Zeta.

Fraternities were strictly prohibited by The Citadel and had it been found out that Michael, Stewart and Craig had been trying to get into one, they would have been expelled. Kevin and I ran the same risk at the College because although we could pledge fraternities, the school would have surely sent us packing if its officials had found out how we were going about it. None of us cared. The five of us were willing to risk life, limb and our academic careers to be Zetas because we loved her that much. We'd do it again in a heartbeat.

To be a Zeta meant respect. It meant notoriety. It meant power. After we became Zetas, we were kings. The five of us became Kings of The College of Charleston and The Citadel. The guys knew it and they wanted to be us. The ladies wanted to sleep with us because G Dingoes were legendary for their bedroom prowess. At the College, my first semester, I was a nameless, forgettable face in the crowd. After I became a G Dingo, everyone knew who I was and I loved it. After what I endured at Sky High, I loved being cool and popular. I loved being what my daddy was. He told me that after he crossed the burning sands of Zeta, he had sex with seven different women on the same day just a few days following. He told me that he and his L.B.'s were a force to be reckoned with on South Carolina State's campus.

I became obsessed with women and power just like my father had become years earlier. I didn't even realize it until I had both in my grasp at the College. I was a G Dingo and I was going to show the world that I belonged. The only hitch in my giddy up was the fact that G Dingoes were known for being heavy drinkers. It was a minor hitch because I knew that I'd never drink; come hell or high water.

G Dingoes had a well-deserved reputation for throwing the livliest bashes on campus. A G Dingo party was an event not to be missed. After our pledge process, it was time to live it up. The night of our first step show, we were euphoric. Stepping is a tradition that traces its roots back to African dance. While other African-American fraternities and sororities may have stepped, we leaped. Leaping is stepping the G Dingo way. We emphasized a military style of precision and call and response as we jumped in the air, stomped our feet, clapped our hands and slapped our bodies in rhythmic synchronization. We'd spent months practicing. We passed out flyers inviting the world to the soiree and the entire campus was buzzing about it.

The gymnasium at The College of Charleston was packed that Saturday night of February 22, 1997. They were there to see us. The new G Dingoes. We entered through the back of the gym and came out in a line from shortest to tallest. It was the exact same sequence we were in when we were pledging. We were shirtless accoutered with Army dress white pants, white suspenders and silver boots. Kevin was the ace dingo, or the number one on the line, and I was number two, the deuce dingo. Michael was number three, or the tre dingo, and Craig was the four dingo. Stewart was number five, the last and tallest one on the line. In Zeta Rho Xi, he was referred to as the tail dingo.

Kevin was a stout, toast-colored teddy bear. The women loved him because he was a dead ringer for the popular R & B singer Gerald Levert. Michael was the star wide receiver on the football team at The Citadel. He was exactly six feet tall and just two shades darker than Kevin. He was also a preacher's kid. Michael and I used to quote scriptures while we were getting beaten during most sets. I could always hear him mumbling Psalm 23 while the 'rillas were beating the hell out of us.

Sometimes, when the 'rillas were feeling especially truculent, they beat us with a paddle they called "3-D wood." The 'rillas told us shortly after we crossed over into Zeta land exactly why they called it 3-D. They said the disorientation from the pain it caused made the vast majority of pledges hallucinate with visions of holograms and other three dimensional pictures. More than a few times, in high definition detail, I saw pink hearts, yellow moons, orange stars and green clovers. One night, I saw the leprechaun jump off the cereal box, rip 3-D from the hands of the 'rilla that was swinging it and commence to giving me a good old fashion Irish ass whipping. 3-D wasn't a paddle at all. What it was was a six inch thick, three foot long paddle-esque piece of wood that had to be a California Redwood in its former life. They would hit us on our asses as we squatted in three-point stances; the tips of our left fingertips gripped the floor as our right hands clutched our dicks and nuts for dear life. We would get so thoroughly beaten that our asses would develop black and blue baseball sized welts on them. The 'rillas dubbed these war wounds "ass crust." Ass crust made it next to impossible to sit in class for fifty minutes on Mondays, Wednesdays and Fridays and an hour and fifteen minutes on Tuesdays and Thursdays. Michael would start to mumble under his breath, "The Lord is my shepherd...I shall not want..." *Pow!* "Yea, though I walk through the valley of the shadow of death....." *Pow!* I would always finish up the last part, invariably while one of the 'rillas would have me doing sit ups until I puked, then dry heaved, "I will fear no evil." *Pow!*

Stewart and I never saw eye to eye. He was the middle linebacker at The Citadel. He was muscular and he was so black that he was a shiny hue of violet. I suppose we never got along because he assumed, right off of the bat, that he was the leader of our rag tag group. I've never liked being told what to do, so I automatically imprecated his assertion of authority. The first night that we found ourselves pledging together, I cursed him out. Stewart said that since he was the chief on field play caller of the Citadel's vaunted defense, he was most qualified to lead us. I told him that I didn't play football and didn't give a damn that he did. I could never forget that night. We were all sitting in my dorm room. My twelve-by-nineteen room with the rickety twin-sized bunk beds always reminded me of a prison cell because it was so small. However, we decided that it would be the best place to meet. I didn't have a roommate and we did not want to arouse any suspicion. My dorm was on Wentworth Street on the backside of campus, which made our clandestine meetings less likely to be noticed. Three Citadel cadets walking down Wentworth Street with two College of Charleston guys, on a Friday night, looked odd and we were well aware of that. Any of the black students that saw us together would realize that we were pledging Zeta PDQ. About 99.99 percent of the African-American student population at the College was waiting with bated breath to see who were going to be the next G Dingoes. The five of us together would be all the ammunition needed to start a rumor.

The room fell silent after I cursed out Stewart. He told me to shut the fuck up and I told him that he could and should get the fuck out of my room before I did something to him. The entire notion was absurd because Stewart could have killed me with his bare hands if he had wanted to.

"Y'all brothuz now, cut dat bullshit out! Fuck da dumb shit, y'all stop dat shit or Umma beat both y'all asses!" That was Craig Olivent who broke our silence. He was the eggplant colored reincarnation of the Incredible Hulk. Craig's muscles had muscles. He was not going to let our schoolyard argument prevent him from becoming a G Dingo. I said, "Whatever man," under my breath. Stewart mumbled something, but we dared not let this bald bag of muscles hear us. We weren't afraid of Craig mind you, but we really didn't know him well enough yet to challenge The Hulk. We agreed to disagree. Sometimes, it happens that way with brothers. You can argue with them. You can even fight with them. But, if anybody else even attempts to, they will have hell to pay. Despite our individual personality quirks, when it came right down to the nitty-gritty, Stewart had my back and you better believe I had his. Period.

The five of us crawled into the gym at C of C that night of our probate show, our first leap show, and it was utter pandemonium. We were interlocked like Voltron action figures on our hands and knees as we slithered to the center of the basketball court. We were the new G Dingoes and we wanted to serve notice on that crowd from the word go, that we were going to think, act and operate like our mascot, the almighty dingo, would. The throng was going to see that were willing to become dingoes incarnate to let them know that we were the realest of deals. Blue tarp, from wall to wall, covered the floors and members of our fraternity from North Carolina, South Carolina, Georgia and Florida came out to support us. Smoke from the smoke machine we rented shrouded the gym and *2001: A Space Odyssey's* opening blared over the speakers. And the women screamed! Women and girls screamed our names. Women I didn't even know screamed my name!

Amongst the obstreperous chorus of women screaming and the G Dingoes howling, an avalanche of *MWAN-AMKE's! (in Swahili "mwanamke" means "woman"), the trademark call* of our sisters of Epsilon Lambda Omicron, or ELO, could also be heard in the sonic boom. They were a tidal wave of scarlet and eggshell, their official colors, and were engulfed but not overwhelmed in the ocean of royal blue and sterling silver in that gym. The women of ELO were the most gorgeous and devastatingly fierce sorority on campus, or anywhere else for that matter. When we were pledging, even though the 'rillas implored them not to, the ELO's fed us when we were hungry, helped us study when we were too tired to stay awake and shuttled us around. Most of the time, our asses were too swollen from the beatings to be able to sit, much less sit *and* drive comfortably. I'll love the ELO's until the day I die for what they did for us. Our adoring public couldn't wait for us to start leaping. I think we all realized that night that our lives were never going to be the same. Life is never the same after you realize you're a superstar.

"I know you don't drink, 'rilla, I know dat shit, but you da 'rillas now – take one for da maufuckin' team, 'rilla. I got some fuckin' Crown right here fah you."

A 'rilla I knew from Georgia, who had helped pledge us, shoved a cup of Crown Royal and crushed ice in my face that night after the leap show. It was a yellow Solo Cup and we were at the apartment of an older chapter 'rilla reveling in our newfound fame. As Da Lench Mob harmonized and growled the G Dingoes' national anthem from two huge speakers in the corner of the living room, I stared inside of that cup for a long time. Deep within the depths of my spirit, I begged the Lord to let this bitter cup pass from me. Every image of Daddy drinking that I'd seen in nineteen years danced on the surface of that Crown Royal puddle, topped off with ice. After listening to about one hundred bars of Brother Ice Cube serenade me, I was wired. He pounded me in the eardrums with his rapid fire verbal assault. It consisted of indelible hip hop lines like, *"Swingin' on a vine/Suckin' on a piece of swine/Jiggaboo comin' up from behind"* and *"Wit' da boom- ping- ping/Listen to the ill styles that I bring- bring."* Combined with the song's bombastic bassline, I felt like I could jump off of the steeple of St. Michael's Church at a height of one hundred ninety-three feet. That song had me thinking that I was so *unfuckwit'able*, I would even attempt that swan dive after drinking a gallon of Crown Royal, if someone had dared me. I'd land squarely on my feet, too. Our national anthem, *Guerrillas In Tha Mist*, finally convinced me to give up the ghost.

It was the most unholy of communions. I took, drank ye all of it and remembered that Herbert Gadson's blood was given to me. It was impossible for me to be thankful. The cup of liquid damnation was half full and its contents burned going down. That brown elixir was like nothing I'd tasted before. It corroded my intestines. I loved the feeling instantaneously. The girls that were standing around and sitting, eating and drinking, all of a sudden seemed prettier. They were also friendlier. They were smiling at me now, all of them. They all wanted me. It was because I was more handsome.

I was more charming. An infinite amount of endorphins engulfed all five of my senses. I got so drunk at that after party that I can't swear to you about what I did or didn't do.

I do know that was the night things changed for me. I went from a meek college boy to the one thing in life, up until that point, that was the most unfathomable thing I could picture myself being: a drunk. After nineteen years, the prodigal son had finally made it home. The bottom of that Solo Cup welcomed me into the fold with open arms.

CHAPTER 11

School is for Fools

B y the time the fall of 1997 rolled around, I was having the time of my life at the College of Charleston. I loved college. Everyone knew who I was and I was drinking heavily. I was also having sex with a host of different women. The "C of C" is the thirteenth oldest college in the United States. It is the oldest municipal college in the country and the oldest in the South. The campus is located in the heart of downtown, surrounded by the historic and picturesque mansions and cobblestone streets that were the hallmarks of the pre-Civil War South. The college's backdrop was absolutely resplendent. The school itself, with its buildings that were throwbacks to the Antebellum Period, were exquisite. It had become my personal playground. I loved being a college student. Classes, projects and term papers be damned.

There were many days during my six years in college that I was so drunk when I woke up that I didn't even know what day it was. And quite frankly, for a time, I didn't really care. The G Dingoes would throw a party and I would stagger in the venue and sometimes would have to be carried out. Seems the more I drank, the more I wanted to drink. When

I was drinking, I was Superman. I was full of "liquid courage" and all of my insecurities melted away. No longer was I unsure of what to say to the fairer sex because many times, I would just say something outlandish. For a long time, my opening lines when I was tipsy were, "Hey beautiful, could you please do me the honor of letting me eat your pussy until you come down my throat? Let's not do ourselves a disservice and let this *fuckutunity* pass us by." I knew that if she asked me what a *fuckutunity* was, I'd piqued her interest. When I explained that it was a term I'd invented and it was merely an *opportunity* for us to make love, have sex, or *fuck*, she would ask me what the difference was. I'd then hit her with my personal Gettysburg Address. I explained that the difference was as vast and infinite as the beauty that consumed, yet liberated her being, enough to allow her the freedom to explore a *fuckutunity* with me. I then told her that I could show her far better than I could tell her. The law of averages dictated that because of *fuckutunity's* root word and all the eroticism that my machinations envoked, I had better than 50/50 odds of being taken up on my offer. Ordinarily the young lady would say some variation of, "Oh my God, he's so drunk." Then she would laugh. The women would always sniggle so alcohol taught me that under its influence, it didn't matter that I wasn't the most attractive guy in the room. Hell, my self-esteem was so low anyway that, many times, I felt like I was the ugliest guy in the room. Maybe, I was. Who's to say?

Nevertheless, none of that mattered when I was drunk. I could make any woman laugh and that was how I managed to make myself appealing to the lot of them. I'd get plastered and make them laugh until they cried. I made more than a few of them laugh so violently that they wet themselves. I had a formula: drink the liquor, get the girl to laugh and get the girl. I think I learned more about some of the forces that caused Daddy to drink while I was at the College than at any other time in my life. I tried to have as much sex as I could in school and to drink myself into oblivion because the truth of the matter was – and when I realized this all I could do was cry – I had become just like my daddy. After I had that epiphany, I tried to drown the prospect in more Crown Royal.

The concept of love at first sight was foreign and abstract to me. That is, until I met Felicia Mandissa Crease. I guess the notion is foreign to most twenty-year-olds. Still to this day, almost a decade and a half later, Felicia is the most beautiful woman I've ever met. Now I believe it was love at first sight. Maybe it was lust at first sight. In any event, September 1, 1997, the day I met her, my entire world transformed. I wanted her. I needed her. I did not even know her name.

I was working at the front desk of College Lodge, my dormitory, when she walked in with Crystal, the young lady who I later learned was her room-mate. Two people walked in, but I only saw her. You know the moment in life when something so spellbinding and unbelievable happens, that you feel your heart has stopped beating? That's what happened to me when our eyes locked. We'd already been in school for a week, and I later discovered that she lived in the building, but I guess I hadn't seen her until that moment. At the time, I was having sex with another girl in the building. During this same period, with more than one other coed, I was also trying to effectuate my own version of Christopher Columbus touching down in the New World and the Mayflower and Plymouth Rock meeting. I was feverishly trying to discover and land on the maple syrup coated nakedness of *two* other young goddesses. Maybe that's why my path hadn't crossed with this Nubian queen previously. I don't know. Aphrodite and Nefertiti had nothing on this broad. For every idea of physical beauty I'd ever had, she was the complete manifestation of it. She was about five feet tall and she was the color of an Almond Joy. Her eyes were slanted and mocha in color, which gave her an Asiatic look. Those eyes seduced me from the start. She had long and straight black onyx colored hair that cascaded effortlessly and nonchalantly off of her shoulders and down to the middle of her back like a rich woman's shawl wrap. I would later ascertain that a few negligible pieces were indeed Minky Yaki hair extensions. Felicia wore hair weave from the Korean owned beauty supply store like it was French couture. Truth be told, she rocked weave better than any Hollywood starlet I'd seen in my town or on TV and the movies. She had on a pair of stone-washed jeans that were ripped over the thighs, a peach-colored halter top and a pair of brown and beige sandals.

She was stunning. She was a size twelve and her breasts were two spheres of perfection. Her behind was the subject of the every wet dream I'd ever had. It was dynamic! It was enormous. It was flawless and she knew how to walk with it. She glided with that sumptuous ass. It did not overpower her short stature at all.

The day I met Felicia, I'd had sex with fourteen different women, twelve of them since I'd become a G Dingo. I was doing my damnedest to make up for lost time. Outwardly, my level of confidence had skyrocketed. However, on the inside, I was still the same scared little boy who said utterly ridiculous things to women simply because I did not know how to engage them in meaningful conversation.

As they swung open the big glass doors of the lobby, I didn't see her roommate. This was rare for me. Ordinarily, if I saw a girl I liked and her friend walking somewhere, I always checked out the friend. More often than not, I would engross the friend in conversation to see what the girl I really liked would do. I would then, over time, use the platonic relationship that I had established with the friend to have sex with the girl I really liked, as well as her friend that I'd cozied up to originally. This time was different. Felicia's aura blinded me to Crystal, who was tawny and statuesque. While she didn't look exactly like Naomi Campbell, they definitely shared the same bone structure. Make no mistake, she was indeed a bombshell. On this day however, she was merely Felicia's shadow. I was honed in on my destiny.

"Are you going to stare at me or ask me my name, Mr. G Dingo?"

I liked this girl already. She walked right over to my desk and asked me this without hesitation or trepidation. I couldn't let her punk me.

"I already know your name." I lied.

"Is that right? I don't know how, considering we just met, Shaytee Gadson."

I was shocked that she knew me, but I couldn't let her see that. I had a reputation to uphold. Shit, I was Shaytee the G Dingo; who didn't know me?

"Let's see, you know my name. Um glad because I know every gorgeous young lady on this campus. It's so good tah know dat y'all know me. Dat means Um doin' my job. Now, let me have da privilege uh knowin' yo' number. I want you to write it on my hand, sweetie."

I extended my right hand out to her with a flattened palm. She grabbed my fingers with her left hand, seized the green pen that was sitting on the desk and proceeded to scribble something in my palm. When she touched me, I felt an electric current shoot through my physique and land with a thud at the base of my spine. I loved her supple touch. I could feel and smell the pear scented Bath and Body Works lotion on my hand as she jotted. I never wanted her to stop touching me. Nevertheless, I wasn't about to let her know that.

"I'll write down my number because you already know my name, right? Or were you just runnin' game? I heard about you, Mr. Gadson. I'm a freshman, but I've done my homework. Call me later."

"Oh, and when you talk to me, I wanna talk to the smart guy who answers all the questions in his classes, not the G Dingo. Take care, sexy."

Then she turned away, jumped on the elevator with Crystal and went to her room. How did she know that I participated in class? Evidently, she knew somebody who knew me pretty well. Did we have a class together? Did she just call me sexy? I didn't know this girl from a can of paint and she already had my mind in a tailspin.

Mama Clay was the one person in my life who I knew, beyond a shadow of a doubt, would love me no matter what I did, even if she somehow became aware of how vile I became. We grew up together. I was going through my first childhood. She was going through her second. I never believed that she would leave me. Mama Clay took an early retirement to take care of me as a baby. Undoubtedly, everyone dies. I knew that. Howbeit, I didn't think *she* would. Mama Clay never got mad at me. Even when I kicked her shins with my cowboy boots almost daily from ages five to about ten, simply because I wanted to be a wrestler and she was the perfect opponent, she never got mad at me when her cinnamon colored tibias turned purple. She would just say, "Oi...Oi...Oi...OO-Wee...OO-Wee, boy you done kick me; get me the ankahol." I think Mama Clay believed that rubbing alcohol, or "ankahol," could cure anything from a leg bruise to the common cold. If you got sick in my house and Mama Clay was around, she rubbed you down with isopropyl alcohol. In her later years, even ankahol couldn't do her any good anymore. She would get sick and stay sick for a few days. That was just her way. Her back itched all of the time. She'd always have pain in her lower back. But, she always fought through it.

It didn't alarm me when she went to the hospital on March 4, 1998. I just figured she was going in for a short time to return home as she always did. For most of that weekend, I was passed out drunk and drinking, as I always did. I was too drunk to drive the four blocks from my dorm room to see her at Roper Hospital. The idea that she would die wasn't real to me. I never figured that she would leave me. When I was in college, Mama Clay used to let me pick her up from home and I would take her to cash her retirement checks at Piggly Wiggly. After she would go in to the store, she would come back out to the car and tell me to open my hand. She would then take the wadded up $81.72, exactly half of her $163.44 monthly ransom, place it in my right hand and squeeze my knuckles to close. She would then say, "You's uh growin' boy an' you in school; you got tah have money in yo' han'. I still got mah Social Security [check] comin' so Mama Clay gah be aw'right. Dough tell nobody I give you dis money, ya (you hear). Dough tell Lin, neitha. I dough want she in we business." Then she would laugh and swallow a muffled burp. It always sounded like she was saying "syrup." She always burped after a good laugh. The joke was even funnier because we both suspected Mama knew our little secret, but never let on.

"I'n gah tell nobody, Mama Clay. You know how me an' you is."

Then she would smile as we drove off. I took Mama Clay's money and would buy gas, food and Crown Royal, Canadian Mist, or E&J with it.

You never think that your best friend is going to die on you, even if she is in her mid-eighties. I knew, pronto, that something was wrong because Daddy called. It was Sunday night and I was sobering up because I had decided that I was going to make a rare appearance in my Monday classes the next day. My roommate answered the phone and I could tell he was perplexed by the voice on the other end of the line.

"Ahh- no sir. I'm Jeremy. No sir. I'm not playin' a joke on you. I'm not Shaytee, sir. Jeremy. My name is Jeremy. Ahh, no sir, not Jerry. Jeremy. Ahh, yes sir; it's J-E-R-E-M-Y. You're right sir, they do sound the same. Yes sir, I'll get him. He's right here. Your dad wanna talk to you, man."

Jeremy walked over to my desk and handed me the phone.

"Hey, Daddy."

"Yeah boy, she gone."

"What chu mean, 'She gone?' Who gone where?"

"She pass, Shay, she gone."

Daddy's words were slurred and Mama was out of town so I knew that he was drunk. I was about to faint. The room was spinning. My head was hot. I couldn't even speak.

"Shay, you there? Shay? You want me tah come get chu, bubba?"

All of a sudden, I didn't know where I was. My tongue was as heavy as a brick and the room wouldn't stop doing somersaults. I think I told Daddy that I could make it home.

"No! No son! Umma call Felicia. Then y'all come on out here." Then Daddy said, with all of the sincerity that any drunk man has ever mustered, "Son, Um sorry."

I wanted to die that night. And part of me did. I haven't been the same since.

African-American funerals in Hollywood are joyous and festive. Actually, funerals are more like Pentecostal revivals than interment services. If the person was a well-known figure in the community, it was a certified event. We celebrated the person's life. We sang, clapped, shouted and did all manner of calisthenics. Mama Clay was a luminary in Hollywood. She was the Mayor of Hollywood's mother-in-law and she was Linda Gadson's mother. On March 11, 1998, Wesley United Methodist Church had a standing room only crowd to wish her a fond farewell. People were standing along the walls and standing outside. There must have been about seven hundred fifty or so people in the church, which only had a seating capacity of about five hundred. White, black, Asian and Latino people were there. Even in that crowd, I felt alone. The organist, a well-known local songstress named Christal Brown Gibson, sang like an angel. She was magnetic. She was a rich shade of chocolate. Her hair was in a graduated bob that accentuated her round face. Her Mac Makeup was impeccable. She had on an understated shade of coffee brown lip gloss and her eyeshadow was burnt umber. I was entranced by her as she sang.

"When I see Jesus....Amen....When I see Jesus......Amen...All of my troubles......All of my disappointments, all of my pain.....Amen......When I see Jesus.....AAAAA-AMEN." Amidst the contralto voice coming from the organ, all you could hear in the congregation were muzzled sobs and sniffles. The crescendo was building.

Mama and Daddy were sitting on the front row and I could tell that everyone, to a person, was waiting on Mama to break. At black funerals in my town, no matter what kind of hullabaloo is created with the singing and shouting, there is always an unspoken contest going on. As with any bet, there are always wagers being placed. No money changes hands mind you, just a knowing nod from one funeral goer to another of, "I told you so" or an, "Ah huh", resonating in the congregation is the reward for winning. The hedge is who is going to be the first person in the family to break. Breaking could mean a deep guttural and uncontrolled cry, sob or body jerk. The ante can include who is going to pass out and have to be carried out of the church first. You could almost feel the satisfaction and relief in the congregation when the first person in the family lost it. And losing it would always be followed by a chorus of, "Dass all right chile, you kin cry. Dat was yo' Mama. Iss all right," or "God knows bess chile, He dough nevah take nuttin' but E own," and "She in uh betta place now. Ress easy, ya mama watchin' ovah you now, bay'bee."

I held out for as long as I could. From the time that we walked into the church, I believe that every child, grandchild and great-grandchild of Mama Clay's was crying. Her pastor, The Reverend Joseph L. Speights, a heavy man who shook like a bowl of jelly when he laughed and whose walnut-colored face became contorted into an almost hellish look when he preached, cried as he was trying to eulogize Mama Clay.

"Now, Mother Clay was an upright woman. She loved her children, her grans (grandchildren), an' her great-grans. Mother Clay was not a woman to put on no airs. Oh no! What chu saw is what chu got."

The crowd was whipped into frenzy as he spoke.

"Preach, Preacha! Yes she was!"

"I know you knows it!"

"Say that! Say that! You betta say that!"

He continued. "She was a woman of faith and Mother Clay loved da Lawd. She didn't know no otha way." That's when the congregation became unhinged testifying.

"No, she din know no otha way! You talkin' right, man'dove Gawd! Yes suh!"

"All her life, Clay was upright!"

"Doozy taught her, yes she did!"

"Ahh, Glory God!"

"You talkin' right, preacha!"

"Yes, she was! Clay was light an' salt uh da earth!"

Reverend Speights was on a roll. "She took me in like a son when I first come to dis community, so many years ago. I din know nobody an' I din have nothing. She become my mama. Lawd, look uh my mama in dat casket! My mama gone on to Jesus!"

No sooner than "Jesus" rolled out of his chubby cheeks, he started crying like a baby. I'd never seen a preacher cry during a eulogy. His tears spoke louder than his words. I thought I even saw Mama Clay crack a smile in the casket.

When I saw my best friend in that mahogany casket with the gold plated bars running along the sides of it, all the time we spent together came rushing back to me like a flood. I thought about how she sacrificed so much to make sure that I knew what uncontrolled, unrestrained and unconditional love was. I thought about how she got me hooked on soap operas as a little boy. I thought about how she told me that no matter what life throws at you, you have to wear the circumstances, both good and bad, like a loose garment.

"You dough nevah want life bad tah cling tah ya soul an' ya dough want da good tah make ya soul too comfortable, because dat devil is uh mean man. You gaht tah wey (wear) dem things like uh loose gahmit." She'd tell me that all the time when I was little and hurt myself, and she said the same as I got older and other people wounded me. I envisaged her words as it was my turn to walk up and view her body. Then I kissed her face. Through my tears and guttural moans, I whispered to the best friend I ever had in this life, "I love you Mama Clay...Ya boy gah be aw'right, okay?...I gah carry you wit' me...I aine nevah gah fahgit chu...Please dough fahgit me, okay?...Ya boy gah always love you, my girl...You gah always be my girl...Watch out fah me...I gah always love you, my baby...O'wl always be yo' boy an' you gah always be my baby..."

I waited for her to tell me that she loved me back, but she didn't. She couldn't. If only I could have heard my girl tell me one more time that she loved me. I would have given anything to hear that old lady say, "I love you, my boy," just one more time. When I waited and she didn't say it, something came over me. At first, I just stroked her cheeks. Seemingly, from heaven's pearly gates, a voice emitted that because other family members wanted to visit the casket, I had to shuffle on back to my seat. I paid no attention to the opine. I kept on rubbing her cheeks. I felt someone, maybe it was Reggie, come up beside me. He try to pry me away from the casket.

"No! I aine movin'! Get off me!"

It was my voice, but I couldn't believe what I was saying and just how loudly I was saying it. It was at that moment, I realized I was climbing into the casket with her. Amidst the sniffles and the tears of my family seated on the first three rows, and in the middle of the congregation frenetically dancing and singing, "When we aaaallll git to heeeeaaaaven, what uh day of rejoicing dat will beeeee....When we aaaall...Seeeee Jeeeee-sus, We will sing and shout uh-victor-reeeee", spontaneous aphonia paralyzed God's house.

Reggie and Daddy descended on me in a millisecond.

"Reggie, help me git him outta here! Ya bubba done loss e mine (mind)! I figga'ed (figured) dis was gone happen!"

"I got his legs, Daddy; git his arms! Come on, Shay...don't fade on me now! Wake up, lil' bubba. Come on, now! Come on, baby! Wake up!"

I don't know if I passed out, but I do remember Reggie telling me that as he was gently slapping my face. I'm not sure what my response was. Daddy, Reggie and four active pallbearers had to forcibly remove me from Mama Clay's casket and take me out of the church. As they moved me to an undisclosed location, the disquieted congregation awakened from the slumber my rampage induced. They started signifying almost as loudly as they sang just moments earlier.

"Lawd, dat boy know e love e gramama."

"You know, he was Clay heartstring."

"Clay take care dat boy from uh baby, ya know..."

"Lawd, I pray fah dat boy 'cause e prob'ly gah go fool now 'cause Mama Clay done leave ya. Lawd, hammercy on dat po' boy, Jesus..."

Maybe I did "go fool" after Mama Clay died. I'll never let go of her memory. I've reflected about her just about every day since she transitioned. Some days, she still brings me to tears. I drank every day for a month after Mama Clay died. I'd mulled over icing myself so that I could be with her.

As time and chance would have it, Felicia and I were doing all of the things that people in a relationship do, minus the title, before Mama Clay died. We slept together, we dated, we talked about everything and we fought. After Mama Clay went on home though, she became my rock. I needed a stabilizing force and she was it. I don't quite know when it happened, but in almost nothing flat, after Mama Clay went on to glory, we officially became a couple, and beyond.

"Shaytee, I'm pregnant."

Now I don't care what any man tells you, but if he says that he is anything but scared to death when his wife, girlfriend or random sexual partner tells him that she's pregnant, he is lying. It was March 19, 1998 – my D-Day. It was my own personal Normandy. I'll never forget it because I haven't been as tempestuous as I was on that date- before or after.

Felicia and I were thick as thieves. Everyone who saw us together knew it. Granted, I was in love with her, but I cheated on her every chance I got. I know she was in love with me, too. I *knew* that. But I abused her love by not being faithful. I didn't even try to be. She did, in fact, catch me on video utilizing my tongue and penis, and necessarily in that order, administering a deep tissue full vaginal massage to a single black female. The young lady and I decided that it would be a great idea to record our lurid romp. We wanted to keep it as a momento of our weekend together. We engaged in acts of debauchery the likes of which would make my mama ashamed to say that she knew me, much less admit that I was her baby. Well, on this video, I was Morgan's baby. At least, I think her name was Morgan. I can't say that I remember with one hundred percent certainty. That weekend was the weekend of a G Dingo party, so I was quite intoxicated and thought it would be a good idea to stash the video in the console of my truck where Felicia would never think to look. I reasoned in my drunken stupor that it was an ingenious idea. Even though she drove my truck just as much as I did, she only had two eyes – and who can multitask well enough to drive, text, talk on their cell phone, put on make-up and be fully aware of everything going on around them in the cabin of a car – and still have time to look in the console? Thus, I reasoned in my inebriated mind, the video was safe and damn near invisible. It didn't register with me that she kept her charcoal black Gucci sunshades, Mac Full For You Plushglass and work identification in there.

Well, she looked. And we fought. She told me that she'd invested too much time and too much of her heart into "my Shay" to let some dirty slut, whose name she was certain that I didn't remember because she could tell just how drunk I was by the spaced out look in my eyes and the slurring of my words in the video, ruin our relationship. Felicia knew me better than I knew myself. Then we made love. And even after she saw me committing those lewd and lascivious acts, she stayed. God only knows why. Love conquers all, I guess.

I drank every weekend, and at The College of Charleston the weekend starts on Thursday evening. I partied with my G Dingo brothers. On the weekends that we happened to be throwing a party, I became especially frowsy. I'd leave the dorm on Friday and if Felicia didn't come to the party on Saturday night, she just wasn't going to see me that weekend. At one party, a party that I knew that she and her friends were going to be in attendance, I got a number from this young lady and she saw me procuring it. It must have been about four hundred people in the Stern Center ballroom that night. We were packed into that place like sardines. Out of all of those people in there, Felicia saw that one girl in that pitch black ballroom, made even more murky by the sea of black people, bequeath me her number. I say "bequeath" because I'd have been better off taking that slip of paper, crossing out her number and writing my last will and testament on it. On the one wall that I picked to hold myself up because I was so tipsy that I would have fallen down if not for the wall's assistance, the love of my life had a clear view of me. From where she was standing across that overcrowded and enormous ballroom, Felicia was able to not only catch me with my hand in the cookie jar, but she also saw me groping around in it to pick the biggest and most delectable looking one.

She ran over to where I was standing and snatched the young lady's number out of my hand. Felicia Crease wasted no time dealing with the situation.

"Shaytee has a girlfriend; I don't know if you knew dat, but he does."

"He didn't tell me that he did. I was walking by and he pulled me toward him." The girl was petrified. She would have told Felicia that she was deaf, dumb, blind and gay if she figured that it would get her out of the thrashing that she knew she was about to get.

"I know. I saw the whole thing. Um not blamin' you, Um blamin' his drunk ass. You uh freshman, right?"

"Yes, I am. I swear to you that he didn't tell me anything about his girlfriend."

"It's not your fault, he preys on freshmen 'cause he knows dat y'all dough know no betta. Y'all see dese Zeta letters an' y'all lose y'all mind. It's okay. Now you know."

Just like that, that nameless, statuesque, beige and milkshake thick young lady walked out of my life. Felicia dragged me out of that party by my arm and I was too drunk to protest. At that moment, I wasn't the loud and boisterous big man on campus that I portrayed myself to be. At that moment, I felt I wasn't worth shit.

On this night, I was a drunk who couldn't even stand up on his own. It's a good thing that Felicia dragged me out of the Stern Center because there was no way I could have walked that half a block from there back to my dorm if she wouldn't have lugged me. I spent the rest of that night on my hands and knees, hurling out every drop of Crown Royal and Coca Cola I'd consumed just a few hours earlier, into my commode. Felicia sat next to me, Indian style on my cold bathroom floor, rubbing my back and patting my shoulders into the wee hours of the morning. Little did I know, in the very near future, our positions would be reversed on that chilly congoleum floor that had seen better days. I was going to be a father and neither of us knew it.

"Felicia, are you sure?"

"Yes, I'm sure Shaytee. I missed my period."

"Well, maybe, it's just late. Just 'cause you missed yo' period, dat dough automatically mean you pregnant."

"I know my body. I know my cycle. I know Um pregnant. Plus, I took uh pregnancy test this mornin'."

"Oh yeah; an' what did it say?"

I guess in the heat of the moment, I became so bewildered, I asked perhaps the dumbest question I could have. We were in my dorm room standing across from one another and listening to each other's heartbeats, too scared to breathe, waiting on the other to say the next thing.

"It said that I was pregnant, jerk!"

We both laughed at that because if it was negative we wouldn't be having this conversation.

"Look, those things are wrong all of the time. You aine pregnant." I kept saying to myself that this couldn't be happening. As we stood there in front of my TV, with the Cartoon Network braying in the background, I had to laugh to myself at the irony. I was going to be somebody's daddy and I was still watching *Ren and Stimpy*.

That poor kid. With me as a father, he was surely doomed. I was irresponsible, feeble minded and probably the best example of immaturity that C of C could have ever concocted. I was twenty years old but in reality, emotionally and mentally, I was maybe sixteen. Maybe. I had to talk some sense into this girl's head to make her see that she was not pregnant.

"Look, all you gotta do is take anotha test, dass all. You aine pregnant. Your period will prob'ly be on tomorrow since we done talked it all up." I actually believed that stupid shit.

"Shay, listen to me. I've never been late; not one time in my eight years I been gettin' uh period have I been late. Ever."

"You on da pill; so, dat means you aine pregnant, right?" If I was nothing else, I was logical. "Besides dat, if iss mine, you already know dat you gone have tah git rid of it. You do *know* dat, right?"

What the hell possessed me to say that? I knew as sure as the cafeteria at C of C served Mahi Mahi every Friday night that Felicia had absolutely no intention of having an abortion. She had grown up in Mullins, South Carolina. Mullins was a small town in one of the poorest counties in the state. What the people of Mullins lacked in financial capital, they more than made up for in family values. It seemed to me that by the stories Felicia told me, everyone in her town was related to each other in one way, shape or form. It was the tightest of tightly knit communities. She was the first person in her family to attend college. She was raised in a strict Christian home by her grandmother, who was almost as strong willed, opinionated and outspoken as Mama. Felicia's grandmother passed down those traits to her. I guess that's one of the things that attracted me to her in the first place. On the surface, Felicia was a lot like my own mama. She was smart, tough and determined. I was equally as determined. I was determined that I was not going to be a father at sixteen. I was going to say anything to convince her to kill this baby so that I could get my life back. End of story. And at this point, I really didn't give two shits about how she felt about it. Felicia was just going to have to abort the baby. There was no other way around it.

At that point, I said something really asinine. Looking back on it, I should have known it was going to start our own personal World War III.

"Well, you might be pregnant. You might be. But, how I know iss mine?"

Felicia became unglued.

"Mothafucka, I been fuckin' you and only you since September 8, 1997!"

I couldn't believe that length of time had passed. My mouth flew open from the shock that we had been having sex that long or that she remembered the exact date that we'd started having it.

"You uh sorry ass, stupid ass bastid Shaytee Herbert Abraham Gadson!" She knew that I abhorred being called by my full government name. "How da fuck you gone fix yo' dumb ass mouth tah tell me dat you dough know if iss yours?! You are sooo damn trifling and oh sooo fucking ignorant! Oh, my God! You make my asshole hurt wit' all yo' stupidity, boy! When ya punk ass snuck into my room at night tah fuck, ya wasn't questionin' shit! When ya happy ass nutted in me, ya wasn't questionin' shit!"

"I only nutted in you 'cause you was on da pill!" I was getting desperate and sounding more and more imbecilic as this conversation progressed.

"Dis yo' baby! Da pill is not one hundred percent, you fuckin' asshole! People *DO* get pregnant on da pill, dummy! I can't believe you tryna treat me like Um some hoe off da street!" She was crying real tears now.

"All Um sayin' is dat I dough know if you pregnant or if iss even my baby you pregnant wit'!" We were screaming at each other and no one heard a word the other was saying. Somehow, I pondered that my doddering attempt at reframing the argument would help matters. It did not.

My small dorm room was at the corner of Saint Philip and Calhoun Streets. The street was named after the former Vice President of the United States, John C. Calhoun. The walls felt like they were closing in on me. I wasn't feeling presidential at all. I was feeling downright nauseous. Felicia's father had spent most of his adult life in prison. Her mother was so young when she had her, they were more like sisters. She'd told me, too many times to count, just how important family was to her. Be that as it may, her moral stance on when life begins had about as much chance of softening my position as a one-legged man in an ass kicking contest. I was too busy trying to extricate myself from this quagmire that I was stuck in to think that compassionately or abstractly. If she didn't care enough about me to sing this kid a lullaby and put his ass to sleep for all eternity, I wasn't about to care enough about her to seriously entertain this baby bullshit. *Rockabye baby.*

"I ain't fucked nobody else since I been in Charleston, you fuckin' asshole! I hate chu, Shaytee!"

Despite her best efforts to the contrary, I was the picture of serenity and grace under fire.

"How I know dat fah sho'? Huh?! You tell me you pregnant an' Um jess 'sposed tah take your word for it?! Yeah right, bitch! What chu need tah do is git rid uh YOUR baby, goddammit! Dass what da fuck need tah happen! You must be outta yo' rabid ass mind if you think Um gone be dis baby daddy jess 'cause you say iss mine. Piss pregnant on uh million sticks but dis one nigga you aine gone trick! Bitch, please!"

Felicia stopped crying long enough to punch me in the face. Hard. She hit me with such force, I estimated that she'd sent me careening into the next seven days and had extirpated the taste from my mouth. My mama had been threatening to "knock" me "clean into next week" and "slap the taste" outta my mouth for years whenever I did something on the extreme end of defiant. Felicia did in seconds what my mother didn't manage to do in two decades. I staggered into my TV and she pounced on top of me hitting me in my neck, back and shoulders as I fell to the ground.

"I didn't make dis baby by my fuckin' self! I ain't some hoe! Um yo' girlfriend, mothafucka! How can you say dis cruel shit to me?! I hate chu, mothafucka! I hate chu!"

I was well within my right to defend myself, and I'll accept the label "pussy" if necessary, but there was no way that I was going to hit this pregnant woman. As she hovered over me screaming and punching, I just covered my face as best as I could.

When I felt her land that second blow to my face, I could feel the most temporary of insanities inundating my consciousness. I choked her.

"Bitch, git off me! Umma kill yo' ass! You betta leave me da fuck alone!"

As I was liberating the air from her windpipe, I managed to turn her off of me and over on her side. I felt Felicia gagging and coughing. I should have stopped, but I just kept choking her. I must have held her by the neck, hands wrapped around her throat, trying to squeeze the life out of her and my unborn child, for what seemed like an eternity. When I saw this pulchritudinous woman that I loved more than life itself's color go from chocolate to violet, I let her neck go as she gasped for air. I jumped up off of the floor from on top of her and watched her cough and spit and cough until she started to breathe normally again. I almost killed my child's mother. I wanted to act like a grown man and did not want to accept responsibility for what happens to grown men sometimes when they become reckless. When I finally realized what I had done, I ran out of my room leaving Felicia and the baby on the floor in a heap. I needed a drink.

The officials at College of Charleston probably allowed me to remain a student at their venerable institution far longer than they should have. I dropped out of college when I reached my sixth year. I realized that after way too many instances of getting drunk every weekend, having sex with a gaggle of different girls, skipping classes and generally wasting Mama's and Daddy's money, college wasn't the place for me. Long before I quit school, I think I engaged in all of that self-destructive behavior in the attempt to get myself kicked out. I was such a good student in the beginning of my college career, it took way too long for the wheels of college justice to complete the "eradicate Shaytee from the College of Charleston" process. My grade point average was so high initially in fact, that when I started messing up, it took one semester of straight "D's" and another of straight "F's" before the College finally decided to put me on academic probation.

When I finally did get placed on probation, Mama and I went around to all of my professors for that prior semester and got them to change all of my "F's" to "W's" because of "extenuating circumstances". They were better because it meant that even though I had withdrawn from these classes, I would incur no penalty. W's just looked bad on your transcript. As far as I was concerned, they looked a hell of a lot better than F's. Mama was convinced that my academic collapse was due to the fact that very early in the semester, Mama Clay had died. So my mama, being who she was, walked with me around the campus of the College of Charleston after that spring semester ended. We paid a surprise visit to the Chancellor. Then, we went to each professor individually. Mama stressed to these powers that be that because my grandmother had died, I could not be held responsible for those abysmal grades. I was depressed and grief stricken, therefore I was incapable of any reasoned thinking. She told them that I was the Mayor of Hollywood's son. She expatiated that my father was extremely disappointed in me; which only added to the severity of my situation, which had already been duly exacerbated because I was on probation, which was a direct result of Mama Clay's passing. Mama explained that each of these factors added to my stress level. She made a great argument, and the defendant, yours truly, got all of his grades changed for the previous semester by those esteemed professors at the behest of the Chancellor of The College of Charleston.

It happened just like that. I was the Mayor of Hollywood's son and that got me out of a semester full of F's. Hell, I don't think anyone even asked me to produce an obituary as proof. Daddy being Mayor got me out that pile of shit I'd jumped into. Now you see why I loved the fact that Daddy was The Mayor of Hollywood. As the Mayor's son, I had power. I had authority. I had a name. To this day, I believe that Mama was able to get those white professors and the white chancellor at the predominantly white College of Charleston to change her black son's grades for an entire semester not because her mother had died, but because her husband, my father, was who he was. I was a drunkard and a whoremonger. My grades were wretched. I was well on my way to getting kicked out of school before Mama Clay died. Albeit, it took just a few more years for me to fully complete the process, but after she left this side of the Jordan River, The College didn't have to fire me. With remorse that cut me to my very core and a heavy heart, for all intents and purposes I told C of C, "I quit."

After I, for the most part, dropped out of school, Felicia followed suit. I say for the most part because I did manage to hang on to a semblance of my academic career by duping myself to believe that taking one class a semester, and barely attending it, still classified me as a "college student." I loved that label and every connotation that came with it, so I found it oh-so-difficult to part with it.

We found ourselves living in an off-campus apartment while awaiting the arrival of our baby. I was panic-stricken. I had no money and I could not keep a job. Felicia was working at Comcast Cable and keeping a roof over our heads and food in our stomachs. I've never had a job I liked or was good at. A couple years before, when tax time rolled around, I had twelve W2 forms. That calculates to one job a month. I had no passion for anything that I'd ever done for a living. I wasn't proficient at anything. No boss I ever had liked me. I'm going to go out on a limb here and assume that no supervisor I'd ever had held me in very high regard because I absolutely sucked at the jobs they assigned me to do. I'd done everything from signaling traffic on the side of the highway with an orange flag to calling people and telling them that their DirecTV was going to be shut off if they did not pay their bill. Nothing stuck. The more I tried, the more I got fired. I had a child coming and I knew that I had to think of something to do with the rest of my life.

Quati LeNay Crease Gadson was born on Nov. 22, 1998. Felicia's pregnancy was relatively easy. No morning sickness. No midnight cravings. No complications. No nothing. She was pregnant for nine months and then one day just popped out a baby. I was grateful to God that He allowed me to be in the delivery room holding Felicia's hand when Quati came out of her birth canal. I was so grateful, in fact, that I fainted. After the nurse revived me, I saw that my baby girl was was precious and bloody. She weighed seven pounds and fourteen ounces. She was angelic. It was in that moment that I cut the umbilical cord, the full gravity of what I had done to all of the girls that I'd taken advantage of or cheated on Felicia with, truly hit me. I saw some of their faces in my mind. I saw the places I'd been with them. The things we had done and how I used their bodies for my own sexual gratification suddenly filled my soul with mortification. Perhaps, they used me as well. I don't know. But, in that moment, I was sorry for the devious things I'd done and the misguided intentions I'd had where they were concerned. I now had a daughter. The hunter now had as flesh of his flesh and bone of his bone someone, someday, who would surely be hunted. I snivelled and moaned when I went to the neonatal unit of The Medical University of South Carolina because of how I'd mistreated those girls. The thought that some boy or man might one day have the same intentions toward my daughter made my psyche and mortal body go numb.

I secretly said a prayer for Quati and begged God not to allow her to find a man like her daddy. I begged Him not to let a man take advantage of her. I asked the girls for forgiveness in my mind and heart. I didn't have sense enough to know that treating women that way was wrong. It was cruel. Sure, on the surface, they didn't seem to mind. They loved me. They loved the G Dingoes at the College of Charleston and at The Citadel. I realized when I saw that little girl laying in that incubator, helpless and taking in the brightly colored elephants on the wall, the red, green, yellow and blue balloons on her blanket, and the nurses' uniforms, that I was going to have to ameliorate. I was going to attempt to become a better man. I wanted this girl child to not have to pay for the sins of her father. I wanted this baby to be proud of me.

Because I had trouble keeping a job, it was decided that I was going to stay home with the baby. Unsubstantial as it was, I did work as a substitute teacher when I could. Basically, this only amounted to one day a week. On those days, Luci our next door neighbor, would watch Quati until I got home from school. This arrangement was especially strenuous. Luci, even for one day at a few hours a week, wasn't free or cheap. Felicia worked marathon hours. So, me working one day a week proved to be the wisest choice for us given the circumstances. Plus, we saved a ton on daycare. She was an excellent mother. She breastfed Quati. She'd read to her during her pregnancy, but after Quati was born, she read to her voraciously. *The Bible. Curious George* books. Self-help mothering books. She read them all to our baby. She was the most read-to baby in the world. Quati and I had a ball during the day. We watched *Sesame Street* and *Kenan and Kel*. I made her formula and we took naps together. She peed on me, shit on me and retched on me, and I basked in every second of it. I took to fatherhood like a duck to water. Actually, the only thing I've ever been good at was nurturing Quati. It was like Mama Clay and me all over again. But, as always, Felicia and I still struggled. We never had enough money because I couldn't hold down a job. Nurturing your child is good. However, I've learned that unless you're bringing in a steady income of some sort, regardless to whether you're being the best stay-at-home dad in the world, fatherhood and its sometimes precarious dynamics is a tenuous proposition.

Felicia suffered from postpartum depression, I think. She was never diagnosed with it or anything of that nature. But once the daily grind of caring for a baby, then a toddler, kicked in and the constant pressure of trying to keep a roof over our heads continuing to gnaw away at her, she became sad all of the time. And rightfully so. She had little financial support from me; who could blame her for breaking down?

"Shay, you gotta help me. Baby, you have to find uh job. I kan' do this by myself no more. You takin' care uh Quati during the day is good, but we need uh second check."

Every day, without fail, after she got home and rested for awhile, I'd go into our bedroom and massage her back and feet; invariably, after she was sufficiently relaxed, I'd get some variation of that recapitulation. I wanted to help. You couldn't have convinced me that I wasn't helping. Quati and I had become a well-oiled machine, I tell you. At a year and a half, she could identify objects and colors, her gross motor skills were great and she was a well-adjusted baby. But, Felicia was tired of fighting the good fight alone. She was moody and sullen. Working those long hours had made her so tired, she didn't have the energy to deal with our child when she got home. She arrived late to work often enough that over the course of a few years and more than a few reprimands, her tardiness became a deal-breaker for the giant, multinational cable conglomerate. She was trying to stay resilient, but she just couldn't get past this great black cloud that had seemingly hovered over our lives. Then it happened. It wasn't like it caught me by surprise. For years, I thought that wishing the notion away would work.

"They fired me, Shay. They said that I couldn't be late no more, but I just cun get up. I couldn't get up."

Felicia came home that day in 2003 without a job. Little did we know that that pink slip would send our lives careening down a path that we were just not ready for. We had a two-bedroom, two-bath apartment. The rent was far too exorbitant for the part of Charleston where we were living. The light bill was already late, not to mention food and the other things that we needed for the baby. Mama was helping us out, but I knew that if I didn't figure out a way to get us some money really fast, we were going to be homeless. As Felicia sat and cried on our old yellow and brown couch with various Quati stains on it, I just held her tightly in my arms. I tried to console her. The grim reality was I needed someone to console me.

"Everything's gone work out, baby. You just wait an' see. I'll find some-thin'. We gone be okay."

I didn't believe a word of any of that malarkey. I sat there on that couch with Felicia's head buried in my chest and a Hanes undershirt soaked with her tears as I stared off into creation, dazed and confused. I wondered if she'd bought that crock of bullshit I'd told her about us being "okay." I know for a fact that I didn't buy it. I didn't know what to do.

It started off innocently enough. We had endured about six months of living off of Felicia's unemployment check and my meager earnings as a subsititute teacher. We were getting by, but just barely. Felicia men-tioned to me in passing that she had spoken with Mama who had talked to one of her friends about a job that Felicia would probably do well at. It was a position as clerk for the Town of Hunter's Point, which is located just on the outskirts of Charleston County. She would report directly to the mayor and her duties would include clerical work, office management and any other duties not specifically enumerated, but deemed important by him. Felicia was excited because the job paid well enough so that all of our bills would be taken care of and we would still have a little left over at the end of each month. Mama's friend, who was extrememly well connected in Hunter's Point, set up the interview and Felicia interviewed with the mayor.

Peerless Humphries Davier was mayor of Hunter's Point. Davier, in addition to being mayor, owned several businesses. He parlayed his real estate ventures into a three-million-dollar-a-year empire. He was a civil rights legend in Charleston and he and Daddy went back quite a ways. He was rangy and had wavy jet-black hair. His skin was puerile, clear and the color of banana nut bread. And he always smelled like Cool Water Cologne. The man was well into his sixties, but he could have easily passed for forty-five. He had a wife and four adult children. He was a devoted husband, father and grandfather. He used his wealth to feed the poor of Hunter's Point. During election season he even kissed babies. And, regrettably, he needed a clerk.

The Town of Hunter's Point may have been just a fishing village, but Town Hall was an ultra-modern government building. The people of Hunter's Point were very hardy and they sustained themselves by living off of the land. Just about all of its eleven thousand residents loved their mayor. The charismatic Mayor Davier took care of his people and, thanks to his prominent friends in the federal government, made sure that the Town Hall was a well-funded and deft political engine. It was a two story, 8,500-square-foot café au lait brick facility. It was the only seat of government outside of the City of Charleston that had thumbprint recognition technology. In order to gain clearance into certain areas of Davier's acropolis, it was essential. The floors were marble and the ceilings were vaulted. The building had three elevators and two stairwells. On the second floor in the far right corner of the building, Mayor Davier sat aloft his perch in his office. It had a fourteen-foot solid oak conference room table and bathroom with a shower. He designed the chocolate-and-mint-themed office himself. He ran the town from his customized leather chair. It came with a price tag of just over two thousand dollars. The driver's seat was a gift to himself, from himself, for his sixty-fifth birthday. In no government building were you allowed to smoke. Anywhere. Mayor Davier smoked Cuban cigars in his office whenever he damn well pleased. Who was going to tell him that he could not?

The mayor had been interviewing for the city clerk position for the better part of two and a half months. No one, not one person, was qualified enough in his estimation. Geneva Stanislowsky had been his clerk for the last quarter-century and knew him better than his wife. Unfortunately for the mayor, Geneva had grown tired of the cutthroat world of politics and had decided to retire back to Mother Poland. She was a steely-eyed Slavic immigrant from Warsaw and she would have done anything for Mayor Davier. The mayor gave her her start in life and they built Hunter's Point government from the ground up. The petite brunette with the gray eyes finished the mayor's sentences. She sent his wife two dozen long stemmed yellow roses and a heart shaped box of Godiva Chocolates every year on her birthday, Valentine's Day and their anniversary. The super-efficient Slav was proving to be irreplaceable. Felicia was the sole interview that the mayor was going to do for the day before his tee time at 4 o'clock. And he was only doing this as a favor to his friend who said that her friend had the perfect young lady for the job. The mayor just didn't conduct the interviews on Friday afternoon. He'd ask her a couple of questions and send her on her way.

The mayor was dressed that day in a navy blue Armani suit with powder blue pinstripes, thousand-dollar cufflinks and navy blue Ferragamo leather loafers. He emanated of Cool Water. He was brushing his hair and looking in the wall-to-wall mirror when his secretary buzzed him, "Felicia Crease is here to see you, Mayor." He cleared his throat ostentatiously. "Send her in."

"How are you? I'm Mayor Davier."

What was that alluring scent she was wearing? The mayor almost pondered this aloud. Felicia's signature pear scent wafted in the air, then danced in his nose. He couldn't help but marvel at how soft and smooth her hand was as he shook it. He held it for a half second longer than he should have, and wondered if the temptress noticed. He stared her directly in her eyes the entire time as he looked in his periphery at her left ring finger. It was naked.

"I'm Felicia. It's an honor, Mayor. Your reputation precedes you."

"Oh, does it now?"

"Yes sir, it does. You were fighting for civil rights in Charleston when the fights were the most brutal. You were a key organizer of the 1969 Charleston Hospital Workers' Strike. You kept developers out of Hunter's Point until they showed you that their long-range plans would be beneficial to the people who have spent their lives here. You have been a titan in the African Methodist Zion Church for over four decades. I know you, sir. You are a legend."

Mayor Davier didn't impress easily, but Felicia impressed him. She walked into his office, shook his hand, took her seat and gave this man a short synopsis of his life before he had a chance to seat himself. He chuckled and regrouped quickly.

"Well young lady, seems you know all about me. Let's see what I know about you. Your resume said that you attended The College of Charleston. Communications major. So what have you been doing since you graduated?"

"I didn't graduate, sir."

"Oh really now, smart young lady like yourself? What happened?"

"I had a child, sir. In trying to care for her and working, school was no longer feasible."

"I see. Is her father around? Does he help out?" The wheels had already started turning in the mayor's head.

"Yes sir, we're still together. He also attended The College of Charleston. He's an excellent father."

"Is that a fact?"

"Yes, sir."

"Well, I'll be the first to tell you, I'm not the easiest person in the world to work for. I demand excellence. I believe in accountability. There will be long hours. Some days, between dealing with citizens' concerns, my demands and the folks from the state in Columbia, you will want to quit. Will you quit on me, Ms.Crease?"

Felicia smiled at his statement. She knew she'd won him over. The job was hers.

"If I'm hired, I will not sir."

"Okay, Ms.Crease, my secretary will notify you of my decision no later than Monday via email."

"Thank you, sir."

"I trust you will see your way out."

"Absolutely, sir."

He watched the sway of her hips in her chocolate business suit, with the pink pinstripes, as she left his office. He couldn't take his eyes off of her. He watched her walk down the staircase and out of the building. The mayor laughed to himself, "How could she have known that I love chocolate brown?" He chuckled again already thinking about his golf game at 4 and how he was going to give this ambitious young lady a chance. "Monday morning indeed, Ms. Crease. Monday morning, indeed." Then, he swung his imaginary nine iron in the direction of one of the stairwells.

After Felicia had been working at Hunter's Point for a while, everything was, "Mayor Davier this" and "Mayor Davier that." Day after day, she would talk about some new deal that her conquering hero, Mayor Davier, was closing, or some huge purchase that he'd told her to make for his wife. Please don't get me wrong, I was grateful to the man for allowing us an avenue to be able to eat and to survive. But as a man, when you hear your woman talking about another man like she worships him, it's only natural that jealousy was starting to turn my brown eyes green. I mean, sure it was only her boss, but from everything that I had heard about him from other people and from what Felicia said about him herself, I couldn't compete with the man on any level. He was an attractive, sophisticated, well traveled and very wealthy older man. He also controlled her job, which controlled her money.

The lesson I had yet to learn in life at twenty-something is that when any man, especially if he is boss or husband, controls a woman's money, that woman tends to look at him with either a sense of reverence or antipathy. Depending on that man's psychological profile, that woman's repugnance will be masked as adulation. And most of the time, that man's personality quirks are indicators as to how well he will treat that woman. If that man happens to be a mature, decent and self-actualized individual, that woman will love and honor him. Conversely, if that man happens to be a dictator, her sense of inward recalcitrance for him will outwardly be obfuscated as love. She will continue to fake it until she can make it without that man.

Disastrously for me, all things considered, Davier was an okay guy. So, guess who became a virtual demigod in my house? And who was I to Felicia? I was her underemployed, substitute teacher baby daddy who was at home watching the baby more often than he was in a classroom because teachers are not sick most of the time. More often than not, their children are well. The vast majority of the time, they don't take vacation days. Subsequently, most days I was at home with the baby. One day, I overheard her talking on her cell phone with her homegirl as she came home from work.

"That man is amazing," she was saying. "I truly believe that he can do anything. Uh huh. Girl, I know. An' girl, he be tellin' me 'bout how when he an' his wife were startin' out, how they din have nuttin' girl. Mmm hmm. She dough appreciate him. Tammy, I know how hard dat man work to give her da good life so she can spend her days in da spa gettin' mani's and pedi's. He say most uh da time, when he come home, ain't nuttin' on da stove fah him. Say he gone have to hire uh cook it done got so bad. Girl, he say all he is is her ATM. He be sayin', dat she be sayin', dat he don't spend enough time wit' her. Bitch, he out here tryna make a livin' fah yo' ass! Girl, an' he be lookin' so sad sometimes. Yeah girl, Um gettin' ready tah go in da house right now. Dey prob'ly sleep. Yes, girl! She gettin' so big! Yeah girl, he here. He right here. Tammy, you stupid! You know dat, right?! You is too crazy, girl! Okay, girl. Holla back at chu, later. Love you too, Tam. You know you need to stop, crazy. Bye, bitch."

Our bedroom window was right by the front door of our apartment. It was tinted, but it wasn't soundproof. I was lying on the queen size bed that we'd gotten from Mama and Quati was resting on my chest. She was sleeping. I was not. Felicia was talking on her cell phone to a friend about the mayor while she was at the door putting the key in the lock. She was talking to Tammy, her bestie; that wasn't unusual. The fact that she was talking about the mayor wasn't particularly unusual, either. As a matter of fact, he had become the standard topic of discussion in our tiny apartment. However, what did color me curious was the fact that she was talking about the man's home life and his wife. It became glaring to me, that day, that they were more than employer and subordinate. They were friends. They were *great* friends. A Siberian chill shot through me that turned my blood into ice water. I was so naïve. When Felicia pushed the door open, she turned the corner, walked into our bedroom and found me and Quati sound asleep.

Later, though: "Shay, I am SICK of facing eviction every fuckin' month! Um tired uh bein' the one that gotta get up every mornin' an' doin' what I gotta do to keep uh roof over our damn heads! When you gone get up outta dis house, *every* day an' do what chu gotta do?! Um not gonna be tossed in da streets because you don't wanna work!"

"I have uh job! Um doin' da bess I can, Felicia!"

"No you ain't, Shay! Da best you can? Da best you can?! Substitute teachin' one day uh week is not the best you can, Shay. You one uh da smartest people I know. Why can't you keep uh job, baby? What's wrong with you?!"

I couldn't answer that one. "I jess need some time tah get myself tagetha on uh job, dass all." That one was wearing thin.

"Shay, you been sayin' dat for da longest. Quati is almost six, man! She aine gettin' no smaller. Every day I find uh pair of shoes for her dass done got too tight or uh pair uh jeans dat she's outgrown."

"Felicia, Um tryin'!"

"Tryin' aine gettin' it no more, Shay! You gotta do somethin' baby. Um tired uh havin' to handle all dis shit by myself! I need you to be uh man, Shay!"

When we began to talk about bills and the money that we didn't have, our conversations always commenced with placidity and mutual restraint. Then, when Felicia started to think about all the money we were bereft, she'd start yelling the paint off the walls.

"Shay, I love you with all uh my heart an' soul! Um not gonna live in da streets for you, dough! Um not! I work too hard not tah be able la pay my damn rent, Shay!"

"I saw the eviction notice. I called Mama an' she said dat she would help us and..."

"No, Shaytee! Every month yo' mama helpin' us an' Um tired of it! I need for you to be uh man an' get uh *real* fuckin' job!"

"I am uh man!"

"No, Shay; uh man is willing to do whatever it takes to feed his family! If you had to take uh job as uh fuckin' janitor to feed your child an' keep uh roof over her head, you would do it if you were uh man! I kan' take dis hand to mouth shit much longer! Iss killin' me on da inside!" She started pacing the floor as she anathematized underneath her breath: "Felicia always gotta find uh way. Felicia always gotta handle shit. I'll handle shit like I always handle shit. I've handled it. You betta know Umma rider for mine, buddy. I got dis under control. I got dis. Dass aw'right, Shay. Dat is aaaw'right.

Normally, whenever we'd have an argument, we'd try to make sure that Quati could not hear us. We would turn the television volume up in our room and double and triple check to see that she was watching TV in her room, which was on the other side of the apartment. Looking back on it, considering the apartment was only about seven hundred square feet, I guess if we got loud enough, which we almost always did, Quati could hear us, which I guess she almost always had. I'd made Felicia cry because I'd disappointed her. Again. She'd placed a lot of trust in me when she decided to have my child. When a woman decides that she is going to have a baby with a man, she is entrusting that man with her life and the life of that child. She is telling that man that I trust that you will be a man. I trust that you will ensure that the lights remain on, rent is paid, this child's back is clothed and stomach is full. I was failing my woman and my child. Miserably. She was sitting on the edge of a bed that I didn't buy, crying about money that I didn't make, to take care of the rent that I couldn't pay. Wait a minute, she said she'd handled the rent, right? Isn't that what she said? I walked over to the bed to console her and to ask her about the rent. I wish I never would've opened my mouth.

As I was standing at our room door watching my girl cry, I meandered over to the bed and sat beside her. Between the tears, I was telling her that everything was going to be okay. I kissed her on her cheek and tasted her salt water tears. As I pulled her toward my chest, she buried her head there and I rested my chin on her head. I finally worked up the nerve to ask her the question that I'd already known the answer to.

"Baby, where'd you get the rent money?"

I'll never forget the look she gave me as she lifted her head up off of my chest. It was a strepitous glare. It spoke in a very loud and violent timbre a million words that she'd already said; and a million more that she could not give voice to because she didn't want to shatter me.

"You know where I got it from, Shay."

I broke down crying. I slid off of the bed and got on my knees in front of her.

"You take dat mothafucka money, Felicia?!" I was wailing uncontrollably now. "How you take dat mothafucka money?!"

She was crying and screaming at me through her tears.

"I took his money because we needed it, Shay! This ain't college no more; this is real life! We are drowning, Shay! Dass why I took it! He offered it to me! I didn't ask him for it!"

"How da fuck he offer it if you didn't invite da mothafucka in our business?!"

"Dass my boss and my friend! I was asking him if he knew of anybody dat would hire you!"

"I don't need dat mothafucka tah find me no fuckin' job, Felicia. I don't need dat shit!"

"He asked me if I needed anything and I told him about the eviction notice, Shay!"

"What da fuck did you say to him?!"

"I told him that we were four hundred dollars short!"

"An' da mothafucka gave you four hundred dollars?!"

"Yes! He went into his wallet and gave me four one hundred dollar bills! Yes!"

We were screaming at each other so loudly that at first, we didn't hear Quati knocking at the door. By the time we did hear it, my little girl was standing there crying.

"No fighting! No fighting! I don't want my mommy and daddy to fight!" I was enraged. I was mad at Felicia for taking her boss's money. I was mad at myself for not providing for my family.

"You fuckin' him, Felicia?! You an' dat mothafucka fuckin'?!" I read her face for a twitch or a quiver or some kind of movement that would give me the answer. Her face told no tale. Her lips didn't, either. She didn't answer the question. "Felicia, are you fucking that man?!" Silence.

Quati started screaming. "Daddy, don't yell at my mommy! Please!" I was enraged and outraged now. "Ansa me, Felicia!"

By this time, she'd run over and picked up Quati by the door. She thought I was going to hit her so she picked up the baby. Quati was screaming and hollering. Felicia was boohooing. I was shrieking. I did want to hit her. Instead, I punched a hole in the two-bit, cheaply painted, milk colored bedroom door. Felicia jumped back.

"Shay, please leave before I call the police! You scarin' Quati!"

My child was screaming hysterically so I left the house. As I jumped in my truck and drove off, I met a squad car pulling into our complex. Our nosey neighbors had beaten Felicia to the phone. I drove around for hours hoping that the police weren't given my license tag number by her or the neighbors. When I realized that I wasn't going to jail that night, I figured out exactly what I needed to do to make myself feel better. At ten minutes before seven, I found myself parked outside of a dingy white building with three red dots on it, which in South Carolina denotes a liquor store. It was sorrow-drowning time.

"No, Felicia! Fuck no! Anything dat bastid tell you to do, you do! I am so tired of this bullshit!"

"Shay, don't start dis shit again. I do what he tells me to do because that's my boss. Somebody in dis house gotta work. You show as hell ain't."

"So, you an' him goin' outta town? Tagetha? An' by y'allself?! Y'all mussy think people crazy! Tah some Suburban Cities and Rural Municipalities Consortium meeting, that you just *now* gettin' 'round to tellin' me about- that 'bout right?"

"Yeah. That's exactly right. I told you about it months ago, Shay. He told me right after I got hired that we would have to travel out of town together sometimes."

"You didn't breathe uh word tah me about none uh dis shit. You really dough give uh damn about me, do you? Um just da damn babysitta. Ansa me dis: how long y'all been fuckin? Huh?!"

"Shay, he's uh married man an' Um tired uh you askin' me dat."

"You tie'ud uh me askin', but for months now I been tie'ud uh you not answerin' with uh straight yes or no."

"What chu need to be tired of is not pullin' your weight around here, Shaytee. I've been askin' you fah months now tah git anotha job 'cause da subbin' aine cuttin' it."

"Any other job I get will barely be enough to cover daycare for Quati an' you know dat. You always thowin' dat shit in my face. You know we come out far betta an' far cheaper with me stayin' home wit' her. If it wasn't fah Quati, I'd uh been gone." Because Quati's birthday didn't meet an August deadline prescribed by the Charleston County School District, we had to wait to enroll her in kindergarten just a few months before she was to turn six. Now we could have enrolled her in Evangel or the exclusive Porter-Gaud School in Charleston, but there was no money pay the expensive tuition. Money was our Achilles Heel, even when it came to an issue as rudimentary as to how best to facilitate the formal education of our baby. It never failed. It seems like every day when Felicia came home from that job that I hated with that boss that she loved, or was in love with, we fought about it.

In late 2004, our fighting, arguing and general discontentment with each other came to a head. It's not like we didn't see the finish line in sight; I guess it's just after seven years and a child together, no one was ready, seriously ready, to say that it was a dead end ahead. Finally, one day in November, Felicia gave up trying.

"Shay, maybe iss best dat you go back home to Miss Linda. You not workin' an' bein' depressed about not havin' money all da time is wearin' on me. Quati gettin' to da age now where she knows when we are genuinely happy wit' each other an' when we puttin' on a show for her sake. You know what she axed me the other night?"

I was waiting for this. I knew it was coming because I'd heard Quati and her talking in the kitchen when I was in the bathroom scrubbing the tub. Perpetual underemployment had turned me into quite the domestic.

"She axed me why we keep makin' each other sad an' mad. She said dat she loved Daddy, but she wondered why every night I'm in the room by myself an' Daddy in her room with her and Brother Flukey." Brother Flukey was Quati's stuffed panther and by this point, even he probably wanted me gone because I was taking up an awful lot of space in his bed. I'm sure Brother Flukey had thought about mauling me in my sleep more than once. I know his love for Quati was the only thing keeping me alive.

"She aine say dat shit. You jess want me gone so dat you kin bring da nigga ovah here. I pay bills ovah here, too. Damn if Umma leave my house!"

"Shay, you need tah go. Um not yellin an' Um not screamin'. Um not happy an' I haven't been for a long time. Yeah, you pay bills. But it ain't enough, Shay." I'd never seen her so tranquil and halcyon during one of our arguments. I was in the living room and she was in the kitchen, which was really one room. Felicia was serious and she wasn't shouting or angry. She just wanted me to go back home to my mama. I wasn't going to leave that easily.

"Lemme tell you something: ain't no other man raisin' my chile, you hear me? I'll die an' go da hell before I leave Quati here wit' chu!" She was frying chicken and she was as cool as a cucumber. She barely looked at me. I was fuming because she hardly wanted to engage me in conversation and it appeared as though I was being kicked out. She continued poking the chicken as the grease popped her on her hand.

"Shay, listen. This is my house and my name is on the lease. Not yours. Mine. I don't want you here. I want to be wit' uh man who gone make me happy. I want to be happy. Um tired uh fightin'. I want to be happy; and I'm going to the meeting with the Mayor. It's for my job and I will be back on Sunday. Will you please keep Quati until I come back?"

"I keep my child every day. I'll be gone by the time you come back, Felicia, dass cool." I had gone from angry to serene. I was going to win the contest on who could be most equanimous on the outside while most volcanic on the inside. "But I bet chu if I gotta leave, Quati damn sho' comin' wit' me."

She didn't even look at me. "Okay, Shay, we'll see."

No one said another word for the rest of the evening. The chicken grease popped as Alex Tribek grandstanded with answers from the TV. Oh, how I wished I was Alex Tribek at that moment because I had nothing but questions in my mind and on my heart. It was Tuesday, November 3, 2004. I had five days to plan the greatest escape ever.

I was packed and waiting when Felicia got home Sunday from her trip to Hilton Head for the meeting. I calmly anticipated the ambuscade as I sat in very plain sight on the couch. Quati was bouncing like Tigger on my lap when her mommy slid the key in the door.

"Hey, Felicia."

"Hey, Shay. I see you packed, huh?" She looked genuinely hurt.

"Yup."

Then I did what I hadn't planned to do at all. All weekend long, I had contemplated how I was going to make a huge scene when she walked in that door and how I was going to take the baby to live with me in Mama's house, in the same room I grew up in. I was going to slap the taste out of Felicia's lying face as I was walking out, too. She'd been lying to me for months. Of course she and this affluent and efficacious man, who *always* got what he wanted, were having a dalliance. I didn't know it for sure, but I knew it in my heart. I couldn't blame her. If I were a smart, young and attractive girl who worked with a man of that caliber every day, then had to come home to a sack of shit whose biggest decision of the day was whether or not to let the baby have another apple wedge or apple sauce, I would have cheated on me too. Maybe I would have done what Felicia did for months: neither confirm nor deny. In the end, after all of the mental scheming, I got up off of the couch and sat Quati down. I turned on ETV so that she could watch *Reading Rainbow* while I took my suitcases and Hefty Garbage Bags to my truck.

Felicia was sitting on the edge of our bed crying. These were probably tears of unspeakable jubilation because she was finally going to be rid of me. I don't know. After I took the last garbage bag out to the truck, I went into the room and kissed her. We hugged for a long time sitting on the edge of that bed.

"Shay, I love you. We just need some time apart to see what happens next."

"Yeah, take care uh yourself."

The tears were welling up in my eyes. I had a baseball sized lump in my throat that I couldn't swallow. I walked out to the living room and kissed Quati while she was totally engrossed in the book Lavar Burton was talking about. It was called, *The Giving Tree*, by Shel Silverstein. It was a book about a little boy who planted a tree. The tree and the boy grew through different phases of life. As the boy matured, the tree provided him shade and he even used the wood from the tree to build himself a house. When the boy became an old man, he used part of the tree to fashion a walking cane out of. And when the old boy/man died, someone in his family, I imagined, decided to use the tree to construct his casket. As I watched, I wondered if my family would bury me in a pine box or a nice and expensive mahogany sarcophagus like Mama Clay had. I also wondered in that moment if Felicia would attend my funeral. I realized that because of the current circumstances in which we found ourselves entangled, the only reason that she would show up to my home going service would probably be to make sure that the bane of her existence had finally bit the dust. Quati was fascinated by this story. For some reason, so was I. I was sure going to miss our television filled days. I was going to miss living here.

"Quati, Daddy gotta go, okay?"

She looked puzzled. "But why, Daddy?" Her tears were already starting to form.

"Well, Daddy gonna go to Gramzy's house for awhile, but I'll be here every day to see you. 'Member what we talked about this weekend?"

"Yeah. You gotta go to Gramzy's house to stay so you and Mommy won't be sad anymore, right?"

"You got it, Quati! Who's da smartest lil' girl in da world?"

"I am!"

"Who's da prettiest lil' girl in the world?

"I am!"

"Who loves you big as da sun?"

"My daddy!"

"That's right, girl! Always!"

"Always?"

"Always, forever and a day!"

"I love you, Daddy!"

"I love you too, my baby."

I could hear Felicia sobbing. I could see her shaking. It looked as if she was almost to the point of seizure with her head buried in a pillow in the room so I didn't bother to say anything to her as I walked out. I left the house key on the coffee table right next to the plate of Quati's Chef Boyardee Ravioli. Felicia would see it when she got up, I guessed.

"Friends to know'ah, ways to grow'ah, ah Reading Raaaaainbooooow!...." *Reading Rainbow*'s theme song was my fade to black. That was the last sound I heard before I walked out that apartment, for the last time, as a resident. My baby was transfixed on the TV amidst the background noise of Felicia's moaning and the show's soulful ode to the joys of reading. Even now, whenever I see Lavar Burton as I channel surf, I get a knot in my stomach. I walked down the cement path leading from the apartment and I saw Felicia on the couch holding the baby through the slits in the venetian blinds. Quati was singing along. Felicia was wiping tears from her cheeks. I was walking aimlessly with a purpose. I was headed back to Hollywood. I was on my way home.

CHAPTER 12

Banned from Hollywood

Linda Dingle Gadson is Rural Mission. Rural Mission is Linda Dingle Gadson. Quite simply, the two are inextricably linked. On paper, Rural Mission is a non-profit ecumenical organization. It fosters, promotes and ministers to the spiritual, economic, social, educational, medical and housing needs of the five Charleston County Sea Islands: Johns, James, Wadmalaw, Yonges and Edisto. Mama's been called the "Mother Teresa of the Sea Islands." But in reality, Rural Mission is an idealistic society of sorts. White volunteer work teams come from across the country and descend on the five-acre campus, which is on Johns Island and faces a large saltwater creek and a lush marsh front. The volunteers come each year to work on the homes of poor African-American, white and Latino people from the aforementioned five Sea Islands. Rural Mission has been around since 1969 and has been building and repairing homes since its inception. It was doing the work of Habitat for Humanity long before Habitat existed. The glaring difference between Rural Mission and Habitat is that when the Mission erects or repairs a home, the people who live there are not burdened with a mortgage. I am of the opinion that Jimmy Carter is one of the most well-intentioned and compassionate presidents, and effective statesmen, these United States has ever produced. I never really grasped why though, while Habitat has done so much for so many, it saddles those who can least afford it with a mortgage. If I could, I'd ask the 39th President that.

Rural Mission operates on the thinnest of shoestring budgets. Their money to operate comes primarily from donations by churches and private donors. This Shangri-La is run by African-Americans who serve poor African-Americans. Perhaps it is because of this fact that "God's Little Soul-Saving Station" hasn't gotten more exposure, notoriety or credit for the people they've touched. And the lives they've changed. Perhaps. The affluent work teams, constituted of doctors, lawyers, engineers, CEO's and many other professionals, for one week during the summers, come to serve the poorest of the poor. The people who they serve live in the type of unrelenting squalor that, if you have not been exposed to it on a regular basis, would physically sicken you. Mama has been in charge of this outfit for twenty-five years, but she has been there since 1972. A summer job turned into a thirty-year plus mission from God to help hurting, impoverished and spiritually depleted people.

On Tuesday evenings during the summer, the native islanders gather together at Rural Mission for the legendary Seafood Jamboree. The Jamboree is part gospel music show, part soul food and seafood smorgasbord and part church service. Mama has everyone to align themselves in a big prayer circle where the African-American locals and the white volunteers introduce themselves and tell where they're from. Over the past three decades, people with mind-boggling wealth from all fifty states and at least twenty different countries have intermingled and socialized with local people who are absolutely destitute.

I get the distinct impression that the Seafood Jamboree looks exactly like heaven must look. The Mission is just across the Bohicket Creek and is less than a mile away from two of the most exclusive and pricey resort communities in the United States: Kiawah and Seabrook Islands. Oprah Winfrey once owned a home on Seabrook and Kiawah is world-famous for its golf courses, especially the Ocean Course, home the 1991 Ryder Cup and the 2012 PGA Championship, among other tournaments. Celebrities from across the globe routinely flock to the islands because of their world-class amenities and unparalleled ambience.

Rural Mission isn't exclusive at all. It's all-inclusive. It makes room for the rich, the poor, Latinos, whites, blacks, Native Americans and Asians – anybody and everybody. On Tuesday nights, we all get together to partake of the boiled Lowcountry blue crabs, fried shark, fried chicken and a virtual cornucopia of other Lowcountry dishes. Homemade okra soup, cornbread, red rice, watermelon and "sweet tea" [sweetend iced tea] also grace the menu of these feasts. You can see practically see the mouths of the swarms of the out-of-state teenagers, who come to the Mission, water. They anxiously anticipate the moment that they partake of the food for the first time. Okra soup is similar to gumbo and the wonderful concoction consists of okra, shrimp, sausage, crab and any number of vegetables blended together in a tomato based soup. Those kids always consume every drop. Red rice is really white rice that morphs into red when it's mixed with tomato paste. The rice and tomato paste are slowly and expertly cooked together. In my mind's eye, I can taste those bits of celery and sausage embedded in those fluffy and pillowy beds of rice. I smell the salt coming off of the black water of the Bohicket Creek as we stand out there on the pier, nestled on the property between thickets of green and yellow marshland and the Atlantic Ocean.

We always gather in a circle around the wood-planked, seven-foot-long, six-inch-tall stage with the moist island dirt under our feet and a song in our hearts. We wait for Mama to get on the stage and facilitate the singing, the praying and the meet-and-greet that are all a part of this mountaintop experience. The orange and blue horizon above our heads coalesces with the sky, which goes from henna to cerulean to periwinkle as the sun sets. The sky that becomes a veritable rendering of a Basquiat canvas, right before your eyes, gives your five senses a feeling of serenity like nowhere else on earth. That gentle sea breeze blows just off the Atlantic, which flows into the Intracoastal Waterway, which swells into the Bohicket Creek. This life affirming deluge becomes the water by the pier. It always makes you feel like God is truly amongst us. The massive oak trees on the property seem to forever look down approvingly at the sight that they see at the Jamboree.

White hands calloused from the week's work, interlock and overlap with gnarled, knotted and grubby hands of Mexican migrant farm workers, whose hands mesh with the worn and wrinkled hands of local black islanders. They come to the Mission on their weekly pilgrimage to experience, almost as if it was the first time each time, this unparalleled phenomenon.

An added bonus of the Seafood Jamboree experience, every bit as transformative and transcendent as the Jimi Hendrix Experience, is the sights, sounds and the looks of astonishment on the faces of those white children and teenagers. The kids watch the native islanders dexterously break open the blue crab shells. On the heels of that, they suck the orange eggs out of them. They go on to pick clean the creatures. And the islanders repeat this process until the volunteers get the hang of it. Much like spying the spellbound audience at Woodstock as Jimi lit up the Star-Spangled Banner, watching these kids intently study the island natives as they perform this lesser known Lowcountry blue crab concert is a joy to behold.

Before the eating begans, Mama makes sure that from the makeshift stage, as she looks out over that massive prayer circle that sometimes includes upwards of five hundred people holding hands together, we stop and introduce ourselves to one another. The adult chaperones of the work camp volunteer teenagers serve as spokespeople for the various work teams. They always tell us what particular group they represent, where they're from, what church they attend and just how fulfilling their work week has been. After the volunteers introduce themselves to the locals, the locals introduce themselves to the farm workers, the farm workers introduce themselves to the volunteers and the volunteers introduce themselves to each person they may have missed in the other two groups with a handshake and a hug, Mama shouts, "Hallelujah!" She goes on to tell the crowd just how grateful she is not only for their presence on that Tuesday evening, but for God's presence amongst all of us. After the introductions and salutations, The Rural Mission Prayer Group takes us to glory through song. The Prayer Group is a covey of elderly ladies and a few elderly gentlemen. They meet at the Mission every Tuesday for prayer and have done so since Mama founded the holy platoon in 1986. They sing and chant gospel songs, hymns and old Negro spirituals. The Negro spirituals are derived directly from slavery and were taught to them by their grandparents and great-grandparents who were trapped in the "peculiar institution." Mama sings, "Have you gaaaaaaaaht (got) good relig'jaaaaaaaahn (religion)?" and her band of prayer warriors who are seated in steel folding chairs behind her on stage warble, all twenty in unison, "Certainly Laaaaaaawd." "Have you gaaaaaaaaht good relig'jaaaaaaahn?" "Oh, Certainly Laaaaaaawd, Certainly, Certainly, Certainly Laaaaaaaaaawd!" The women clap and the men stomp their feet to provide the percussion. Mama beseeches the crowd to start singing as she sings, "Is Your name on hiiiiiiiiiiiiigh?" "Certainly Laaaaaaaaawd!", would be the crowd's instinctive response. It was utterly amazing to me, but a flock of the volunteer kids would always end up singing and shouting on just the second chorus of one of the Prayer Group's songs. The Holy Ghost would always come upon them.

But, prior to the singing and certainly before the eating, we always pray. Mama prays and thanks the Lord for His majesty, for His bringing together of so many different races and colors of people, for us loving and understanding one another and for His Holy Spirit. Under the canopy of live oaks and caught up in the smooth caressing sea breeze of Bohicket Creek, visitors and locals alike sit in steel folding chairs, at plastic folding tables, on top of wooden benches and even on the cool dirt ground. If it starts to rain as we stand outside, as it sometimes does, Mama just steps off the stage. She proceeds to kneel on that dirt ground that she spontaneously makes her altar and begans to pray: "Lord, we trust that the good work that You have started here on this evening, amongst Your people, will be allowed by Your hands to continue. We humbly beseech You, Master, to allow us to sup with one another on Your holy ground. So Father God, if You only so please, hold back the rain. Hallelujah!" If it looks like it's going to rain, it will not. If it has already started to rain, the rain would stop. Many people have witnessed Mama turn away the rain over the years. We would see latecomers to the festivities experience utter befuddlement when they enter the gates of the Mission. Water from the rain that they just came through having thoroughly soaked their cars, only feet outside of the campus, compels them to marvel at the fact that there was no rain to be seen falling on Rural Mission's real estate.

Rural Mission, Inc.: ANSWERING PRAYERS

Since 1969, Rural Mission, Inc. has taken citizens in South Carolina by the hand as they endure difficult times in their lives. Linda Gadson, executive director of Rural Mission, is the embodiment of that dedication.

"We try to look after the whole person, whatever their needs may be," says Gadson, a 25-year veteran of Rural Mission. Those needs come to her in the form of migrant children needing basic necessities, families that have had their utilities disconnected, and a stack of prayer requests that she bundles with her well-used Bible—only an inkling of the overflowing filing cabinets and boxes that she keeps in her prayer room at home.

Powered by a staff of more than 100, and a volunteer presence that numbers at least 1,000, Rural Mission is addressing two specific needs through Roper Foundation-funded programs—the distribution of prescription drugs to those who need but cannot afford them, and the addition of bathrooms to homes that don't have indoor plumbing. Gadson motions to the cracked walls and broken windows around her as an example of situations the Mission comes into contact with everyday.

A minimum of 5,000 people receive assistance from the Mission every year, says Gadson, and with an ever-growing list, every little bit of support counts. "We have no problem with people reaching us, the problem is having the resources to take care of the need," she says. "Roper Foundation has really been a blessing to us."

HOUSE CALLS · 33

Mama featured in House Calls Magazine.

Mama praying with volunteers as they began construction of a home.

*Mama front and center at the Seafood Jamboree making sure that **everybody knows everybody**. The meet-and-greet is one of the highlights of the evening.*

A volunteer work team at the Seafood Jamboree singing and praising the Lord on stage under the majestic oak trees.

Volunteers connect hands, pray and partake of the mouthwatering Sea Island cuisine at the Seafood Jamboree.

The soulful ladies (and gentlemen) of The Rural Mission Prayer Group pictured on the pier at Rural Mission.

As people were coming to the Jamboree after Mama opened her holy parasol, they talked about how badly it was raining, thundering and lightening as they came down Bohicket Road, which is the road that runs contiguous with Rural Mission, Kiawah and Seabrook. The latecomers were amazed at the fact that right outside Rural Mission's tract and as far down the highway as their eyes could see, it was storming. Inexplicably, as soon as they landed on the Mission's property, it seemed to cease. Mama would just effervesce on that stage and smile. People would stand in stupefaction of her as they jumped out of their cars, joined the food lines and relayed their individual stories to each other about this weather anomaly. She would just continue to beam.

All are represented at those Tuesday night gatherings. We get a chance to truly understand and communicate with one another. For some of us, it's a new realization that we are more alike- than we are different. It was on those balmy Tuesday summertime nights between 6 and 9, where wealthy and poor, black and white, old and young, business executives and day laborers, country folk and city slickers, all come together to pray, praise, sing and eat. I learned at a very young age that if heaven didn't look and feel like a Seafood Jamboree at Rural Mission, it had to be pretty close.

Linda Dingle Gadson is an irresistible force and an immovable object. If there were no Linda D. Gadson, you would have to create one. I have seen this woman care for the children of migrant farm workers, provide human services for the poor and indigent of our community, pay bills for people who have had their lights and their water turned off and feed people when food was nowhere to be found. I've witnessed her feed mobs on what amounted to "food fumes." And in a fashion similar to how Christ asked God to multiply the five loaves and two fish to feed the multitude, she has been on her knees in supplication at 4 o'clock in the morning in her prayer room, for over two decades, asking God to multiply scarce resources to help a hurting people.

She has petitioned God perpetually to divinely increase Rural Mission's stake, as the mission has been on the brink of closing its doors for lack of funds far too many times to count. Her faith and belief that God would give her what she needed, to keep the doors of the Mission open to serve His people, have made her an icon.

The Jamborees were Mama's time to pray, sing, shout and feed everyone that came there for those Tuesday night fellowships. Anyone who has ever been touched by them will carry the memory for a lifetime.

I have those memories, too. Notwithstanding, I will always remember the Seafood Jamboree and those Tuesday nights for a far more sinister reason. After we'd had a joyous and festive time one night in the early 1990s, Daddy tried to kill Mama.

Because we would normally arrive home from the Jamboree around 10 or 10:30, Mama would always make sure that she would get one of the cooks in the kitchen to prepare a plate for Daddy. Like everyone else, he was fond of the food. He knew that on Jamboree nights, Mama didn't cook. When we got home, as was customary during the week, Daddy had on his sober glasses as he sat in his recliner waiting to graze on the food. Because the juices from the boiled crab seemingly

would seep through our skin causing us to smell like the critters themselves, it was always a race for us to see who would get in the shower
first. Telley was helping Mama bring the food out of her van, so I ran to
the shower. I was grateful that I had beaten her there on this particular
night. Normally, I would have to stew in my own crab induced funk
while she used the shower first. But on this particular evening, the inver-
sion of our normal shower sequence almost got Mama obliterated.

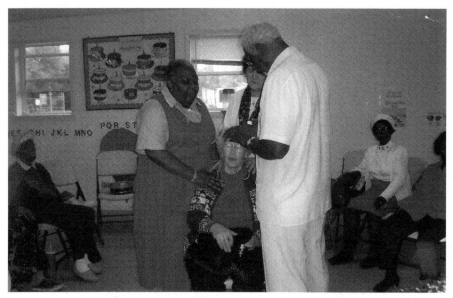

*Mama as she prays for and uses **Hallelujah! Oil** to aid a Seabrook Island resident during a
Tuesday afternoon prayer meeting held at Rural Mission.*

For the longest time – and nobody ever really knew why – Reggie,
Telley and I never used the blue bathroom's shower and bathtub. We
christened our comfort station "the blue bathroom" because everything in
the lavatory, from the walls to the toilet water, was some tranquil shade
of blue. You couldn't find a more relaxing environment to, in Daddy's
words, "take a cool shit." We shared a bathroom, but we three kings of
Orient minus one, plus a princess, were guided to the perfect light of
Mama and Daddy's shower and bathtub. When I went to use their shower
on this particular Tuesday, it didn't dawn on me as abnormal, nor did I

give it a second thought when I heard Mama close her bedroom door that was in relative proximity to her shower door. What was disconcerting was the ferocity with which she slammed it. It was a thunderous "I'm mad as hell" slam. That much I knew. What I took for granted was that Daddy, as was his normal procedure, left his wallet on top of the television. The TV was only about two feet from the bathroom door that led into the shower. When I shut the bathroom door, the loud thud and the vibration from the door slamming to close knocked his wallet onto the floor. When Mama came into the room to get settled for the night, she observed his wallet was on the floor. When she bent down to pick it up, she noticed something. She then raced down the hall toward the den where Daddy was satiating himself. After I heard the bedroom door crash, all I heard was Mama screaming.

"Herbert, do you think I'm stupid?! I know you fuckin' da slut! I been known, but now I got my proof, nigga! Herbert, you uh damn dirtbag; you know dat?! I got tah look at this whore every Sunday in church an' she always grinnin' in my face! Man, when you gone stop doin' dis to me?! If you dough want me, gimme uh damn divorce! You can have the house; I just want my children! Herbert Gadson, you dough want me and I damn sho' dough want chu! Nigga, you make me sick! If you wanna continue to fuck that Lafayette Muldrow slut, you can do that! Just gimme my damn divorce!"

Mama ministers to a young man during a prayer meeting.

BISA's Distinguished Black Women

1981
Harriet Tubman*
Shirley Chisholm*
Marva Collins
Wilma Rudolph*
Nan Brown
Mary McLeod Bethune*
Barbara Gardner Proctor
Hazel W. Johnson
Frances C. Welsing
Marian Anderson*
Yvonne B. Burke
Rosa Parks*
J.C. Hayward

1982
Ida B. Wells*
Lorraine Hansberry*
Yvonne Young Clark
Althea Gibson*
Fannie Lou Hamer*
Barbara Jordan*
Rosemary Reed-Miller
Phillippa Duke Schuyler*
Phyllis Wheatley*
Leontyne Price
Carolyn Payton
Judith Jamison

1983
Mary Church Terrell*
Louise Diagne
Jeanne C. Sinkford
Katherine Dunham
Charlotte H. Brown*
Sadie M. Alexander*
Helen Simth-Mason*
Althea Simmons*
Freddye Henderson*
Eloise Greenfield
Maya Angelou
Renee Pouissaint

1984
Augusta Savage*
Brenda Swann Holmes
Daisy Bates*
Lena Edwards*
Janet Collins
Annie Woodridge*
Ophelia DeVore
Willie M. Whiting
Gwendolyn Brooks*
Dorothy Bolden
Esther M. Kpor
Ethel Lois Payne*

1985
Madame C.J. Walker*
Sojourner Truth*
Gladys Scott Roberts*
Cicely Tyson
'M' Alineo N. Tau
Azie Taylor Morton
Goler Teal Butcher*
Vera C. Edwards*
Deborah P. Wolfe*
Ruby Dee
Charlotte K. Brooks*
Susan L. Taylor

1986
Patricia R. Harris*
Dorothy Ferebee*
Lois Mailou Jones*
Marion Jackson
Mary H. Futrell
Ruth Bates Harris McKenzie*
Pam Johnson
Maxine Waters
Jennie Patrick
Floretta Dukes McKenzie
Vernice Ferguson
Falaku Fattah

1987
Bessie Coleman*
Anna J. Cooper*
Zora Neale Hurston*
Clara M. Hale*
Selma Burke*
Michele C. Boyd
Edith V. Francis
Carmen Turner*
Joyce F. Leland
Yvonne Walker-Taylor
Pauli Murray*
Ernesta Procope

1988
Maggie L. Draper Walker*
Madame Lillian Evanti*
Helen G. Edmonds*
Marian Wright Edelman
Norma Merrick Sklarek
Hilda Howland M. Mason
Addie L. Wyatt
Mary Grayson*
Sybil Mobley
Ruell Cone
Arnette R. Hubbard
Yvonne Kennedy

1989
Hatshepsut*
Winnie Mandela
Delilah W. Pierce*
Roselyn P. Epps
Doris W. Jones
Lena Horne
Margaret T. Burroughs
Era Bell Thompson*
Phyllis Wallace*
Wyvetter Younge
Alyce Gullattee
Beatrice Gaddy*

1990
Unita Blackwell
Nannie H. Burroughs*
Johnetta B. Cole
Meta Vaux Warrick Fuller*
Kimi Gray*
Ethel Harvey
Ruth Wright Hayre*
Juanita Jackson Mitchell*
Constance Baker Motley*
Arline Neal
Eleanor Holmes Norton
Marta Gabre-Tsadick

1991
Oral Lee Brown
Mary Schmidt Campbell
Elizabeth Catlett
Barbara L. Harris
Jean Blackwell Hutson*
Jacqueline Joyner-Kersee
Jessye Norman
Gloria Randle Scott
Pat Tobin
Dorothy Porter Wesley*
Vera T. White

1992
Margaret W. Alexander*
Byllye Avery
Cardiss Collins
Dolores Cross
Christine Darden
Hazel Nell Dukes
Mae Jemison
Genevieve Johnson
Sharon Pratt Kelly
Eula H. McClaney*
Dionne Warwick
Lillian Lincoln

1993
Madeline Cartwright
Alice Coachman Davis
M. Joycelyn Elders
Ella Fitzgerald*
Bertha Knox Gilkey
Hannah Hawkins
Joanne Martin
Njinga*
Niara Sudarkasa
Alice Walker
Flavia B. Walton
Princess Whitfield

1994
Debbie Allen
Etta Moten Barnett
Willie Barrow
Theresa Brown
Emma C. Chappell
Evelyn Davis
'Sweet Alice' Harris
Edith Irby Jones
Georgia McMurray*
Carrie Meek
Carolyn Reid-Wallace
Donna Jones Stanley

1995
Juanita Kidd Stout*
Cynthia A. McKinney
Bettye Collier-Thomas
Shirley Clark-Franklin
Joyce E. Oatman
Carol Moseley Braun
Rita Dove
Mona Lake Jones
Frances M. Plummer
Joyce Roche'
Louise Jackson
Hazel R. O'Leary

1996
Beverly J. Harvard
Mahalia Jackson*
Leontine T.C. Kelley
Ida Van Smith
Shirley A. DeLibero
Frances L. Murphy II
Marcia Ann Gillespie
Carrie Saxon Perry
C. Vivian Stringer
Dorothy West*
Carolyn Jordan
Joann Horton

1997
Rebera Elliot Foston
Osceola McCarty*
Helena Ashby
Benita Fitzgerald
    Mosley
Deborah Hyde
Leah J. Sears
Lena S. King Lee
Carol Doe Porter
Mary Hill Johnson
Regina Benjamin
✱ Linda Dingle Gadson
Ruth J. Simmons

Mama was honored in the 1997 edition of the Black Women In Sisterhood for Action Calendar. Icons such as Dr. Maya Angelou, Rosa Parks, Ruby Dee, Winnie Mandela and Zora Neale Hurston are amongst the world changers that have also been featured in the calendar. A few of my heroines are highlighted (denoted with an asterisk). You may recognize some of the names on this illustrious and star-studded list.

Honorees

July, 1994

LINDA DINGLE GADSON

Social Worker

Linda Dingle Gadson is an unusual person who is a master of all trades. She serves as Executive Director of the Rural Mission on Johns Island, where she is counselor, doctor, minister, teacher, lawyer and real estate agent for her spiritual values, caretaking skills and the importance of education. Gadson graduated from the College of Charleston with a major in political science and a minor in sociology. Although she was planning to to enter law school at the University of South Carolina in 1972, she got sidetracked by a part-time summer job coordinating one of the projects at the Rural Mission of Johns Island, Inc.

Over thirty years later, she is still there. "The Rural Mission, Inc. fulfilled the need for me to help otherd," Gadson explained. "The mission fosters, promotes and ministers to the spiritual, economic, social , educational, medical and housing needs of five Charleston County Sea Islands: Johns, James, Wadmalaw, Yonges and Edisto." The Rural Mission, Inc. is an ecumenical, non-profit organization founded primarily to care for migrant farm workers and needy families. It is located in a small community on Johns Island and is supported primarily by a network of churches and congregations throughout the United States. The mission is constantly expanding services and projects.

Gadson oversees the coordination of services and the operation of the facility. Serving more than 250 children, the Migrant Headstart Program is one project that cares for migrant farm children in four location. Migrant Headstart has helped to rescue children between six weeks to five years from the fields and to provide them with a healthy environment where learning is

Mama was honored in the 1994 edition of The South Carolina African-American History Calendar. This calendar shines a spotlight on black South Carolinians who have made significant contributions to our state and our world. Jazz great Dizzy Gillespie, former World Heavyweight Boxing Champion "Smokin'" Joe Frazier and former House of Representatives Majority Whip and current Assistant Democratic Leader James E. Clyburn, are among the calendar's previous honorees.

*"Servanthood is my thing;
I was sent here by God to be available
to touch the lives of his people."*

Faith

Mission Impossible?

Linda Dingle Gadson
Executive Director, Rural Mission

Not to Linda Gadson, who oversees a
staff of 100, backed-up by at least
1,000 volunteers. Together they
make the impossible happen,
distributing prescription drugs to
those who need but can't afford
them, adding bathrooms to homes
without indoor plumbing, and
supplying migrant children with the
basic necessities of life. Busy as she
is, she doesn't neglect her faith or
that of others—beside her Bible are
a stack of prayer requests she tends
to daily. "She's one of God's
dynamos," said a colleague. "She
lights up many lives." Amen to that.

PHOTOGRAPH BY WILSON BAKER

Mama featured in Charleston Magazine.

Daddy never looked up from the plate of Seafood Jamboree food that Mama brought for him until he heard her maniacal rodomontade stop. Now, it was his turn.

"Linda, I dough know whah you talkin' 'bout. I aine fuckin' no damn Lafayette Muldrow. I see dat woman in church, jess like you see her in church. The only thing I know is that all uh us go to da same damn church. That's all I know about the woman. I dough even know no damn Lafayette. Linda, I dough want no damn divorce, but you keep pushin' me an' fuckin' wit' me! You make me wanna go in da street and find uh woman! But I'm tellin' you Linda, as sho' as stink stuck on shit, I dough know no Lafayette an' I dough have no damn woman! Linda Gadson, you outta yo' fuckin' mind! You done stan'nup ya an' done become deranged right before my damn eyes! Lawd, *please* help my crazy ass wife 'cause dis woman done gone bucking damn fool!"

Would you believe that years later, a guilt-ridden, remorse-addled and tear-soaked Lafayette appeared at our doorstep? She almost gave Mama a coronary when she came to her door, asked who it was and discovered that it was Daddy's former mistress standing on the other side of it. As soon as she pulled open the door, Lafayette commenced to sobbing and saying that in the years since she and Daddy had their tryst, her life was reduced to rubble. She lost her single wide trailer, the job that she'd worked as a home health nurse for twenty-two years *and* her husband. She told Mama that on that very morning, the Holy Spirit spoke to her very clearly and told her that the reason her life had taken a nose dive was because she had terribly wronged Herbert's wife. The Lord Thy God then intimated to a contrite and repentant Mademoiselle Lafayette Antoinette Zja'Nele Muldrow that the only way she was going to recover any semblance of the life she once knew was to go to Linda Gadson and beg her forgiveness. It seemed only right to me, that because of Lafayette's French Creole ancestry, the only response she *could* have articulated to the voice of the Lord was, "Oui Oui, Jesus! Oui Oui!"

Before Lafayette could utter another word, Mama grabbed her by the hand, embraced her and guided her into the house. They made a beeline to the prayer room and the two ladies kneeled at the prayer stool simultaneously. Mama then proceeded to pray for Lafayette as fervently and passionately as Billy Graham, T.D. Jakes or Joel Osteen would have. After Mama finished praying a prayer that made Lafayette weep as bitterly as The Apostle Peter, immediately after the cock crowed, she removed Lafayette's shoes. Then, she purposefully and deliberately extracted Lafayette's socks from her weary feet. Mama, then anointed and washed Mademoiselle Muldrow's feet in her special *Doozy, Mama and Me Oil.*

But on that Seafood Jamboree night that she discovered Lafayette's number, had she paid Mama a visit, Mama would have taken her Bible and beaten Lafayette Muldrow senseless with it. As a matter of fact, Sister Linda Gadson *told* me that she would have beaten her church sister like she was Kunta Kinte. The First Lady of Hollywood admitted that she would have then made Lafayette tell her that her name was Toby.

"I'm not outta my mind Herbert, an' I'm not crazy! If you don't know da bitch, den how you get this?!"

Mama threw his wallet at him. When Daddy picked it up off the den floor, he got a load of his "Town of Hollywood" business card with "Mayor Herbert Gadson" embossed on the front of it. His heart dropped into britches and subsequently plummeted into his drawers. He knew what was written on the back of it – Lafayette Muldrow's name and telephone number – and he knew Mama had seen it.

As Mama turned around and started to leave the room, Daddy sprang from his chair. He hurled his porcelain Corning Cookware plate, still full of Mama's Seafood Jamboree food, straight at the back of her head. Telley just happened to be coming down the hall at that exact moment. She flung her arm up and deflected the heavy plate. It was an arm flung up to heaven. That arm must have been a prayer because that plate was mere inches away from meeting its mark.

There was no doubt about it now: Daddy was having another affair. And neither was there any doubt that the mother of three and the First Lady of Hollywood, South Carolina, would have been a corpse had Telley not been there at that precise moment. The same Seafood Jamboree that brought Mama so much joy, and that was interwoven into the very fabric of who she was, almost contributed to her demise.

Daddy walked outside and lit a cigarette. Mama dropped to her knees where she was. And there, in the midst of the fried fish, fried chicken, macaroni and cheese, red rice and okra soup that were splattered all over the walls, TV, fireplace and floor, she began to pray.

"Praise You, Father! Hallelujah! God, I thank you for sparing my life! The devil tried to kill me in my own house, Master, but You saw fit to let me escape death because I know You love me so. Thank You, Jesus! Hallelujah!"

I was standing there in the den, mouth agape, naked and covered in Dial Soap. Dial kills 99.9 percent of bacteria and 100 percent of crab. As all of this happened, I was in the shower trying to take the smell of the delicious crustacean off of me. I am still bowled over at the carnage that met my eyes when I ran out of the shower, through Mama and Daddy's room, down the hall and into the den: Telley's arm was bruised and already starting to swell. Seafood Jamboree piquant fare variegated the room. Mama was on her knees praying and interpolated in all the mess. Tears streaked down my face at the sight of the delicious conglomeration of the foods we loved. That savory heap was to be a testament to the mama I almost lost.

Even today, tiny specks of that food are still lodged in a little corner of the left wall of our den, because try as we did, we just couldn't completely scour all of it. That little corner is now a memorial to the remnants of a love gone sour, or that maybe never even existed. I can't speak for Telley or my mama, but for me, Seafood Jamborees never quite seemed the same. The food never quite tasted as good after that.

Mama and Daddy should have gotten divorced long before they officially decided to call it quits. They were never happy. Just three short years after they were married, an unsaved Mama took the butt of Daddy's loaded rifle and smashed out every window of his 1971 Chevrolet Monte Carlo. She found a motel key in Daddy's pants pockets after he came home drunk. He reeked of Smirnoff Vodka, another woman's perfume and her womanhood. Mama once said, "Out of the thirty and a half years that we were married, me and ya daddy may have been happy two of those years. Maybe."

Daddy would tell me that he was only happy one day – the day they got married. I would always wait until he started drinking and goad him into telling me the story of how he and Mama ended up betrothed. Over time, and after I got over the devastation and dolefulness of situation, it amused me. Daddy always made a grim situation even more indecorous with his poignant obiter dicta. I'd be sitting on the couch while we watched TV and say something like, "'Ey Big Herb, how you an' Mama en'nup marrid?" Because I knew the story inside and out, I'd start laughing even before he'd start talking.

"Boy, lemme tell you somethin'. I married ya mama so dat I wun be homeless. I aine had no place tah go an' Doozy say dat in order fah me tah stay wit' dem, I had tah marry Linda. She say we aine been gah live in sin unda her roof. So yeah, I was uh happy ass somebitch, bubba. I been happy as uh pig in shit dat I wun gone be homeless."

When he came back from a teaching assignment in North Augusta, South Carolina, he saw that his room at Grandma Arthelle's house had been pilfered by his cousin. Chitney told him that he had "squatter's rights." Daddy understood that, by any reasonable definition, he was in fact homless. He knew he had to do something.

"Boy, look ya (here): I had tah find me uh place tah stay so I axed Linda tah marry me."

Daddy always told me that verbatim when I asked him, from the couch, if there was a big courtship between him and Mama. Drunk or sober, his statement never changed or wavered. The story was just that simple. However, it was far from an open and shut case for Daddy. You see, he was already engaged to another young lady. Maybe he actually loved the other girl. Maybe he didn't. Daddy would palaver for hours on end about it when he was drinking and when I asked.

"Man, Shay, I took my damn ring back from dat damn gal because I loved my family. I also liked da fact that dey (Reggie and Mama) had four walls an' uh fuckin' roof over dey heads, even if it was in Doozy house. I wun gone be outdoors for no damn body. Man, damn dat shit."

Mama said that ever since Reggie was conceived on a blanket on a grassy knoll at State College, about a month after the Orangeburg Massacre, hers and Daddy's relationship was off and on at best. When she was in the kitchen, and Daddy and I were in the den strolling down memory lane, sometimes Mama would chime in.

"Shay, me an' Herbert were going together since high school. He aine nevah been serious about no relationship or family, so even after I got pregnant an' had Reggie, I never really expected us tah be together. I do owe yo' daddy. If he had never gotten me pregnant, I would not have become the first black woman to graduate from The College of Charleston 'cause I would'na had no reason tah come back home. So, I guess I owe him. But son, yo' daddy been playin' games uh looong time. You hear me? A looong time."

Then Mama laughed a hearty laugh. "Shay, the more I think about it, Herbert Gadson an' I shoulda nevah happened. Reggie was almost four when we got married- when I made the biggest mistake of my life. Man, me an' ya daddy shoulda just stayed friends. Dat man aine nevah care 'bout nobody 'cept Herbert Gadson. Ween nevah been on da same page."

It would be right around that point in the conversation, Daddy would jump up from the recliner with feigned indignation and say, "Man, Linda, please wit' all yo' bowshit. Marryin' me was da bess move you evah make. Y'all aine even had taulit in Doozy house. Y'all po' ass niggas been pissin' an' shittin' in da damn shit house. Y'all was some impoverished and destitute ass somebitches if you look at the sitcha'ation objectively, Mrs. Gadson. Y'all aine had pot tah piss in an' couldn't afford da winda tah throw it out uh (of). Ya broke ass mothafuckas, you. You see how she do me, Shay? Ya mama is uh ungrateful ass heffa. You see how she talk 'bout me afta I put her in dis damn palace?" Then Daddy would laugh his signature cackle. Daddy's laugh sounded like the noise the TV makes when the wind knocks out your satellite or when the cable service is interrupted and there's nothing on the screen but snow. Whereas the sound of the snow is continuous,

Daddy's laugh had clipped pauses in between. UH/KE/KE/KE/KE/KE. His laugh was one of a kind and I loved it.

Mama's feigned indignation would always be just a bit more dramatic. She'd look at him over the kitchen counter as he was holding court in the den and say something like, "Herbert Gadson, if I'd uh knew da hell I woulda caught wit' chu, me an' my chile woulda stayed in a manger before I agreed tah marry you. And if memory serve me correctly Mr . Gadson, y'all was usin' outhouse facilities, too. Was y'all not? "Oh, man Linda yo' ass! See, we had da two seater shit house. Dass 'cause we was some biggity, rich ass po' niggas. Y'all was jess regular po' niggas, ya'undastan'. We had da Cadillac uh (of) shit houses. Y'all shit house aine been nuttin' but uh damn sloppy jalopy."

Then they'd both laugh hysterically.

For the last fifteen years of their marriage, my parents went from a healthy toleration of one another, to merely paying bills together and passing each other in the hallway en route to their regularly scheduled daily programing. Between Daddy's alcoholism, infidelity and the fact that he resented Mama deeply for getting saved, he would often quip, "I aine marry no damn preacher. I jess married uh good woman. I din sign up for all this prayin' an' *'God- from- da- time- ya (you)- open- ya (your)- eye- in- da- mahnin'- til'-da- time- ya-close-um (them)-at-night' mess you got goin' on."*

The last five years of their marriage were pure hell, but by that time Daddy and Mama were living totally separate lives, including sleeping in separate rooms. Their relationship was totally financial. And it was actually working out for them. Daddy still had his women. Mama still had her Jesus. Things were going along fine. Then, out of left field one day, Daddy just up and moved out. The Mayor of Hollywood had found true love.

Daddy divulged that he didn't have any other choice but to move out. Specifically, he evinced that, "da betch turn my black ass *cleeean* out, son." I was chauffeuring him one day and he broke the entire situation down for me.

"Man, dat damn Vivian did things tah me I ain't nevah had done tah me before in my whole fifty somethin' years uh livin' on dis damn earth!"

What he discovered was that Mama had finally had enough. He found himself in front of a judge in divorce court. He left her high and dry and the Mayor of Hollywood had finally crossed the line. For years, Mama had erased and redrawn said line, like a gerrymandered district, to make allowances for his infidelity. Daddy couldn't help himself. The man was a pathological line crosser. He did the inexcusable in the eyes of not only God, but of the greater Hollywood community. He left Mama in the house by herself. The phrase that I kept hearing over and over again by the townspeople was, "Man, Herbert mussy aine know whah da shit he doin'. Shaytee, yo' daddy done gone fool fah sho' now. Da Mayor done plumb loss e mind." If my Daddy had any idea what lay ahead for him, Mama said, "He woulda left dat slut right under the rock whay he found her."

In my town of Hollywood, it is almost acceptable for a married man to have affairs with other women. Depending on the man and his stature in the community, sometimes it's even kosher for him to have a whole other family, complete with children, outside of the confines of his marriage. These facts are just embedded in our subculture, I guess. What *is* totally unacceptable is to physically leave your family even if emotionally, mentally and psychologically you had been gone for years. You especially didn't leave your house. You never, in my town, as the man of the house, voluntarily leave your house. In Hollywood, as a husband, you left your house only through court order or at the point of a gun. You absolutely never left your house if you were the Mayor of Hollywood. You committed political suicide if you, as Mayor, left the domicile that you shared with the patron saint of Hollywood herself, Saint Linda of Pineland.

Daddy told me, on that car ride, because he was in the drunkest of states and most introspective of moods, that he did in fact regret the relationship with the woman he left Mama in the "house by herself" for. Shortly after he had purchased the woman a new couch, china closet, bed and dining room suite, he caught her in that bed with another man.

"Man Shay, dat thing hurt me goddamn. I come home early from Town Hall one day thinkin' I was gone surprise her wit' uh midday screw, ya'undastan'. Goddamn, I walk in da fuckin' house, right? All I hear was dis betch talkin' 'bout, "Oh, shit. Oh, shit! Damn, you fuckin' dis pussy! Gate (Great) God, you know you fuckin' me right!"

I was speechless as Daddy and I were driving through Hollywood that day. He liked for me to drive him around town when he was drinking. I enjoyed it because contrary to popular belief, it was Herbert Gadson, not Will Rogers, who was America's greatest storyteller. The Mayor of Hollywood used words like Monet used oil paint. He knew I liked to hear his stories so I didn't mind driving at all. I learned a lot about what made him the man that he was on those drives.

"Goddamn when I gone up da stairs, who I see wit' she damn legs up in da air but dat damn gal wit' some nigga on top uh her, fuckin' dat sweet ass pussy. I just stan' in da doorway lookin' fool. An' you know what dat nigga say tah me when he stop fuckin' her long enough to realize dat I was standin' right dey, huh Shay?"

Years of growing up in a home where dysfunction and insanity were the rules of the day, and the unchallenged laws of the land, had rendered me insane as well. Here my father was telling me about his infidelity and instead of being mortified and crestfallen, I was laughing to the point of tears. Through the laughter and the tears, I managed to ask, "Whah e say, Daddy? Whah dat nigga say?" I loved egging him on. I lived to set up his punchlines. I was the best straight man in the history of Hollywood. Over the course of years, we'd become quite a comedic juggernaut. Abbott and Costello. Martin and Lewis. Richard Pryor and Gene Wilder. Chris Farley and David Spade. The Mayor and The Boy. We were definitely in that pantheon.

"You know whah dat mothafucka say? He say, 'What da fuck is you lookin' at, nigga? Get da fuck outta here, dis my pussy now!'" So naturally I inquired, as I was deliriously laughing, "So what chu do, Daddy?" He broke out in a drunken snigger and said, "Da fuck you think I did, boy? I leave dat betch right dey! I run downstairs an' grab some uh my shit I already had done pack up. Vivian lil' girl let me know da score one day when she got mad at me fah drinkin' her damn Sunny D. Sheen nevah like me. I'n nevah like her lil' funky attitude havin' ass, neitha. It was da fuckin' Sunny D I bought, mind ju. She gah tell me talk 'bout she kan' eat her grits an' eggs if she aine got no Sunny D. Da fuck she think she is?! I tell her lil' black ass she betta chase da grits an' eggs wit' some milk an' git da hell out my damn face! Eat some cereal uh some shit! Nooo! She too good fah Tony The Tiger. Her stomach mussy line wit' gold an' kan' digest Lucky Charms an' shit, enny?! I done tell her ass da shit is magically delicious! Grits an' eggs ev'ry damn day. Da fuck! I know dat lil' spiteful ass betch been in school all damn day plottin' how she been gah git even wit' me, ya'undastan'. Maaan Shay, time dat heffa git home dat evenin', she gah tell me talkin' 'bout, 'You know my mama got another boyfriend right?' So I aine say shit, but evah since dat day, I had me uh pack duffel bag wit' most uh my essential shit in it so it aine been shit fah me tah just get up an' go. I say man mothafuck uh Vivian Dumars, Shay! Fuck dat dirty, damn crazy ass betch! I aine talk tah dat dirty betch since dat day I left dat damn house. Lawd, I miss dat betch dough. Vivian was tall, yella, dat pussy was smokin' an' dat thing had stay weeet (wet) up; I miss fuckin' dat thing. Dat mothafuckin' gal fuck me on uh dime an' I make dat pussy spit out nine cent uh change. Yes suh! Shitch'yeah boy; sweet pussy Viv!"

I had to pull over to the side of the road because I was laughing so hard, I couldn't drive. By this time, Daddy was laughing at me laughing at him. He looked over at me and said, "Boy, you one crazy ass somebitch." I looked over at him and said, "Yep, jess like my ole crazy ass Daddy." We were both doubled over with laughter at this point. I guess after all we'd been through, we were all crazy.

The timing of Mama and Daddy's divorce was only advantageous for Daddy sexually. Not only did Mama hire a private detective to put him under surveillance and found damning evidence of him coming in and out of Vivian Dumars' house, but the really terrible part was that Daddy was in the midst of mayoral campaign. He had weathered many political storms over the course of his fourteen years in office. Besides the attempted rape charge, he had a very public affair with his secretary where her "Dear John" letter was leaked to the media. In an ironic twist of sexual fate, Reggie had quite a few libidinous rendezvous with her before she started working for Daddy. Reggie used to work under her, literally and figuratively, while they were in Kiawah's employ. It later surfaced that she embezzled five thousand dollars of town funds while she, literally and figuratively, worked under Daddy.

Daddy was not only used to Hollywood's obtrusive perlustration regarding "all things Mayor Gadson" and the controversy that generally resulted from it, he thrived on it. He paid little attention when people started talking about how wrong he was to "jess leave Linda in da house by eself." Daddy would always say, "Boy, dey can't tell me shit 'cause dey can't outthink me. They can't fuck wit' me, Shay. My political enemies can't fuck wit' me 'cause I da black Bill Clinton. I can't be stopped. I can't be touched. Nobody can touch me." Nobody touched Daddy to make him fall from the top of the political totem pole in Hollywood. Everybody just kind of talked him down.

We gave Hollywood back to the white people on June 6, 2003. Herbert Gadson's tenure as the Mayor of Hollywood was done and there was nothing that anyone could do about it. Quite simply, the townsfolk had grown tired of Daddy's antics. I was standing outside of C.C. Blaney, which on Election Day served as a polling station. I clearly heard this lady, who just so happened to be one of Wesley's octogenarians say, "Um so damn tie'ud uh Herbit an' his shit, an' Um so goddamn tie'ud uh dat nigga jess makin' we so damn shame in dis town. I hope everybody in dis town git some sense in dey head da'day an' do whah I jess did an' vote fah dat cracker runnin' 'gence Herbit ass. Man, we gotta git his black ass out dat office. I dough like dat cracker runnin' 'gence um, but lease he whoa make we shame tah say we from Hollywood. Who I feel sorry fah is Linda an' dem chern dough; dass who I feel sorry fah. God knows I love Linda, but Herbit wit' all dat drinkin' an' bein' drunk up in Town Hall gotta go. Herbit ass got tah leave dat Town Hall da'day! Put da white man in da office. Lease we know he whoa make we shame."

It was unbearably hot that day. Besides the looks of heat aggravation I saw on people's faces, I observed another look. It was plastered on the faces of the black people who came out to exercise their civic duty and moral obligation. It was the "Herbert-Gadson-with-all-of-his-drinking-is-going-down-today" look. Along with beads of sweat, I could see the vengeance rolling off the brows of very angry black folk. Black folks in Hollywood had had enough. He had made them utterly ashamed to admit they lived in Hollywood. It seemed that everybody in Charleston County and many people from well beyond had heard of his many scandals. If you lived in Hollywood, you knew someone was going to laugh as soon as you admitted it. You also knew that they would only want to talk about that "Mayor out there" and his latest shenanigans. The Mayor had made Hollywoodians – black and white – feel worn down, dejected and downright mad.

Reggie and I stayed out there from seven that morning until seven that evening. We hoisted signs and passed out flyers trying to convince people to vote for Daddy. We distributed the propaganda in 100-plus degree heat as we screamed "VOTE FOR MAYOR GADSON" and "VOTE FOR OUR MAYOR." But even my brother, who was sober that day because he wanted the one hundred dollars that Daddy paid all of his campaign workers so he could buy crack that night, knew what we all were thinking. Roundly, we were far too nervous to verbalize those thoughts. But when Reggie said it, I knew Daddy's time as Mayor was up.

We were relaxing outside of the school, taking a break from toting signs, passing out flyers and shouting campaign rhetoric, when Reggie was struck with a bit of philosophical inspiration.

"I think damn near everybody wake up dis mornin' wit' Daddy on dey mind, man. Dey got on dey knees and said, 'Lord, please dough let dis day pass an' dat nigga still da Mayor uh Hollywood.' Den dey call all dey friends, family an' church members an' axed all uh dem tah pray dat exact same prayer."

We laughed a long time about that, but Reggie was right. It was going to take an act of God to oust Daddy from office. The good black *and* white Christian folks of Hollywood were going to help the Almighty out with the miracle.

I kept hearing black people say, over and over again, almost as if the town had developed the mantra, "We love Linda an' dem chern, but Herbit black ass got tah git out cha. Man, people tie'ud uh seein' Herbit on da news. Herbit should'na leave Linda in dat house by eself."

Ironically, what those people were most livid about on that day wasn't necessarily the fact that Daddy had taken up residence with the woman he left Mama for, or that his public drunkenness had become more and more visible, or that he had brought shame to himself, his immediate and extended family. No, what angered folks the most was that he had left Mama home alone.

The people got what they asked for. Hollywoodians spoke in a collective voice as bombastic as the one Mama says "Hallelujah!" in. After fourteen years, they sent Herbert Gadson packing. But what exacerbated the situation, at least for Daddy, was how he lost. It was rumored that the other black man in the election's three-way race was "placed" there solely to siphon votes from him. Many people, years later, still do believe this to be true. Even with that, Daddy still only lost by eight votes.

That June day, he lost much more than an election. That day my father lost his identity. He lost every bit of his sense of himself. He left the Mayor of Hollywood in the polling place that day. On the morning of Election Day, he sauntered into Town Hall as the Mayor. That evening, by the power vested in the votes of Hollywoodians, he was deported back into private citizenship. He hadn't ventured into that country in nearly two decades. He was just Herbert Gadson again. Regular Joe. Daddy lost his soul that June day.

I really think the Vivian fiasco wounded Daddy far deeper than even his most drunken moments will ever allow him to admit. Daddy was proud of three things. The first was that, at more than fifty years of age, he didn't "need no damn Viagra" because his "dick worked fine." The second was that he was The Mayor of Hollywood. And the third was that he could do anything that he wanted in the streets, as far as infidelity was concerned, because his "damn wife wasn't gah damn divorce" him. Out of the three, he lost his office and wife within a six-month span. The effects, politically and psychologically, castrated him.

Half a year after Mama divorced Daddy, he lost the closest election he had ever been involved in. This was in large part the result of the fact that he did not have Mama's public support. She didn't give any rousing speeches for him at church. She didn't hold court at the Hollywood Post

Office, where people congregated to pick up and drop off mail and gossip. She wasn't at the Piggly Wiggly or anywhere else imploring people to vote for him. But, despite her lack of public endorsements, every morning before the sun rose, she was on her knees at home praying for him.

Daddy's loss of his wife and his election virtually ripped his heart out. Herbert Gadson was done, and he'd ended up sticking the fork in himself.

In the first few years after Daddy was ousted as the Mayor of Hollywood, he spent much of that time drinking or drunk in an apartment in Charleston. He utilized most of his days trying to convince himself that he cared little about Hollywood politics. It was a different couch, recliner and venue, but his vitriol and my level of interest in his sermons remained the same.

"Shay, I dough give uh shit whah da people do in Hollywood. You see how dem niggas did me with dat election shit? Man, damn uh Hollywood! I gave dem niggas water an' sewer when da city uh Charleston been fightin' Lela Dickerson (the mayor he defeated) about dat shit fah years. I let a lot uh dem niggas put trailers on land dat legally, not so much as a doghouse should'na been ney (there). I fixed dem niggas houses. I brought development, industry and jobs to dat town, an' you see how dem niggas thank me? You see? Dey replace me wit' dat goddamn demon. Dey put uh demon in office because I drink too much. Man, fuck uh Hollywood! Dey gah see whah happen to dey ass once dat demon ass cracker staht puttin' his *white* foot up dey *black* ass. Dat demon shit (fooled) all lem niggas, Shay. Every lass one uh um. Hollywood is uh poor an' workin' class community an' dat demon whole goal is tah disenfranchise da same people who put him into office – black people!"

To add insult to political injury, days after the election, Daddy was charged with burglary and the unlawful use of a telephone. In a drunken fit of rage, he barged into a woman's home and accosted her, accusing her of causing him to lose the election. Mayor Gadson, according to the reports, said he was going to take her to an area of Hollywood where people have been known to disappear. Later on that same day, he called the Town Hall and threatened the new mayor and his administration. He was arrested a couple of days later and had to appear before the same judge he and my brother had faced years earlier for their Christmastime debacle.

This time, Judge Guedalia was not as lenient. This time he threw the book at Daddy, and rewrote the history books in the process. On August 7, 2003, he banned Daddy from entering the Town of Hollywood. This ruling made him the first elected official in United States history to be banned by a judge from the place that had elected him.

When the story hit The Associated Press newswire, The Orlando Sentinel, The Boston Globe and The Los Angeles Times wanted to add their own spin. It was during that same time that Californians recalled Governor Gray Davis. California Lieutenant Governor Cruz Bustamante and iconic actor Arnold Schwarzenegger were squaring off to see who would replace Davis. Each of these publications wanted to juxtapose our Hollywood and Mayor against Schwarzenegger and his Hollywood. I thought it was poetic justice that they wanted to compare and contrast The Mayor and The Terminator. We declined the offers because we didn't want to compromise Daddy's case because we were not sure how it was going to end up.

After the divorce, my daddy bounced around from apartment to apartment in the greater Charleston area. The only thing that he was able to find in each of the various complexes he inhabited was shelter but not refuge, dwellings but not a home. He lived from drinking binge to drinking binge, alternating between sober private citizen and drunken former Mayor of Hollywood. He became a shell of his former self, a million miles removed from his past political glory.

Daddy would binge for an entire month on a cocktail of Schlitz Malt Liquor Bull and Crown Royal as he tried to salve the pain of a royal crown lost, one that would never again be his. He filled the days evangelizing about national politics as C-SPAN blared in the background of his two-bedroom apartment.

Each day that I would go to visit him, he'd start talking politics. It was in his DNA. Much like when I was a little boy, he'd be in his recliner and I'd find myself intently listening to the undisputed first and last political genius Hollywood ever produced. "See Shay, the Republicans done been rocked by scandal an' dey done let da Democrats peep dey hand; dey just as morally bankrupt as dey claim the worst Democrat ever was." An epiphany such as that would always be followed by maniacal drunken laughter. "Man mothafuck dem hypocritical ass, intrusive ass, invasive-done-declare-war-on-the-poor-ass, wanna-try-an'-tell-uh-woman-what-da-fuck-she-can-an'-can't-do-wit'-her-own-vagina ass Republicans, Shay! Them mothafuckas party just as much as me an' Um one uh da staunchest Democrats walking!"

But on his sober days, when the pain of a loss too fresh to bear and a political wound too deep to relieve really started to get to him, Daddy would shut down and shut everybody out. He became a recluse, barricading himself in his man cave because he just couldn't cope with not being the Mayor. I would visit him just about every day just to check on him and see how he was doing, and The Mayor of Hollywood was just as unpredictable as he'd always been. I didn't know when I walked up the steps to his foxhole and turned that key whether or not I'd meet him on one of his drunk days or one of his sober days. But just like when he was Mayor, I'd just have to wait until I opened the door and wait for the show, whether it was a comedy or drama-filled tragedy, to begin.

The common denominator, and the reason why Daddy escaped all of those previous scandals virtually unscathed, was because Mama stood by his side. She was the pillar of strength for our town. Mere months prior to his final election and right before he abandoned his Hollywood cruise ship for his concubine Vivian's rowboat, while Mama may not have been publicly "all in" for Daddy during the campaign, she never stopped privately praying for him.

But when Daddy left Mama, I believe that the divine covering she had petitioned God to put on his life was torn to shreds. Their divorce meant not only the end of a marriage, but in Hollywood, it was the end of an era.

Former mayor's arrest sparks surprise, relief

Thur, 8-7-03

BY GLENN SMITH
Of The Post and Courier Staff

HOLLYWOOD—Former mayor Herbert Gadson was charged Wednesday with drunkenly barging into a woman's home and accosting her for failing to support him in the June election that cost him his job.

Karen White told sheriff's deputies that Gadson, the town's mayor for 14 years, was extremely intoxicated and reeked of alcohol when he entered her Scott White Road home uninvited on Tuesday morning.

Gadson, 54, reportedly yelled at her for not voting for him, grabbed her arm and threatened to try to shut down the daycare center she runs in her home. Children were playing outside, but they did not witness the confrontation, said Sheriff's Capt. Dana Valentine.

Investigators say Gadson appeared to be drunk when they caught up with him shortly after noon on Wednesday sitting in his pickup truck outside a friend's Johns Island home.

Gadson was expected to spend the night in the county jail on charges of second-degree burglary and assault and battery. His bail hearing was delayed until today to give White an opportunity to attend and Gadson a chance to sober up, deputies said.

White could not be reached for comment. A woman who came to the door of White's home on Wednesday peeled back a corner of a shade and shouted "No comment."

Gadson, who was a councilman for six years before becoming mayor in 1989, lost his bid for re-election in June by just eight votes to former councilman Gerald Schuster, a West Ashley doctor. His presence, however, lingers over the town.

The town's main intersection on S.C. Highway 162, which boasts its only stop light, is named after Gadson. The mere mention of his name is guaranteed to spark debate around town. At Town Hall on Wednesday, one employee even stumbled when a reporter asked to speak to the mayor.

"He wants to see Mayor Gadson... I mean, Schuster," she said with an embarrassed laugh.

Among the locals, reaction to Gadson's arrest ranged from surprise to relief.

Herbert Gadson

"I'm shocked."
Lisha Robertson

"It's been too long coming. (Gadson has) gotten away with things related to this same behavior time and time again."
Buster Herrington

See GADSON, Page 6B

Former mayor Gadson arrested

Thurs., 8-7-03

GADSON from Page 1B

Some see Gadson as a visionary leader who worked to improve water and sewer service and pushed for affordable housing and development. Others recalled a man who was prone to irrational behavior when drinking and quick to play the race card, which created divisiveness in this town that is 70 percent black, according to the Census 2000.

"I'm shocked," said lifelong resident Lisha Robertson, 39. "He did a lot for this community. I have to say that. He was a good leader."

Buster Herrington, co-owner of Herrington Equipment in the town's center, said he was pleased to see Gadson held accountable for his behavior.

"It's been too long coming," he said. "He's gotten away with things related to this same behavior time and time again."

In July 2001, local restaurant owner Dean Walker sought a no-trespass order against Gadson, claiming the then-mayor had been "stone-cold drunk" and disorderly in Walker's S.C. Highway 162 eatery. Walker claimed Gadson had come to the restaurant intoxicated about six times in a year and had been difficult to serve.

"We are tired of trying to put up with him and his public drunkenness," Walker said during a hearing before a magistrate.

Gadson, who is black, denied the charge and accused Walker, who is white, of being a "bully redneck." No criminal charges were filed against Gadson in connection with the incident.

Schuster, whom Gadson described as an "evil demon" after the election, said it was clear to him that Gadson had an alcohol-related problem for at least a couple of years. He said his former rival's behavior has been "unusual" at times and has included visits to Town Hall in which Gadson has made inappropriate comments about the town's administration in a "loud and robust voice."

Schuster said Gadson's antics harmed Hollywood's reputation and impeded efforts to bring the community together and progress.

"I think it's a dark cloud hanging over the town and it's something that needs to be cleaned up," he said, during a brief interview in his small, wood-paneled office.

JUDGE BARS EX-MAYOR FROM HOLLYWOOD

Gadson barred from Hollywood

Fri, Aug 1, 2003

GADSON *from Page 1B*

"I really feel that a man who is in the stupor of drunkenness should be held accountable for his actions," she said.

While sheriff's deputies were hunting for Gadson on Wednesday, he reportedly called Town Hall four times in 20 minutes and demanded to speak to Schuster.

Kenneth Edwards, town planning director, said Gadson made veiled threats toward Schuster.

Gadson also appeared at Town Hall on Tuesday, demanded copies of minutes from Town Council meetings and ordered employees to report to him again, Edwards said.

"At this point, the staff feels very intimidated and in fear," Edwards told the judge.

Schuster, whom Gadson has called "an evil demon," said Gadson appeared to be inebriated when he spoke to him by phone Wednesday. Gadson was irritated that the town had failed to pay a $47,000 bill from Frazier Construction of Ravenel for road grading and ditch clearing on private property, he said.

Schuster said Gadson had authorized Frazier to perform work on 10 to 15 roads and properties since January. Schuster said he has no problem with Frazier, but town officials need to know who requested the work, how the projects were monitored and whether it was appropriate to spend public funds on

them before deciding what to do with the bill.

"I've asked the attorneys to look into where we go from here," he said. "It's a very ticklish situation."

Willie Frazier, owner of the construction company, declined to comment Thursday.

Schuster, who is white, said he hung up on Gadson on Wednesday, after the former mayor accused him of delaying payment of the bill because Frazier is black, a charge Schuster described as "ridiculous."

"He said if the person were white that I was dealing with, I would have already settled the matter," he said. "I said 'I don't want to talk to you if you speak in that manner,' and I just hung up on him."

If Gadson, who is black, posts bail, he will be required to attend sobriety meetings and will be barred from contacting Schuster and White, owning firearms or entering a business that sells alcohol. Gadson said he can stay on Johns Island if released.

Gadson, who acknowledged seeking alcohol abuse treatment in 1993, told the judge his achievements should count for something.

"I feel I've contributed a lot to the community," he said.

"Well, it sounds like you've had a little trouble giving up the reins there," Goedalis replied.

CHAPTER 13

A *Hallelujah!* Healing

Linda Dingle Gadson, the former First Lady of Hollywood, South Carolina, was pronounced dead at Roper Hospital on August 6, 2006. She died on the operating table from complications resulting from triple bypass heart surgery.

At least, that's what the obituary was supposed to say. Mama flatlined twice on that operating table, but she didn't stay dead. She knew that she was far worse off than the doctors said she was. God always made Mama privy to information that He didn't alert mere mortals to.

"Doctor, I'm going to get into trouble in there so I want you to use this on me- every hour on the hour," she said as she handed him a bottle of liquid. "Please do it, Doctor. If you don't do it, I'm not going to make it."

My mama was never one to mince words, and she didn't care who you were. I'd once heard that Reggie had stolen Daddy's camcorder for crack money. It was 1991 and camcorders were rare in Hollywood. It was the behemoth first Sony consumer camcorder that sat on your shoulders. It weighed so much that it would break your collarbone if you weren't careful. Mama found out which of our esteemed local drug pushers had it. She

drove her Bonneville into the drug hole where the camera allegedly was
and demanded that the drug peddler who had it give it up. She took her
left palm and put it into his chest and told him, "You know why I'm here.
I want the camera back and I ain't leavin' here 'til I get it. *You* ain't leavin
here 'til I get it. Now hand it over. If you don't, I'll see to it that Sheriff
Cannon, who is a personal friend of mine, is made fully aware of what goes
on back here in this drug hole. *Try me if you want to here*, but you can bet cho
last dusty dollar that not another gram of marijuana, cocaine or heroin will
be bought or sold 'round here. Now I want the camera back, an' I want it
back now! For your own sake, please do NOT play with me!"

There were at least three guns pointed at Mama as she stood in the
middle of this dirt road in Hollywood that you could not get to unless you
knew exactly where you were going. Pot Ash, the guy who Reggie allegedly traded the camera to in exchange for cocaine, his brother Mouka and
their first cousin Dallo, all had guns on their waistlines as Mama verbally
assaulted Pot Ash. These niggas were street-level drug pushers- the most
dangerous strain of distributor. The street level niggas are always looking
to build a reputation or build upon one. Pot Ash glared at Mama for a long
time and she glared right back at him. Pot Ash, Mouka and Dallo were all
big, burly, jet-black and extremely harsh on the retinas. They were ruth-
less. At the time, Pot Ash was out of jail on bond for attempted murder
and Mouka and Dallo were known shooters in Hollywood. I don't know
if Mama knew any of this. If she did, I really don't think she cared. Pot
Ash saw that Mama had more heart than most of the niggas that he dealt
with on the streets every day because she wouldn't allow him to stare her
down. As he continued his futile attempt at launching corneal laser beams
at Mama, he nodded his head and motioned toward the brown-paneled
doublewide trailer the three felons shared. Mouka went into the house and
returned with the camcorder. He gave it to Pot Ash who gave it to Mama.
Pot Ash nodded at Mama with grudging admiration as he handed the camera back to her and said, "Aight Miss Gadson, you got it."

"Thank you, sir. You did the right thing. No need for the wrath of God
to come down on you boys when it didn't have to."

As Mama walked away, Pot Ash touched her on the shoulder.

"Yes, son?"

"You aine been scayed tah come back ya by yo'self? I mean, we coulda did anything to you an' you seem like you aine been scayed uh us. How you know you been gah git dat camera back, Miss Gadson? How you know if *you* been gah git back [home]? Huh? How you know?"

Mama looked at Pot Ash lovingly and said to him, "Son, I trust God wit' everything. I trust Him with my very life, an' because I trust Him an' love Him the way I do, why should I fear death? Huh? Y'all couldn't do no more to me than the Holy Spirit would have allowed y'all to do. Dass why I wasn't scared uh bit to come back into this dungeon to get my camera. Son, the fear of death ends at the outstretched arms of Jesus, an' that's where He keeps me- cradled in His arms. You boys please take care of yo'selves. Hallelujah!"

Mama walked off, hopped in the car and drove away. It was just that easy for her. Her life was in danger and she still effortlessly took control of the situation. She coerced those young and very menacing dope boys into doing exactly what she wanted.

And on the day of her surgery, she would do the same thing. She told another person, whose occupation was dispensing drugs and presiding over matters of life and death, exactly what she wanted and that she expected to get it.

Dr. Sherman Tims was the lumbering anesthesiologist with caring eyes. He was a dirty blonde with Mediterranean features. This allocator of drugs, like Pot Ash, did not take long to feel my mother's power of persuasion.

"Well Mrs. Gadson, what do you mean? We're gonna take good care of you. The surgery is gonna take about three hours and there will be a few hours of recovery time. You'll be in the hospital for about ten days after that and then we'll send you home. You are going to be just fine, my dear."

It was plain as day that he genuinely believed that. Telley, Mama and I looked at Dr. Tims. He was beaming with that wide Kool-Aid grin that assured us that his words were not just schtick. That pre-op room, with its sterile white walls, beeping machines and monitors could have been a church for as safe as Tims made us feel.

Well, he made two of us feel that way anyway. Mama wasn't at all convinced. Tims may have consulted Mama's charts and medical records, but Mama had already had a talk with Dr. Jesus. She lay on that bed as calm and as cool as if she were lying on the sunwashed sands of Edisto Beach.

"Look Doc, I hear what you're sayin', but I know what the Master has already told me. I had a talk with the Man in my prayer room before I left home this morning. I am far sicker than you all realize."

"Aww, Mrs. Gadson, I can assure you, this is a routine bypass surgery. All your records indicate that we'll have no problems. Once we actually get inside of your heart, you are going to be fine, sweetheart. The lead surgeon, Dr. Spriggs, is the best in the business; you will be in and out before you know it."

Tims beamed and his eyes radiated. He'd seen many a timorous heart surgery patient in the pre-operation room before he injected the anesthesia into their bloodstream. He knew that Mama just had a case of nerves and that his bedside manner and charm were irresistible. He'd make Linda Gadson feel comfortable. Oh, how wrong he was.

"Dr. Tims, listen to me. I have this oil that I use that I call *Doozy, Mama and Me Healing Oil* . I named it after my mother and my grandmother who raised me. Its base is olive oil and I also add my own ingredients to it that the Lord gave me."

"Oh, that's wonderful dear."

Mama motioned to me as I was sitting at her feet at the foot of her bed.

"Shay, look in my pocketbook and pass me a bottle."

I dug in Mama's pocketbook and pulled out the plastic burgundy bottle. I handed it to her.

"Thank you, son. Read that label, Doc."

Mama shoved it in his face for effect as he stood over her.

"Okay, my love. Let's see. '*Doozy, Mama and Me Healing Oil*. Behold, I will bring health and healing – Psalm 23. Directions: Apply daily with prayer as needed.'"

Tims seemed stunned, but not bewildered, and very interested all at the same time. I could tell he wanted to know more about this oil.

"What is this, my love?"

Mama was all too happy to explain. "This is *Doozy, Mama and Me*, Doc. I created it in my prayer room in an Igloo Cooler in 1986. I pray every morning beginning at 4."

"Really?"

By this time, Tims was sitting at Mama's feet, fully engaged. She had him right where she wanted him.

"Yes, really, Doctor. I pray at 4 o'clock in the morning in my prayer room that I have in my house. It is good for eczema, psoriasis, sunburn, diaper rash, nausea and a whole lot more."

Tims smiled. "This is quite interesting!"

"It is interesting Doctor. People have used this oil for all sorts of things. We've had people that have had the worst type of sunburn. I mean sunburns where they could not move or walk. They put this oil on and the next day that sunburn was gone. Babies with diaper rash; I mean the sort of diaper rash that was eating away at the skin and they cried like crazy when their mommies would touch it."

I started to smile as Mama spoke because I knew for a fact that some men used her oil to help their erectile dysfunction. Had Mama known that, she would have had a stroke. I didn't want to kill my mama before Dr. Feel Good could get the drugs into her. I kept the details about how Linda Gadson's oil hardens flaccid penises to myself. So, I just kept listening. And smiling.

"Their mamas would use the oil on them and the next day the diaper rash would be gone. We've had women who have had breast cancer to use it, Doc. After they did, the cancer was stopped dead in its tracks and their doctors couldn't explain why. Doctor, that stuff you have in your hands works wonders."

Then, Mama took the oil from Dr. Tims. She continued.

"See Doctor, it's harmless."

She sat up in the bed, turned the bottle up to her head and drank some more of it. Dr. Tims was in shock.

"If it was something to hurt, I wouldn't drink it. HA HA HA."

Then Mama drank some more. Tims, Telley and I remained astounded, motionless and silent at her bedside.

After listening to these stories of people whom he'd never met before, being cured by what Mama indicated was a miracle in a bottle, he laughed. Then Mama laughed. Telley and I played Goldie Hawn and Arte Johnson and joined in the laugh in.

In the blink of an eye, Mama got deathly serious. The smile on her lips went from wide and boisterous to pursed consternation in less than a heart-beat. She looked Dr. Tims deeply in his aqua blue eyes and said:

"Listen to me closely, Doc. I am in worse shape than you all could ever imagine. I know what I'm talking about. If you don't use this oil on me every hour on the hour, I am going to die on that operating table. There ain't no two ways about it."

Dr. Tims got it. He got it right then at that moment. This man of science was fully aware that hospital protocol everywhere, at any hospital you could name, prevented him from taking this *Doozy, Mama and Me Oil* into an operating room. He knew that. But there was something in her eyes that made him understand. He knew that in that very instant, that my mama was fully cognizant of the ramifications of this Moira. He had an epiphany. He couldn't fight fate. He didn't want to become a modern day participant in what had all the makings of an antiquity style Greek tragedy. If he didn't use her oil on her, every hour on the hour as instructed, he would be as responsible for her death as any heart attack. He *understood*.

"Mrs. Gadson, let me tell you something. I wasn't supposed to be your anesthesiologist today. Dr. Cromwell was supposed to be the anesthesiologist working with you. He called this morning, at the last minute, because his mother had a massive stroke. I was assigned to you just this morning."

"Is that right, Doctor?"

"Yes ma'am, that's right. There is no way that Dr. Cromwell would have taken this *Doozy, Mama and Me* into that operating room. No way in the world. Number one, you can't take non-sterile equipment into an operating room. And number two, he's an atheist."

We were shellshocked. Telley was holding Mama's left hand and I was holding her right. Dr. Tims saw the look of horror on her face and he started to rub Mama's left foot with the fuzzy orange sock on it. Mama was going to have an atheist operate on her. This was rich. Dr. Tims proceeded.

"However, Mrs Gadson, I am a Christian. I know I don't look it, but I am Greek and I attend the Greek Orthodox Church."

"You sure don't look Greek, Doc. I just thought you were white with a George Hamilton tan. HA HA HA HA HA."

Mama could always make herself laugh. Dr. Tims roared with laughter.

"Mrs. Gadson, I believe in the power of prayer and I could not do my job without it. I know that. The entire time that you were talking, I was debating in my mind about whether or not I should take this *Doozy* into surgery with me. There should have never been any debate. I am going to take this in there and I am going to use it on you- every hour on the hour. Kids, we are going to take care of your mom."

Mama then said what we knew she was going to say:

"Hallelujah! Praise You, God!"

She was so excited that she was going to jump out of her skin.

"You see, Doc, I knew that there was something special about you. You were sent to me. Hallelujah! Thank You, Jesus!"

"You remind me of my mom, Mrs.Gadson. She was very spiritual and she used olive oil for everything. She was Greek so I know what olive oil can do."

"Doc, the oil is going to save my life! Hallelujah for you, Doc, for hearing the word from on high!"

Dr. Tims smiled. "Well, Mrs.Gadson, I'm going to give you a few more minutes with your children, then I'm going to come back and administer the anesthesia and then we'll carry you down to the O.R.- okay?"

"That's fine, Doctor. God bless you!"

"God bless *you*, Mrs.Gadson."

With that, Dr. Tims got up from Mama's bedside. Twenty minutes later, they were rolling her to the O.R.

I don't think I fully appreciated just what kind of impact that my mother's life had until the day she flatlined. I mean, what child of a saint is truly able to comprehend how that saint's life impacts people?

Long before that day Mama died though, while I was still in school at Baptist Hill, Daddy realized that he wanted to live and live a long time. Because he was a rabble-rouser and in many circles was referred to as, "that outlaw Mayor of Hollywood", he decided to wage war against his weight. This was a lifelong battle. Cowboy or no, Daddy figured that he should at least look his best for the TV cameras that always found their way to Hollywood when he decided to run amuck. He was always rotund, and in 1986 he decided to start jogging. He became an avid runner. He eventually lost over one hundred pounds, so he just kept on running. The kids teased me mercilessly for it. Daddy's favorite running course happened to be Highway 162 and Baptist Hill Road. It was also one of the main school bus routes. Seemingly, every kid in school saw him running in the mornings. In the mornings when I got to school, the kids regaled me with their epic tales of Daddy's morning jogs. Their commentary was classic. We'd be sitting in homeroom at the beginning of the day. Shortly after the morning announcements, the pledge of allegiance and the homeroom teacher's droning on and on about why it was important for us to join those lame school clubs that people only ever really join to get out of class, when the room got semi-quiet, someone would start in on me.

"Shaytee, boy yo' daddy got some big ass nuts, boy. Dat nigga nuts be flyin' from side to side in dem damn short ass Bill Clinton jogging shorts he be wearin'." Then, somebody would start singing, to the tune of The Farmer in the Dell of course, "Da Mayor got big nuts, da Mayor got big nuts, Hi ho dat nigger-o, da Mayor got big nuts."

By some sick, twisted and anguishing trick of the gods, Victor, my torturer-in-chief since Timmy Sky High days, and I ended up in the same homeroom in our ninth- and tenth-grade years. We probably would have ended up in the same homeroom the next two years of high school, but Victor got kicked out on the very last day of our sophomore year. Apparently, his entrepreneurial spirit picked the final day of the school term to imbue his soul. The great spirit told his brain, to instruct his hands to distribute a controlled substance near the proximity of a school. Mrs. Eager caught this fool selling reefer. This happened during the third lunch period. He was standing outside of Building A, which was right next to the cafeteria. This Einstein was serving out in the open, damn near in broad daylight. But before he left school unceremoniously, his play-by-play commentary of my father's daily jogs became the stuff of urban legend, but with a decidedly countrified spin. Day after day, it was the same thing.

"Boy Shaytee, I see yo' daddy dick in dem short ass shorts, boooy! Dat nigga dick *big*! Yo' daddy dick an' nuts too big tah be da fuckin' Mayor! We gah impeach e ass; den we gah *assassinate* e ass 'cause e fuckin' nuts an' dick too big tah have dat damn Mayor job!"

I'm still not fully aware who deemed these kids the official governing body that adjudicates genital terms and conditions for public office. After a while, they even had me convinced that my father's penis and scrotal sack exceeded acceptable standards and practices for Hollywood's highest political office. Despite the taunting and constant verbal abuse, I made good grades. Even in the face of what was going on in school and at home, I managed to excel academically. I had to. I was the Mayor's son.

What can I say? I was an easy target. Everything that Victor said about me, even from Sky High days, was true. I *did* have a larger than normal size head and my glasses *were* huge. I loved to read. I loved studying. I *was* a *nerd*. I had a locker, but I walked around school all day long with a shit-load of books in my bookbag. I showed my peers I had to be the smartest person in the school. Who else toted each of their books around all the live long day? Mine were welded to my back like a JanSport/Houghton Mifflin tumor. I knew exactly how many pounds the books weighed- twenty-four- because I plopped them on Mama's bathroom scale one day. By the time I graduated, I knew exactly how Diogenes must have felt. I was Nigganes.

In addition to everything else that was going on by the time I got to high school, the sale and consumption of drugs, and the violence it always perpetuates, had nearly ravaged the place. The prevalence of the drug sub-culture created an overarching school culture of crippling instability. I had three different principals during my four years of high school. No administrator wanted to come to Baptist Hill; subsequently, none wanted to stay. If Baptist Hill was a teacher, he or she would have most assuredly been branded *persona non grata* as far as the Charleston County School District was concerned. We understood why. We were an African-American, countrified, underprivileged and drug-addled school. With the exception of the rise in the popularity and availability of cocaine and marijuana, it was the same old story since Mama and Daddy walked its hallowed halls. I was a freshman and we were in Mrs. Jones' World Geography class one day when we saw two students running around the school shooting at each other. This wasn't the other Hollywood, mind you, where shoot-'em-up and bang-bang movies were made every day, and gun play outside of a school may not have even made the evening news. In my Hollywood, this was unacceptable. Baptist Hill had officially become a war zone. Somebody had to do something. Enter Saint Linda.

I don't recall exactly when it happened, but Mama just kind of showed up at school one day to pray for the students and she never left. Nearly every day for four years, she was there praying. I can only remember a few times that she didn't come. That's only because maybe there was a meeting or other matter at Rural Mission that required her immediate attention. She prayed and laid hands on the kids who were attempting to cut class so much that after a while, they just figured it was less of a downer to stay in class and sleep if the teacher would let them get away with it. The unpleasant alternative was to walk the halls and risk having Mama perform exorcisms on them. I'd be in the middle of changing classes at the bell and the thugs would track me down in the hallway. They were all too eager to tell me about some latest attempt at a good time that they were to have that Mama thwarted.

"Man, Shaytee, yo' mama aine no joke, my nigga. Miss Gadson come in da C buildin' wit' her Bible an' we haul ass. Shit, I been cuttin' [class] an' Carlos been cuttin', too. Carlos had uh blunt in e han' so when we see yo' mama, we git da fuck out da C buildin'! Boy, Miss Gadson da truth!"

I remember one day we were changing classes and Mama and her prayer partner, Doris Dennis, walked up on a drug deal. I saw Mrs. Dennis whisper something to Mama. In a flash, Mama walked up on the guys who were too preoccupied to realize who was standing in front of them. She bellowed, "In the name of Jesus, put down the drugs! Right now! Hallelujah! Praise You, God!"

"Miss Gadson, we aine got no drugs; I sway we aine got no drugs." The young man, from what I could see, had dropped what looked to be a piece of crack on the ground and stepped on it hoping that Mama wouldn't see it. She did. By this time, a crowd had gathered around Mama, Mrs. Dennis and the two guys. I was in the mob of rubberneckers. I was embarrassed. I was also terrified. I didn't know what those guys were prepared to do to my mama for trying to stop their transaction. I was going to fight both of them if they even looked like they were going to hit or curse her. They were probably going to stomp me to death but they were just going to have to get their Timberlands bloody. I didn't know what they'd planned to do. Of course, whatever their plans may have been, Mama would have been totally unmoved by them. Why couldn't I have a normal mama? Out of all those people in that murder of crows, Mama's eyes locked in on me. She simply looked in my direction and smiled. She knew that I was prepared to kill or be killed if this exchange between her and these juvenile delinquents went bad. She kept looking at me and smiling. My stomach was in knots. My fists were balled up at my sides. Mama gave me a look as if she was as unconcerned and gay as the breeze blowing through Palmetto trees on the Battery in June. Almost as if on cue, she gave one of her patented Linda Gadson afterschool special speeches to the miscreants. They, and the flock, stood paralyzed, curious and confounded.

"I'm sure that y'all know that the piece of crack y'all are selling will get y'all expelled. What's worse, the man y'all are selling it for probably doesn't even know you boys exist. In fact, in a few years, y'all will either be dead or underneath someone's prison cell. While y'all are rotting in a cage, that nameless and faceless man that y'all are selling for will be living on a resort somewhere in the lap of luxury. He gone be sipping on a Tom Collins and as unconcerned about you boys as John C. Calhoun is overlooking the green on Marion Square. I don't know either of you, but I look at both of you as my sons. In the name of Jesus, please put that crack away before y'all get challselves involved in something y'all can't get out of. God's invested too much into you boys' eternal souls for y'all to continue to allow a man that you will never see, or hear from when you guys' get locked up, to continue to get rich off of your labor. Hallelujah! God bless you boys. Please, do the right thing."

That was it. Mama turned and walked off. Mrs. Dennis did so as well. The boys were blown away. The one boy picked up the crack and threw it in the garbage can when he was sure that no one was looking. By this time, the perplexed crowd had dispersed. No one said a word. I don't think anyone could believe what had just happened.

The one guy told the other, "'Ey, you know Blue? Dass *Blue* mama."

The other guy said, "I know man; I know."

Then, they both walked away. In later years, the boy who was selling the crack never forgot about that day. He has been in and out of prison for selling crack and a host of other felonious activities, but he always remembered Mama. He would ask me whenever I saw him, "How Miss Gadson doin', Shay?"

"She doin' aw'right," would be my response.

"Tell her I love her and I axed about her."

"I will, fam'ly. I sho' will."

Mama's praying at Baptist Hill High School got me teased and ridiculed at the time. I know now she probably saved a lot of lives during my high school years from the early to mid nineties. I know this for a fact because a few of those kids that she prayed for and talked to have told her and me that, because of her, they realized someone cared.

To me, Linda Gadson was just Mama. To the forty people that packed that waiting room at Roper Hospital that day waiting for her to come out of heart surgery, she was counselor, confidant, minister, lawyer, social worker and friend. The waiting room at Roper seats twenty-five people. The walls are a shade of green that was somewhere between pea and sea. It was a cozy little space on the seventh floor. It could have been a great room for a Thanksgiving or Christmas gathering. It had two large TVs on the walls. Instead of showing the Macy's Thanksgiving Day Parade or *A Christmas Carol*, it put on full display to us just how long Mama had been in surgery. Everyone who was family to us, either because Mama was their mama, sister, aunt or friend, was in that room. There were white people sitting on the floors when the seating space ran out. There were Latino people pacing back and forth. There were black people looking out of the big window that covered a wall and provided a great view of the Charleston skyline. They were praying both silently and vociferously that God wouldn't take Mama from us. There were Asians on cell phones giving hourly reports, to voices on the other end, that alternated between concern and fear. Telley, Reggie and I sat next to each other holding hands, praying and hoping for the best.

At some point, Dr. Spriggs walked in. Dr. James Spriggs, the lead surgeon working on Mama that day, was discombobulated, puzzled and even a bit frightened when he walked into that waiting room and saw the Rainbow Coalition sitting in there. Dr. Spriggs, a white man with emerald green eyes, had long since sweated out his strawberry blonde cowlick sparring with Mama's heart. He had a long angular physique. I think that, if he hadn't chosen medicine, he would have been a power forward. The look on his face when he walked into that waiting room wasn't defeat, but it wasn't far from it. He tried to show a brave front, but he was visibly shaken. No, I'm lying. Dr. James Spriggs was scared as hell. The look on his face and the beads of sweat rolling off it told me that Mama's ticker may have been ahead on points.

"Where are Telley, Reggie and Shaytee?"

My brother, sister and I looked at each other as if we'd never heard our own names before, we were so rattled.

"Right here, Doctor."

Telley was the unofficial spokesperson on all things concerning Mama.

"Would you guys like to follow me into the other room so that we can talk?"

I didn't like the way he said that. He said "talk" like he had awful news that he wanted to alert us to. News that he couldn't do anything about. He didn't want to talk. He wanted to issue an irreversible edict with calamitous ramifications.

"Doctor, everyone in here is family. You can say whatever you want in front of the group." Telley said exactly what Mama would have said. She wouldn't have wanted anyone to be left out, either.

"Okay, family, this is the deal. Your mama's very sick. She's *very* sick. She is far sicker than we originally thought. The preliminary tests did not show the blockages that we found when we *actually* went into the heart. Her condition is very serious. *Very* serious."

"Your mom's very sick." That's what rang in my ear. I didn't hear anything else. You could have heard a rat piss on cotton in that room. Nobody said a word for a long time.

Dr. Spriggs continued, "We are doing everything that we can guys, but we had no idea that the damage to the heart was this severe. The tests just didn't show it. They just didn't show it." Spriggs shook his head and wrung his hands.

You would have mistaken the room for a mausoleum the silence that fell was so deathly. I saw Mike Smith, who was a United Methodist minister and one of Mama's Caucasian sons, out of the corner of my eyes, crying like a newborn. Marisol Concepcion, a Latino woman who was one of Mama's daughters, was sitting in the corner with her head down and her shoulders slumped. When I heard her sniffling, I knew that she was crying too.

Spriggs continued. He looked like he wanted to turn on the sprinklers in his eyeballs right along with everyone else.

"Your mom has an enlarged heart, which exacerbates the situation greatly, but we are doing all that we can. I promise you all that we are working. We are working."

Reggie's eyes were gushing like Old Faithful. My pupils were in Yellowstone right along with him. The babies who weren't crying in that room were simply petrified. They were too panic-stricken to cry. We came here for a routine bypass surgery. Nobody came here for a funeral. Telley was a rock.

"Doctor, Mama is strong and she is going to make it. She is going to make it."

"Yes she is, Telley. I am going to go back in the O.R. now, but I wanted to let you all know that we are working."

"Thank you, Doctor."

"You're welcome, Telley. Family."

Spriggs nodded at us and walked out of the room, and between the sniffling, the crying and the terror, we were all subconsciously trying to wrap our minds around the possibility that we might have to live without Mama.

My sister took control of the situation and did it just like Mama would have done.

"Y'all, Mama is going to make it," she said between the tears. "Mama is going to live because God has work for her to do. We not gone stay at this hospital and wait for them to pronounce her dead. We gonna pray and then we gonna go back and see her and then we gonna go home."

Black hands started grabbing white hands, that started to interlock with yellow hands and brown hands as we made a prayer circle in that overcrowded waiting room. We bowed our heads and prayed through the tears and the wailing and the sobbing.

Two and half hours after we first saw Dr. Spriggs, he appeared just as suddenly as he came in the first time. He looked just as dejected.

"Family, we've finished the surgery, but because of the complications we're going to have to keep her longer than we originally anticipated. The surgery was extremely traumatic. We are going to let her sleep for three days so that she doesn't have to work her body and heart at all. Her body has to rest."

"Can we see her now?" I think those were the first words I spoke since this man walked into my life a couple of hours earlier.

"Yes, but it can only be the immediate family; two at a time for a couple minutes apiece."

Telley and I followed him down the hall and we saw Mama.

Mama was stout. She weighed two hundred forty pounds. Years of an unhealthy diet, three pregnancies and the stress of trying to save everyone from everything changed her once svelt body into what we saw in that hospital bed. The surgery had Mama looking like a beached whale. Her body was swollen and she wasn't breathing on her own. She was huge and grotesque. I broke down when I saw her. I was sobbing almost uncontrollably. I walked up to my mama and touched her face. Her body was cold and went up and down in rhythm with the machines that were breathing for her. Telley was crying as well. Through the tears, I saw Aunt Vi, Mama's sister; her daughter, Trina, who came from Ohio because Mama and Trina were always more like mother and daughter than aunt and niece; Aunt Marti, Mama's other sister who traveled from Philadelphia; my Uncle Tea (so nicknamed because of his affinity for piping hot tea), her big brother, who trekked from Hilton Head; and seemingly two-thirds of the waiting room, standing at the door of Mama's room. We were all just standing there. The nurses, who saw the uniqueness of our situation, were kind enough to relax the hospital rules to let as many people as they could look in on Mama. After about ten minutes, reluctantly, the nurses told us we had to leave. Before we did, we prayed again. Then we left and went home just as Telley had instructed us to do. Telley, Reggie and I kissed Mama's cheek before we left. We had no idea if she was going to live or die.

What we didn't know, what we couldn't have known, is that when Dr. Spriggs came out to talk to us that second time, Mama had already expired. She flatlined twice on that operating table, and Dr. Spriggs was terrified. They were able to revive her that first time, but the second time she registered code blue they spent a good deal of time just trying to get vitals on her. This is why a surgery that was supposed to take four and a half hours ended up taking eight and a half. Mama spent twenty-one days in ICU and another twenty-seven in a regular hospital room. Her lungs collapsed during the surgery and the doctors wanted to do extensive monitoring of her before they let her go home. She was only supposed to be in the hospital for ten days. They kept her for forty-eight. Telley basically moved back home for that entire duration.

The Reverend Telley Lynnette Gadson is simply one of the most dynamic preachers in the United Methodist denomination, end of discussion. She is totally devoted to her flock. Her parishioners were gracious enough to let her trot back and forth the one hundred and eight miles from

Sumter, South Carolina, where she pastored, and she made the trip four times a week. I thank God because if Telley were in another profession that didn't allow her the flexibility to be able to travel back and forth, I would have been a basket case. We would call the hospital for hourly reports on Mama's condition. I could never forget those reports. "She is resting comfortably," or "She is stabilized and resting comfortably."

I remember one evening we called the hospital and they said that Mama had taken a turn for the worse and things did not look good. Telley and I went into the prayer room with a pair of Mama's shoes and we begged God to spare her life. We entreated Him to give her some more years, as Hezekiah in the Bible did when he turned his face to the wall. God gave him fifteen more years when he was on the brink of death. We poured *Doozy, Mama and Me* into her shoes and we prayed and prayed. The next morning when we called, they said that they had gotten all of the fluid out her lungs and we got the same monotone, "She is resting comfortably" from one of the nurses, which was music to our ears. Nobody on earth can convince me that prayer doesn't work. I know for a fact that it does.

Mama could not speak for a month after the surgery. We would go into her room, once she had regained consciousness and she would scribble on a pad what she wanted to say. We'd walk in and say, "Hi Mama", and She'd hurriedly scribble, "Hi stinkers." And then we'd say, "Mama, how did you sleep last night?", and she'd scribble, "I want to go home." I remember that day that we walked in her room and she spoke for the first time after the surgery. She unhesitatingly told us, in a whisper, what happened to her when she perished.

"I was gone. It was beautiful, kids. There was water everywhere – waterfalls and pools of water. I just kept saying that I want my family to come here; I want my family to come here. I remember Savannah….Savannah. God told me to change the name of the oil when I stood around the water. He said that I have to call it *Hallelujah! Oil* and that it's going to be more powerful than ever."

Telley looked at me and I looked back at her and shrugged. Mama laughed because she knew that we could not even began to comprehend what she was saying. She continued:

"Dr. Tims was the one. Dr. Tims using the oil is what brought me back."

Again, Telley and I looked at Mama in disbelief and confusion. Once more, she laughed.

"See, he's a good man. He rubbed the oil on the soles of my feet. He went across the heels of my feet with the oil every hour on the hour. He drew a cross with the oil on my insteps. After I flatlined the second time, he dumped the entire bottle on my feet. They said that about ten seconds after he did that, after a good while of them trying to bring me back, my vitals started coming back and I was alive again. God used that man to bring me back. Just like that. Praise You, God! Hallelujah!" Then she drifted off to sleep.

CHAPTER 14

Little Women

Little did I know at the time, but much like Daddy lost everything in this world that he considered most important to him, I was about to do the same. The nearest and dearest friend I'd ever had was Mama Clay. Felicia had become a close second. My world, which was rocked by the loss of that sweet old lady, might as well have crumbled and swallowed me whole when I lost Felicia.

If I've done nothing else in my life, I've been a loving father. At least I've tried to be. No matter what curve ball fatherhood may have thrown at me, I've done my best to be a nurturing parent. For example, when Felicia kicked me out, she failed to tell me that she was four months pregnant. She conveyed this information to me a month after I left our home. You could have knocked me over with a feather. During the last few months of our relationship we were barely speaking, much less having sex. And at a trimester plus a full month pregnant, I couldn't see where she was even beginning to show. Maybe I didn't *want* to see. Felicia said she waited so long to tell me because it took her two months to definitively decide that she was even going to keep the baby. I could barely provide for the child that I had. The thought of having another mouth to feed gave me a migraine. It was indefatigable. It was unrelenting. It was my constant companion for the entire five months that I became aware that fatherhood, like the postman, was about to ring twice. Who am I fooling? I couldn't provide for Quati without Mama. I lived in her house. I ate her food and every Friday night, like clockwork, I brought my child to her abode. Mama and I spoiled her and made a big fuss over Quati until it was time for her to go back to Felicia on Sunday. Frequently, I got her during the week. I saw Quati every day. I was making but a pittance as a substitute teacher. However, every other Friday when I got paid, I skimmed ten percent off of the top for my tithe. I tithed off the gross that Uncle Sam took his taxes out of. I gave Felicia half of the remainder. I was scraping by to be certain, but what I lacked in money, I tried to make up for in determination. What I didn't have in dollars and cents, I compensated in love and devotion. I adored my little girl. I bought books and read to her. I purchased games and played them with her. We did everything together; me and Quati, Quati and me.

She slept with me at night sprawled on my chest. I'd wake up in the morning with an undershirt full of drool, but I didn't care. I think I've seen *Shrek* more times than any six-year-old on the planet. *Finding Nemo* was our favorite movie. I was determined that what I couldn't provide for this child monetarily, I was going to do my best to make up for with all of the affection a father could muster. But, I was certain that I could not love two children. Quati monopolized every ounce of my attention. I didn't know how I could possibly support, financially at least, another child.

Qynn LeShay Crease Gadson was born on May 1, 2005. Once again, I was right there by Felicia's side in the delivery room. And true to form, I fainted. I was glad that Felicia and I had grown to a place that even though we weren't together, we could present a united front for our children.

Qynn was the perfect little baby. She had ten fingers and ten toes and she looked like a cherub. At least, that was my reasoning after I regained consciousness. Eventually, I got the hang of taking care of a newborn again. I'd forgotten about the 3 o'clock morning feedings and the pee-soaked diapers. I'd also forgotten that sometimes when babies got constipated, you have to go into their rectum and, as Quati would say when she watched me do it, "fish the do-do out, Daddy." That meant I had to hold Qynn's rectum open. I formed my hands as steady and precise as Dr. Vivien Thomas would have. Felicia's dual bedroom chateau may not have been Johns Hopkins, I wasn't by any stretch of the imagination Mos Def, and Qynn wasn't quite a "blue baby," but *she* was something the Lord made. I'd place Qynn on Felicia's bed. I'd take the bulb syringe, fill it with warm water, lubricate its tip with Vaseline and squirt the water up Qynn's little butt. When this didn't work, I had to use my pinky finger and manually pull it out. I used to feel so bad for her because she was constipated quite a bit during the first year of her life. I think I've changed diapers everywhere with Qynn. Unlike her sister, she screamed and hollered when she was wet or had made a bowel movement in her diapers. I changed diapers in bathrooms, on the side of the Interstate, in the backseat of the car, on park benches and on my lap. She remained a trooper. Somehow, we made it.

So now it was the three of us: Quati, Qynn and me on the weekends and sometimes during the week. Raising two children in my mother's house, I developed a new respect for single moms. The ultimate respect. For a year and a half, things went along fine with the three amigos – that's what Mama called us. Then in December 2006, the bottom fell out.

For the record, even before I was purged from our relationship, our home and our life together, I was pretty certain Felicia was having an affair with Mayor Davier. When I got the phone call on December 6, 2006, that she had gotten fired for embezzlement, as far as I was concerned, I'd gotten my proof. I had just hopped into my truck leaving a substitute assignment when my cell phone rang. When I heard Donnie McClurkin's, *Stand*, floating through the cabin of my truck from my cell, I knew it was Mama.

"Hello."

"Shay, where are you?"

"Hey, Mama. I'm headed to Wal-Mart now. I just left work then I'm headed home. Why, wussup?"

"Son, listen, I want you to remain calm." My mama, albeit still recovering from heart surgery not nearly one hundred percent, hadn't lost her flare for the dramatic.

"Son, listen, are you listening to me?"

"Yeah, Mama, whah happen?"

"Son, Felicia was fired from Hunter's Point today. They said that she embezzled money. Nobody knows for sure how much. They're saying it could be as much as fifty thousand dollars."

I couldn't see anything around me at that point. Dorchester Road had become a blur. The trees on the sides of the highway had become a massive green wave and I was about to wipe out. I couldn't breathe. The only thought twirling in my mind at that moment was that my children were not going to have a mother because, inevitably, she was going to prison. Moreover, with that much money involved, she was probably going to rot in there.

"Mama, how do you know what happened? How do you know?"

"Son, how do you think I found out? Kelsey told me. I was the one who told my friend Kelsey that Felicia would be a good fit in Hunter's Point. Kelsey and the rest of the Town Council voted to fire her this morning. The auditor called them and said that there were major discrepancies involving some missing money. She said that they discovered a secret account with only Felicia and the mayor's name on it. I'm sorry, son."

"Mama, where are da kids? Where my girls?!"

"They are with me son. I had them picked up from school when Kelsey called me and told me what happened. Son, she is in big trouble. She's going to be arrested....Shay, you there?"

"Mama, how long was this going on?"

I didn't know in that moment how long her theft had been going on or how long she had been sleeping with the mayor. I really didn't even know *which* of those queries I wanted Mama to put to bed. Linda Gadson, as always, was reading my mind.

"Kelsey said that Davier knew all along and that he allowed her to steal the money. She said that everybody suspected that they were sleeping together, but nobody could prove it. She said that this was probably going on since Felicia got hired. She said everybody in Hunter's Point knew 'bout her and Davier."

At this juncture, I was neither mad nor sad. I was downright homicidal. Felicia and I hadn't been together in almost two years, but she was having an affair with the man while we were together. *That's* why she kicked me out. I wanted to kill them both. It was as if I was reliving the break-up all over again. I was being stabbed in my heart. Again. How could she be so fucking stupid? What in the hell was I going to tell our girls?

As I drove in circles, I thought about the entire situation as objectively as I possibly could. First of all, I had cheated on Felicia throughout the course of our entire relationship. Wire to wire. If she had started having an affair with her boss while we were together, that was just par for the course. I more than deserved that. Secondly, she hadn't known a fatherly presence in just about her entire life. Maybe an older and stabilizing paternal figure is what she thought Mayor Davier would provide for her. I've never been much of a breadwinner. If this man was giving her money or was complicit in her theft of it, could I really say much? The thing that troubled me the most was that since it appeared that they were having an affair, and he allowed her to steal, why was Felicia the only one being accused of a crime?

It was an absolute media spectacle outside of Hunter's Point Town Hall on May 29, 2007. Felicia was officially brought up on embezzlement charges a few months after she had gotten fired. It took investigators that long to figure out exactly how much money she'd stolen. She'd covered her tracks so well that the police and the accountants were sure that they still hadn't come up with the correct total. But enough money was traced back to her for them to charge her. They arrested her at her apartment without incident. She was cuffed and the police officer placed a hand on her head to help her into the squad car. I'm sure that she was utterly humiliated when the details of the story came out. We all were. Almost verbatim, the media told Charleston, and the rest of tri-county area residents what Mama told me months earlier. They said that she'd stolen over five thousand dollars, which was a felony. They said that the theft was discovered during an audit and there was indeed a clandestine account that only listed her and Davier's name on it.

Mayor Davier strutted from his black 2006 BMW 745 IL and walked right into the throng. As always, he was dressed to the nines. Today he was casually appareled in a long sleeve peach-colored Ralph Lauren shirt, tan penguin seersucker pants and chocolate brown Bruno Magli Renegade slip-on loafers. He walked from his car to the steps of his palace right into the firestorm and didn't flinch. The questions flew from the microphones.

"Mayor, did you know that money was being stolen?"

"Mayor Davier, what about the secret account?"

"Mayor, was there an affair?"

Davier, as cool as James Dean looked in *Rebel Without A Cause*, stared directly into the cameras and said, "The sprint of impropriety cannot outrun the marathon that is the rule of law." He sounded confident and reassured. He even managed to sound magnanimous. The prick. Of course, that was just my jealousy and *hateration* rearing its ugly head. Hey, I'm only human. Truthfully speaking, that was some of the coldest shit I'd ever heard any politician say. It was quintessential political doublespeak spoken by a master of the language. It was unnecessarily obtuse, theoretically vague and morally conscientious. How could you not tip your hat to that bullshit? I could see how the woman I loved fell in love with this guy. Davier then walked up the castle steps to a back door that led directly into his office. He placed his finger on the thumbprint recognition technology and walked into the building. He simply said, "The sprint of impropriety cannot outrun the marathon that is the rule of law," and that was that. Poor Felicia couldn't say anything because, at that moment, she was being driven away in a black and white squad car to the county jail.

We tried to stall for time, but the best idea Mama and I could come up with was the library. When Quati asked where her mama was, we said that she was at the library. Quati was eight years old and she was not a fool. She didn't believe us when we said that her mama was at the library, no matter what time of day or night she asked.

"Why is she at the library so much, Daddy?"

"Well, baby, Mommy is getting a lot of books so that she can read to you and your sister so that y'all will be smart."

She would always say, "Oh, that makes sense," but I could almost see the lightbulb shining above her head like in the cartoons when they discover something or figure something out. It was only a matter of time before she found out that her mommy was locked up, if she hadn't figured it out already. Qynn was two years old, and although she asked for her mommy, she was just happy that she got to sleep on my chest every night. The sands of the hourglass that poured and the tea leaves I read said my eldest daughter was going to put the pieces of the puzzle together.

When the phone rang and Quati picked it up, I thought nothing about it. When she screamed out *"Mommy!"* I knew the jig was up. In the five days that Felicia had been locked up, she called Mama and me sometimes three times a day to check on the kids. And so far we were blessed, because Quati never answered the phone, simply because Felicia called mostly at night when the kids were asleep. We had no contingency plan for what would happen if she called one day and Quati grabbed the phone before we did. We simply didn't plan for it.

"Hello. Yes. I'll accept the charges. Hi, Mommy!"

My heart sank. I wanted to tell Felicia that I was going to take care of the kids. I wanted to tell her that I was sorry for not being able to take care of her. I wanted to tell her that I was going to be a better man and that I was going to try to provide for the kids the best way that I could. My heart was breaking when I heard my child on the phone with her mommy in jail. I wanted to tell Felicia that I still loved her. I pushed her into a corner and money became tight for her. Words can't express how sorry I was for her being where she was, but I wanted to tell her that I appreciated her for sticking with me for as long as she did. In my mind, I started writing a poem for her that I finished later that night.

I guess maybe for the seven or so years that Felicia and I were together, I was working on that sonnet subliminally. We kind of grew up together, and the fact is she was my first love. I wasn't taught how or didn't have sense enough to know how to love her substantially. In that moment, I knew Felicia couldn't hear me writing these words in my heart about how I felt about her. Cognitively, I was aware that she couldn't auscultate how my heart bled about the ups and downs of our relationship, our little girls and where this life had taken us. I listened intently to Quati tell her over and over again, just how much she loved her, and how much she wanted her home to kiss her. She *could* hear my words echoing in her spirit through my oldest child. I knew she could. Thank you for pushing me to be a better father and far better person than I thought I could be. Thank you, Felicia, for pushing me to want to be more than what I'd become. I wanted to tell her that the kids and I were going to be fine. Amidst the women in the background at the Charleston County Detention Center Women's Facility yelling at her to get off the phone and screaming that they wanted to go home, I feel like she heard me. I hoped she heard me. I prayed she felt these words:

"Felicia's Navidad"

Part and parcel responsibility
For the maturation of a man
Rests with you
Sweet, sweet Felicia;
I do believe that at will
You can pilfer testosterone from the spirit
Of the father
That deserted you
How else does one explain
This trail of manhood
You placed my psyche on-
To influence my growth
Made your heart as giddy

As a child's six days prior to the New Year
It was you who squeezed my wrist
Making my hands involuntarily
Drop the gauntlet
Declaring war on my frivolity
And gave me the voice
To shout down the walls of my immaturity
Like Joshua at Jericho-
It was then I adopted the Apostle Paul's creed
The childish things withered away
Under your monsoon of encouragement
Eroding away a boy's mentality
Like a beach's sand
To be certain, you were my Damascus Road
The place where I became smitten
The place where my transformation came
You orchestrated the grandest larceny
One could make a case
To banish you to Devil's Island;
Armed with only a machete
Strangely similar to a tongue
You carefully cut away
The gnarled and knotted rope
Attached to an anchor of self-doubt and anxiety
That was weighing down my heart's strings
Then, with the cunning hands of a seasoned burglar
You stole it-
And with those felonious hands
You massaged my heart's muscle
Allowing the blood of life
To circulate through it unimpeded
That day I was reborn
Like Nicademus

Everyday since
Has not been Sunday
But it is because of you
A revival occurred
In my spirt
And I am unworthy of it-
Just as the world is
Of Christmas

✫   ✫   ✫

Epilogue

L et me take this opportunity to apologize to whom it may concern; not for what I've said, but for what you may have interpreted. To be certain, everything that you've read has been the gospel truth, as painful as it has been to share it. I've got the newspaper articles to back up the words I've written; that's for sure.

I'm apologizing for the possibility that you may walk out of Hollywood thinking in absolute terms: that Herbert Gadson is merely a lush, who through sheer manipulation and political posturing, was able to remain Mayor, that Linda Gadson is an overzealous holy roller, that Telley Gadson is a preacher who chose that route because her moral compass was too precise and the pain projected onto her too unrelenting, that Reggie Gadson is just a hoodlum and that I, well, I don't know what conclusions you might have drawn from what I've told you about myself. I almost shudder to think. You also might be thinking that Hollywood, South Carolina, is just some backwater.

Well, from time to time, the truth can sting a little. Okay, sometimes the truth stings a lot. If I were to be frank, all of the aforementioned are quite true. Very true. But truth has components and parts, and it is not always cut and dried. In Hollywood, the truth, unlike the people, isn't even always black and white.

Herbert Gadson is the most skilled politician in the history of my town. Even his most strident foes would lament that. The man who beat him in 2003 called him "brilliant" on the local news. Herbert Gadson is a genius. He can outwit anyone and he is light years ahead of whomever you think has a higher political I.Q.

Before Daddy came along, most black folks, and quite a few white folks, felt utterly disconnected from the political discourse. Daddy changed that. He established a committee specifically geared toward ingratiating these citizens into the decision-making process. He met with these people and implemented many of their suggestions into his agenda. He made folks feel they were included and that their hopes, dreams and ideals meant something in the grand scheme of the town. He brought water and sewer services to a town whose infrastructure was archaic. If you drove through town before Daddy became Mayor, it was common to see people hauling buckets of water from hand pumps in the middle of their yards into their homes. He also fought the drug dealers with every fiber of his being. He could see that drugs and the violence they bred were threatening to tear at the very fabric of our community, because he knew what they had done to his home. He and Mama spearheaded a prayer vigil in the middle of town for a number of years that railed against the drug trade and its purveyors. He also established the Drop a Dime on a Dealer initiative that was highly successful. The premise was simple: you call the police on people that were dealing drugs and you got money for doing so. Both the vigil and the money were effective.

He saw that developers had begun eyeing Hollywood. He rightly predicted that they could fundamentally undermine our rural culture. Daddy knew that he couldn't keep development out of town forever, but he made sure that each project benefited us just as much or more than it benefited the developers. He was bound and determined to ensure that they gave Hollywood more than they took. He saved this town from the gentrification that would have resulted in scores of poor people losing their homes. If developers would have had their way, they would have changed the rural character of this town and most people would not have been able to pay their property taxes. Mayor Gadson kept Hollywood intact because of his unrelenting stance. My daddy did that.

As I am able now to look at my father through the eyes of the man that I've become, I can peer at him through the lens of life experience. And God knows that I do not judge him as harshly as I once did as a boy. I am awed by the Mayor. When I think of how much he accomplished and how much he managed to overcome, there is no doubt in my mind of the man's acumen. He's far smarter and far more intrepid than I'll ever be. When I was growing up, I shivered when people would say, "Boy, I sway you look jess like yo' daddy." I vowed I'd never be like him because of the drinking, the women and, as an unintended consequence of the two, how he treated Mama. A sober Daddy wasn't tender and he wasn't affectionate. If he kissed or hugged us, we were the ones who reached out for the kiss or hug initially. He rarely said "I love you" to Mama, Reggie, Telley or me first. When we said it, he'd say it back, but Daddy just wasn't that kind of man. Our love imprisoned him to the obligation of loving us back. Herbert Gadson wanted to be free.

He wanted to drink as much alcohol and have as much sex with as many different women as humanly possible. Oh sure, for as much as Daddy could conceptualize love, and for as much as he could comprehend and grasp it, he loved us. But at heart, he was a man who grappled every day with the fact that he was a single man trapped in a married man's body. That body made him a caged bird. He was imprisoned by the responsibility of marriage and a family that he didn't necessarily want, yet did his best to cope with. He couldn't wrap his mind around the fact that he'd entered a marriage contract with a woman who was so benevolent and so loving that, over time, probably became to him more mother than wife. He couldn't love his children with his whole heart. Unless he was drinking or drunk, he couldn't, with any real level of comfort, grab us and hold us and tell us that we were special and that we were loved. Nobody – not Granddaddy, not Grandma Arthelle, not Grandma Kayvass, not Murray – ever modeled for him how to do that in a state of sobriety. In spite of this, Daddy loved us as much as he could.

Mayor Gadson was the caged bird that never sang. Not even one out of the four of his parents could manage to give him the voice to sing a melody or whistle a happy tune. So instead he just sat, stood and flew around in that cage. He beat his wings against the bars until they bled. And after years of trying to fly out of a prison that realistically he knew he could never flee, his wings just kind of atrophied. The blood of so many flightless days, that he could count them no more, encrusted on those bruised wings. Of what value is a voiceless and flightless bird than to be trod under the foot of man?

So I look at my father now, not with any hatred, malice or apathy as I once did as a boy. A boy's vision is clouded by a well-founded loyalty to his sainted mother and a keen sense of the right and wrong in the world. Now, I look at the man for who he is and what he became. I marvel at how he was able to make a nest in a cell with nothing but his own old tattered, bloodied and well-worn feathers. After years of useless flapping and trying to fly away in vain, the feathers just formed a cloud around him. They broke off from his body as he beat them into frustration's oblivion. Then, when he looked down and saw that the cloud became a palisade of feathers around him, he just kind of accepted his lot and made a bed out of them.

What his four parents fed him were the worms of confusion, bitterness and anger. Yet, he still managed to do more and become more than they could have imagined. Now that I'm a man, Mayor Gadson is my hero. My daddy is my best friend. And now that he and Mama are divorced, he's the free bird that he always wanted to be. At just over sixty years old, he still lives a hard drinking and hard charging lifestyle.

He may or may not have fathered a child with an eighteen-year-old girl. That will be an issue for a DNA test to decipher. He started having sex with this girl's mother before he met the girl. After he met her, he instructed Reggie to start having sex with the mom because she was only six years younger than my brother was. He told Reggie that it was his job to "keep da betch [the mom] off uh me." Daddy was so eloquent when he wanted to be.

I check on him just about every day. To most people, what I find when I cross the threshold of his apartment may be abhorrent and shocking. I've viewed my father, a man in his sixth decade of life, engaging in sex with girls in their early twenties. My father, as a youth, couldn't stand the idea of implied superiority that "the white man" connoted. As a seasoned citizen, I've seen him having sex with that same white man's granddaughter. Once, I inadvertently walked in on him engaged in a ménage-a-trois with two white girls- whom I later found out were sisters. I assume full responsibility for that incident. My dumb ass should have knocked, or at least announced my presence, before entering his pied-a-terre. I guess time changes people and their perspective. A free bird he is now, indeed. The Mayor's new life would have inspired Ronnie Van Zant to peel off a guitar lick. Mama calls his apartment a den of iniquity. She is fully aware of what goes on there because he tells her. They both readily and gleefully admit, to anyone who will listen, that they are one another's best friend. They talk every day and there are no more secrets now. She often refers to Daddy's personal playpen as "hell." On most mornings beginning at 4, she's in heaven in the prayer room praying that the Lord will have mercy on his soul and that Daddy won't die and go to the eternal inferno of fire and brimstone. She may be accurate in her description of Daddy's apartment as Hades, true enough; but Daddy just calls it home.

I've heard quite a few people tell me that my mother is incredible and that she is special because she cheated death. She, in fact, didn't cheat death at all.

Cheating implies that she finagled her way out of it or that she skirted her way around it. She did neither. She *beat* death. *She beat the hell out of it.*

She looked it dead straight in the eye, stared it down and made it blink. She made it tap out. She cast it back into the pits of hell and used *Hallelujah! Oil* to do it. Over the course of the past twenty-four years, she's helped rich, poor, black, white, believer and non-believer, beat death as well as a host of other maladies.

When Mama came back from the tomb, she rededicated her life to showing folks how to live. Two decades ago, she knew that *Hallelujah!* was going to be the catalyst in allowing folks to reach toward becoming better, doing better and being better. My mother was so effective at doing this, that people are well when doctors said that they should be sick, walking around when they should be bedridden and alive when they should be dead. Their successful lives have become her success.

Having them tell their stories, in their own words, are the best examples of her life well lived. Here are some of their testimonies:

"I entered into the United States Navy in October 1997. I fulfilled many military assignments; my last assignment was in Camp Arifjan Kuwait in 2006 with Navel SG-Echo Rotation. I returned from active duty in 2007 to Norfolk, Virginia, not as I left but with life-changing medical issues. I am now a disabled veteran from the Navy after twelve years as a petty officer. My husband, John Stinnett, is on active duty with the United States Air Force. He has fought in three wars. *Hallelujah! Oil* healed our daughter's eczema.

"In June of 2002, we were blessed with the birth of our daughter Isis. Isis was born with jaundice and started to suffer respiratory failure. She was taken to the neonatal unit and put in an incubator and could only be held when I nursed her. Isis turned three months old and developed eczema. She was given ointments and oral steroids. None of it worked.

"Isis's skin progressively got worse. We took her to all kinds of specialists, but to no avail. I got an email from John that Isis was admitted to the hospital for eczema and was diagnosed with asthma. I returned home in 2007 and started researching every website I could find that was related to eczema. Isis became sad and always wanted to cover her body because kids would stare and laugh at her. She would always cry. One Sunday morning, I got Isis up to go to church and she didn't want to go because her skin was cracking and bleeding. We went anyway. After service, Mother Linda Gadson hugged her and asked me what was wrong with her skin. I told her and she gave me the *Hallelujah! Oil*. She told me to apply it to my daughter's skin. I did just that, and the next day I could see improvement in my daughter's skin. Within a few days, her skin was completely clear! I have been using *Hallelujah! Oil* ever since. My daughter's skin looks so good! She is happy to wear sandals and shorts now! *Hallelujah!* even helped her asthma as she does not even use her breathing machine anymore."

-**Melissa Simmons Stinnett**, 45
United States Navy-Honorably Discharged
Sumter, S.C.

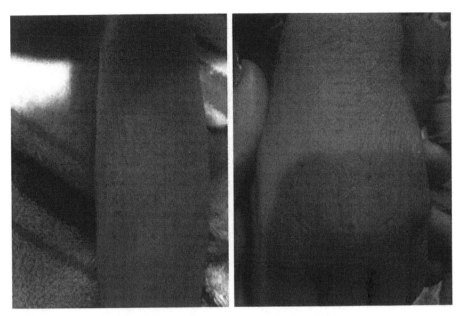

Isis Stinnett before using *Hallelujah! Oil.*

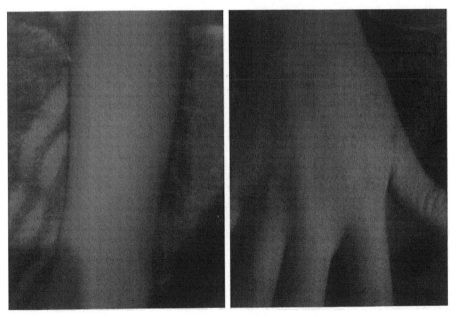

Isis Stinnett after using *Hallelujah! Oil.*

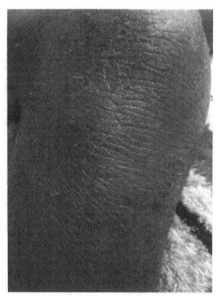

Isis Stinnett before using *Hallelujah! Oil.*

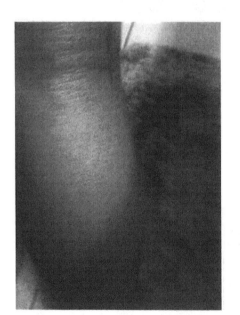

Isis Stinnett after using *Hallelujah! Oil.*

South Carolina United Methodist Advocate

CONNECTING METHODISTS IN SOUTH CAROLINA SINCE 1837

$2   MAY 2008

'HALLELUJAH! PRAISE THE LORD!' – Linda Gadson escapes her companion oxygen tube and gives forth her signature statement at Rural Mission. She was honored April 16 at the S.C. Summit on Women in Columbia as a Woman of Achievement. *Photo by Emily Cooper.*

Keep hope flowing, Linda Gadson asks

By Emily Cooper

JOHNS ISLAND – Rural Mission "is about giving them hope," Chris Brooks said, referring to the hundreds or more people touched each year.

Some of that hope may dry up, however, given the current economy. Brooks, who is charged with helping Rural Mission raise money, said people are telling him to come back later, that their stocks are down and they can't give.

Meanwhile, Executive Director Linda Gadson said, there's a waiting list of 300 families and growing. Brooks would like to see the United Methodist agency increase its help to 20 percent more per year.

"They come in the door, call us on the phone," Gadson said, quoting, "My neighbor's lights are off and I don't know what she and her children are going to do."

"Once people had wells," Gadson said. "Now their water gets shut off, too. People need food, utilities; stu-dents in college need help when their parents don't have the $100 for another book.

"A leak is the beginning of destruction," Gadson said as she and Brooks talked about the mission's ongoing home repairs headed by a 30-year veteran of Rural Mission and licensed contractor, Anderson Mack.

Brooks said Rural Mission coordinates with other church organizations and Habitat on the islands. "Not everyone can qualify for a Habitat House," Gadson said. "We're the safety net for everybody below their level. The need for dollars is urgent.

"It takes the presence of staff to maintain the program," Gadson said. "Rural Mission has always operated on a shoestring; we have to live within the budget. We depend on churches, and churches are affected by the sagging economy, too.

"Helping people is an expensive proposition. When teams come in to work, someone must be responsible."

The staff of 8 swells to 10 in the summer. During Head Start's summer program, part-time helpers are more than 80. "It takes gas, insurance, worker's comp..." she said.

Rural Mission work "becomes part of your heart," said Brooks, a former board member who has returned to help after retiring from state agency work. He began coming as a volunteer with the Rev. Don Britt's team when Britt was pastor of Trinity United Methodist Church in Charleston.

"We see adults who volunteered here years ago now back with their kids," Brooks said. Its work is contagious.

Volunteers have had such life-changing experiences on rural Johns Islands that they've gone home to do mission work in their own inner-city neighborhoods, Gadson said. In that way, they've spread Rural Mission all through the Eastern United States and the Midwest.

See Page 15

State of South Carolina
Office of the Governor

MARK SANFORD
GOVERNOR

POST OFFICE BOX 12267
COLUMBIA 29211

November 11, 2010

Ms. Linda Dingle Gadson
6571 Highway 162
Hollywood, South Carolina 29449

Dear Ms. Gadson,

On behalf of the people of South Carolina, I am pleased to award you the Order of the Palmetto – our state's highest civilian honor for service. This award is in recognition of all you have done to better our part of the world over the years.

It would be easy to point to specific accomplishments that merit the Order of the Palmetto but, in fact, your entire life and career have been marked by a level of commitment and achievement that brings enormous credit to you and to our state. In the world of mission work, you have been an incredibly effective leader. As Executive Director of Rural Mission, you have touched the lives of literally thousands of low-income and migrant families, at-risk children and elderly residents residing on the Sea Islands of Johns, Wadmalaw, Yonges and Edisto. Volunteers have been recruited, funds raised, homes repaired, new homes built, referrals for medical and other services made – and the long list of the countless ways in which Rural Mission has been able to stand in the gap and lend a hand to folks with many needs but limited means goes on. As "The Mother Theresa of the Sea Islands," you wear many hats, "counselor, doctor, minister, teacher, lawyer, real estate agent, and well-known prayer warrior." In all that you do as you wear these many hats, there is no doubt that you look to God for your inspiration and direction. As one who wrote me on your behalf said, "Very few have lived a life so dedicated to serving others…" While it is impossible to compress and describe your lifetime of good deeds and countless contributions in a letter, please know that we are grateful for all that you have done to make a positive difference in the lives of so many in such special and meaningful ways and to make your community and our state an even better place to live, work, learn and play.

What a wonderful model of citizenship you are and an outstanding example to all of us of a life well lived! Thank you for upholding the highest ideals of servant leadership in everything you do.

Sincerely,

Mark Sanford

MS/jbn

Mama's letter of commendation from Governor Mark Sanford. In 2010, he bestowed upon her The Order of the Palmetto- the state of South Carolina's highest civilian honor for service.

December 10, 2010

Honoring the Mother Theresa of the Sea Islands

GOV. SANFORD PRESENTS LINDA GASDON WITH ORDER OF THE PALMETTO

PROVIDED BY RURAL MISSION

On Thursday, November 11, the prestigious Order of the Palmetto was presented to longtime Rural Mission Executive Director Linda Dingle Gadson by Governor Mark Sanford. The Order of the Palmetto is the highest honor given for humanitarian service by the State of South Carolina and the Governor.

Linda D. Gadson, a native and lifelong resident of the coastal sea islands of Charleston County, has served as executive director of the Rural Mission for 38 years. She has given her life to helping impoverished residents, the elderly and migrant families on the sea islands achieve a better life, as well as ministering to their spiritual needs. This amazing dedication and life of selflessness has earned Gadson the title of "Mother Theresa of the Sea Islands".

Thousands have been helped by her dedication and persistence in encouraging others to reach out to those in need. Governor Sanford especially recognized her service to missions and faith, indicating how her leadership has brought thousands of volunteers to the impoverished sea islands to help others in dire need and hardship. Now in its 41st year, the Rural Mission has been gracefully and powerfully guided by Gadson. Under her supervision, the lines of difference and separation have been overcome in making a true difference in the lives of both recipients and volunteers to the program.

The Order of the Palmetto award was presented in a ceremony and special gathering at the Rural Mission with many friends, supporters and appreciative island residents in attendance. Rev. McKinley Washington, a lifelong friend of Gadson's and former State Senator, gave the award to Linda Gadson in a joyous and emotional presentation. Rev. Washington had served on the original Board of Directors of the Rural Mission and he has shared the vision for its success and growth. He joined with Senator Chip Campsen in nominating Gadson for this well-deserved and prestigious recognition by the State of South Carolina.

A LITTLE ABOUT LINDA

Linda Gadson grew up wanting to be an attorney and had planned to go to law

story continued on page 7

The Order of the Palmetto was presented to Mrs. Linda D. Gadson by former State Senator, Rev. McKinley Washington. (l to r: Rev. Washington, granddaughter Quael Woodberry Gadson, Linda Dingle Gadson and granddaughter Quin Woodberry Gadson (front).

"In July of 2007, my father awoke in the middle of the night with a shortness of breath. Although we were used to various diabetic attacks with him, we knew that this was something extremely different. Upon arrival to the hospital, we learned that my father's aortic valve was basically shut down. His heart was operating at approximately thirty percent.

"After speaking with many doctors, we were told that surgery was the only option, but that they would not perform it because he would not survive it. Twenty-one years prior to this experience, my father suffered a massive heart attack and with his history and at seventy-two years old, the doctors were not willing to take the risk.

"Finally, we met one doctor that said that he would do the surgery. After a week or so, the surgery was performed and it was successful. Prior to the surgery though, I recalled the story of Linda Gadson and how *Hallelujah!* brought her back to life. I decided to use it on Daddy.

"Although Daddy's surgery went well, he continued on the ventilator for two more weeks. The patient next to him passed away from staph infection and the doctors decided they needed to go back in to clean the area of Daddy's surgery of bacteria.

"The second surgery was performed and Daddy was okay, but he had a very slow healing time. After various transitions from different hospitals, nursing homes, rehabilitation centers and more, we found ourselves three months down the road and Daddy had contracted staph infection.

"We applied the oil to Daddy every day and sometimes he would even drink the oil. We found out that part of my father's delayed healing was due to the feeding tube being put in incorrectly. Staph infection was present in my father's bowels and the feeding tube went through his colon, however, the infection never spread throughout his system.

"We are very thankful to God for Linda Gadson and *Hallelujah!* We know that *Hallelujah!* prevented the infection from spreading."

Kenda Cooper, *25*
University of Michigan graduate, 2007
Dearborn, MI

"My story was featured on WCSC-TV local news in Charleston, South Carolina (www.youtube.com; video name: "Hallelujah Oil Halts Breast Cancer"). Before I started using *Hallelujah!* every time I went to chemo-therapy, I would regurgitate everything I took in, including water. I started using the oil to calm my stomach, and after that I would come home and eat like there was no tomorrow. With the oil, my appetite returned full force. The oil has gotten me through a lot of physical pain, heartache and depression. I use it every day. My life has gotten better because of *Hallelujah!*"

Claudelle Martin, *46*
Breast Cancer Survivor
Green Pond, S.C.

"In 2010, I was diagnosed with stage IV breast cancer. I had been get-ting regular mammograms, but somehow the cancer was never detected. My doctors began radiation treatment within a week of my diagnosis. I was afraid and I was angry. I was also very discouraged. I began to pray.

I was then introduced to Linda Gadson by my goddaughter. Miss Gad-son gave me her *Hallelujah! Oil* and instructed me to apply it to my breasts twice a day. After treatment and having my breast removed, I went back to the doctor after six months. There was NO sign of breast cancer. In Janu-ary of 2012, my doctors released me- free from *stage IV breast cancer*. I still use *Hallelujah! Oil* daily. I know *Hallelujah!* is a big reason why I no longer have breast cancer."

Janie Hughes, *68*
Breast Cancer Survivor
Charleston, South Carolina

Reggie got clean. My brother actually got clean. I had to say it twice because I'm still stunned by it. On June 17, 2009, my brother said he woke up drinking his tears because he'd cried so much. He'd smoked enough crack for three people the night before and he'd drifted between sleep and unconsciousness. He woke up, ran to the mirror, looked in it and saw tears of remorse and neglect running down his face. The remorse came because of the years he let slip away like sand between his fingers. The neglect came because as he looked at those fingers he noticed, for the first time really, how badly the various crack pipes and soda cans he used to smoke it had burned its tips. He had two twenty-dollar pieces of rock left in his pocket. As he stared in the mirror, he grabbed his jeans off of the toilet, reached into his pockets and did for years what he'd never dreamed he'd have the strength to do: throw the crack in the toilet. Then he flushed it.

Reggie has told me that each day that he spends not smoking crack is a day added to the rest of his life. I'm inclined to believe him. While he says each day does get just a bit easier and the cravings are not nearly as severe as they used to be, they are still there. They wait patiently on him to get stressed. They wait on him to get angry. The cravings eagerly antici-pate any day he gets depressed for any reason. Much like time itself, crack is omnipresent. It lurks in the shadows waiting on my brother to make a mistake. The rock waits on him for the opportunity to turn him back into the old Reggie. So far, my brother daily fights the good fight. He says that he's going to "fight on his soul 'til death." But he knows that once you kiss the bride and lay your lips on that crack pipe or soda can, you marry her. You can never really divorce her. He says that the best you can hope for is a legal separation. She will forever be your bride – 'til death do you part.

My brother did eventually marry Toffee. I'd like to tell you that their story has a happy ending, but it doesn't. Or maybe it does. I guess it depends on how you view life. They got married in 2002 and they're still mar-ried. But, they haven't actually lived under the same roof since 2005. My brother, for better or for worse, is a whoremonger. He can't help himself. Women love him. He loves women. I doubt that will ever change. Now granted, Toffee knew this before she married him. Maybe she reasoned that she could change him or that he would change himself. I don't know. They fought all of the time and they weren't very happy. Toffee left him and she eventually stopped smoking crack too. They are taking recovery one day at a time. They both still love each other deeply; they still have sex with each other and that arrangement works for them.

Reggie lives with his girlfriend and her three children now. He's still as wild as he's ever been. He takes far better care of her children than you would expect and I think that responsibility has in fact made him a better man. All I know is that my brother doesn't smoke crack anymore.

The Reverend Telley Lynnette Gadson must be the most sought-after speaker in the United Methodist Church. She travels across these United States preaching the good news that Jesus Christ died so that a dying world may live. Much like Mama, Telley's mission in life is to save the world from itself. However, in 2005, she decided to save herself. She embarked upon a weight-loss journey that has been nothing short of miraculous. In the past five years, my sister has lost one hundred fifteen pounds. She didn't have surgery and didn't use any fad diets. She simply modified her life. She started to exercise and eat healthy. She got in the gym and worked on improving her body until it hurt. She confronted the demons that made her want to gorge and stuff herself. She examined the factors that made her eat and she decided to change her circumstances. She has inspired many. Her story has been featured in a couple of publications here locally. She is extraordinary.

Just recently, Telley built a church in Sumter and she's totally changed the culture of her entire congregation. Sumter is a working class community and my sister's parishioners have been so inundated with spirits of negativism they thought they couldn't move from the church that they were in. It was a vanilla white cinderblock building that was antiquated and far too small. It was cold in the winter and radiated heat in the summer. It looked very similar to a 19th Century schoolhouse where newly freed slaves would have learned how to read, write and worship. Under Telley's guidance and leadership, they moved into a red brick sanctuary that's about the size of Hollywood's Wesley. My sister did such a good job in changing her congregants' mindsets that she changed mine too. I joined the St. Mark United Methodist Church in late 2009 and it was the best decision I could have made. Now granted, having your sister as your pastor is a bit esoteric at times. Sometimes, I don't think she can tell where the pastor parameters end and the sibling parameters begin, but we do all right. Reverend

Gadson is as good a preacher, teacher and spiritual coach as you will find anywhere in this country. And don't worry that you may not have heard of her yet. Believe me, you will.

By Michelle Greenlee Harris

The Reverend Telley Lynnette Gadson doesn't mind standing "naked" before her congregation. Naked, that is, in reference to her struggle with obesity. "I have been very open with them. Everyone walks with a limp and this one is mine." The 34-four-year-old says she has learned a valuable lesson. "What you can't confront, you can't conquer," she states. So she has taken this lifelong struggle, looked it square in the eye and gone to battle. "I love acronyms so I labeled the last three years of my life as 'SWL 3'," she laughs. That stands for "significant weight loss number three." As pastor of Saint Mark United Methodist Church in Sumter, she is determined to show her

standing next to a normal-sized kindergarten child — we just looked like the number 10," she says. In the third grade, when the class was being weighed, the nurse tried to spare her feelings by weighing Gadson when no one else was in the room. "Still," she recalls, "it made me feel different." She didn't eat lunch in the cafeteria her freshman year of high school because of the other students' reaction when she first walked in.

Home, Church Offered Refuge

While she stood out in school, there were places where she was accepted. Gadson wasn't ridiculed at home. "My

'This Time, I Win'
Busy Pastor Recounts Highs, Lows of Her Weight-Loss Battle

parishioners and herself that, for her, the third time is the charm.

Gadson knows obesity is in her genes. "Both my mother and father have large people in their families so I always thought I was destined to be big," she says. Big is one thing, but morbidly obese is another. Gadson was an obese child. "I remember weighing 75 pounds in kindergarten. That year I won the title of kindergarten queen," she recalls, for raising the most money among the girls. "I had to take a picture with the little boy who raised the most and

family was loving and affirming. I was the middle child and the only girl. I was smart and responsible. It overshadowed my weight." Church was a safe place, too. She was a natural leader, teaching Sunday school at 10 and serving as the church secretary at 13.

But that was nothing unusual for Gadson, who belongs to a family of overachievers. Her father was the first black mayor of Hollywood, near Charleston, serving from 1989 until 2003, and a survivor of the Orangeburg Mas-

Telley featured in Imara Woman Magazine.

sacre. Her mother, an extraordinary humanitarian, is the first black woman to graduate from the College of Charleston. Her younger brother is a writer and an artist. "But my father is also a functioning alcoholic and my older brother is a 21-year drug-abuse veteran," admits Gadson. She recognizes addictive behavior in herself as well. Now that she has gained control of her unhealthy eating, she recognizes her addiction to order and is also a workaholic. At 25, she graduated from seminary and pastored two churches simultaneously.

Gadson now recognizes that at times she was hiding behind work to make herself too busy for some social situations. "I worked all through high school, so on Friday

significant weight loss was when she fell in love. While she was a freshman at the University of South Carolina, she met a slightly older man (6 years her senior) who had come back to school. "We were study partners and when we got our tests back, he had gotten an A while I made a D+ and that wasn't supposed to happen," she laughs. "I knew then that I was gone — head over heels."

It eventually became clear that he did not feel the same way about her, although the two became close friends and he even worked out with her, helping her to lose 50 pounds. But SWL 1 ultimately failed because Gadson still had not faced the cause of her overeating. "I still didn't uncover what void I was trying to fill," she says.

"I haven't set a specific amount to lose; I am just determined to continue to live a healthier lifestyle."
—Telley Gadson

and Saturday nights I didn't have to worry about feeling bad about not having a date, I was busy," she recalls. "Back then, if I did have a crush on someone I was too embarrassed to tell them," says Gadson of her fear of rejection. "Of course, now I know you can reject yourself."

50 Pounds Disappear, but Void Remains

Through her adolescent years, Gadson experienced the rollercoaster rides of yo-yo diets. The first time she saw

"When I tried SWL 2, I was destined to fail again because this time I was determined to do it all on my own. I was going to make it happen myself and God couldn't get any glory out of that," says Gadson. She was successful for a couple of years and had lost about 65 pounds, but then crisis struck and her will power alone was not enough. Gadson's grandmother died and she was having challenges at work. "I was pastoring the two churches, vetting the idea of merger, and dealing with some serious need for conflict

Telley featured in Imara Woman Magazine (cont.).

resolutions," she recalls. Gadson admits she just let go of the discipline.

Epiphany Brings Profound Change

"Then on August 23, 2005, I just had an a-ha moment with God. He showed me that I needed his strength in order to do this permanently," says Gadson. She says she didn't start with a weight loss goal. She just started making incremental changes in food portions and exercise. "In fact, I finally went back to the gym I had joined during SWL 2 and as soon as I walked in, one of the trainers recognized me and said, 'Telley, it's so good to see you. You haven't been in awhile'—— of course, I knew that was obvious. When I got on the treadmill I could barely walk 10 minutes, but I wasn't discouraged," remembers Gadson. She left knowing that she would return the next day.

By using the knowledge she had about nutrition and seeking even more information, she stopped battling with food. "I used intentional portion control and the Lord rescued me from any cravings," she proclaims. Gadson says her saving grace is water. Plus she uses salads, fruits and vegetables as a foundation for healthy eating. The word diet is not uttered.

This worked well until July 2006, when she potentially faced her greatest setback: Her mother developed kidney stones. While treating her, doctors discovered two-and-a-half blockages in her heart, and by mid-July had scheduled her for open-heart surgery. "On Aug. 3, my mother, Linda Dingle Gadson, who is my lifesaver and my best friend, underwent 8-1/2 hours of major surgery, surgery that wasn't supposed to take more than four hours," says Gadson. Her fear and anxiety was exactly the kind of setback that had derailed her weight loss so many times in the past.

"But I heard the spirit of God say to me, 'So what are you going to do now? Are you going to let this throw you or are you going to trust me?'" Gadson resolved to trust Him more than she ever had. "I knew my mother needed me and I had to keep it together," she continues. Gadson stayed on her regimen and even left her mother's bedside long enough to walk around a nearby lake a couple of times a week.

More Setbacks Threaten Her Progress

Her mother was released after 50 days in the hospital and Gadson thought the worst was behind her until she had her own close call in October of that year. "I was told that I had diabetes. I made them test me twice." Gadson admits she threw up her hands in frustration. "I said, 'What am I doing all of this for if I still end up with diabetes?'" The frustration didn't last long, though, and she told the doctor she would give back the diabetes medication in nine to 12 months.

Telley Gadson proclaims that God did even better than that. "In six months, my glucose levels were back within the normal range. The same God that had healed my moth-

> To date, Gadson has lost more than 89 pounds and 45 inches and she is looking forward to even more success. "I can't wait to throw myself a hundred-pound party."

er had healed me," she says. Gadson also credits routine exercise, maintaining a healthy diet and managing her food portions with her success.

To date, Gadson has lost 89 pounds and 45 inches and she is looking forward to even more success. "I haven't set a specific amount to lose; I am just determined to continue to live a healthier lifestyle." But there are several things she is looking forward to. "I can't wait to throw myself a hundred-pound party," she beams. She also looks forward to the services when she tells the congregation that she has a new total. "Now one of the musicians will do a drum roll and the whole church will cheer," she laughs. "I had to apologize to my members for living such an undisciplined life in front of them. I didn't want a young person sitting in the church watching me and thinking it's OK to be unhealthy because that's what Rev. Telley is doing." She smiles as she repeats the title to a sermon she once preached that has become her battle cry along this journey — despite the setbacks, plateaus, injuries, naysayers and past failures — "This time, I win." ▓

Come meet Telley Lynnette Gadson and hear more of her inspiring story at the 2008 Health Ministry Empowerment Tour. Rev. Gadson will be the featured speaker in Allendale, Greenville and Georgetown.

Telley featured in **Imara** Woman Magazine (cont.).

Heroes never really die, right? Well, at least they aren't supposed to. We've all been taught that, almost since birth and certainly since grade school. But what happens when death swallows a hero's shadow and when you look up, you no longer see the reflection of the one you saw move heaven and earth with ease, and where the reflection once loomed, all you can see is blackness engulfing it? What happens when it's your hero? I never thought I'd have to answer that question. One day, the answer became required of me.

My father is more than a man. I learned that a long time ago. What mortal do you know that could have survived the game he's played and lived to tell you the final score? I don't know of any besides the Mayor of Hollywood. No political rival could truly beat him, so over the course of a lifetime Daddy beat himself. Surely, I could have ended this story and put a nice little bow on top of it like the other Hollywood does, but this isn't Tinseltown. And before what happened occurred, I had a totally different way that I was going to end our walk through perdition. But I vowed that I was going to tell you this True Hollywood Story, the events as they unfolded, and that's fully what I intend to do. Just call me the Walter Cronkite of Hollywood. *And that's the way it is.*

Obedience is better than sacrifice. Mama not only told us that, but she told Daddy that as well. Too many times to count. I can hear Mama now, "Herbert, now you kin take what Um tellin' you as uh joke if you wanna, but obedience is better than sacrifice, Herbert." My daddy would respond similarly, whether he was drunk or sober, "Linda, please leave me da fuck alone; I aine in da mood fah no damn sermon." Well, see, the thing about sermons is this: There is always a message to be heeded. There is always a note of caution and a word of warning, even for the heroes amongst us. Stop. Don't do it. Do better. Every sermon has those basic points to ponder, if you're wise enough to listen to the words. Over the years, Daddy became deaf.

The Mayor was as fearless as he was indestructible. Nobody could tell him what to do or how to do it. That's just the way he lived, especially since the divorce. So when he asked me to drive him to Roper on Monday, August 30, 2010, for surgery to remove an aneurysm from the aorta in his right groin, I thought nothing of it. The surgery was supposed to remove it so that he would not suffer a stroke or a heart attack, as the aorta is the main artery leading to the heart. He was going to have a fairly short recovery time and he had already told Aunt Joelle that she was going to have to come and look after him until he fully recovered. Being the genius he was, he'd had it all mapped out.

You ever get a feeling of foreboding that you can't shake? It's a feeling like disaster is eminent, though nothing appears to be wrong. Well, as I sat alone in the same waiting room that I sat in exactly four years and mere days after Mama thumbed her nose at death, I got that feeling. Oh sure, right up until the time that Daddy was rolled into surgery, we were laughing and joking with each other. But as I sat there in that lonely room, something in my soul went haywire. While they were administering the anesthesia to Daddy in what looked to be the same room they doped Mama up in, I stood at his bedside. He told me, "Boy, I done tell da docdah me an' God gah do our job, he betta damn do his." We both laughed. Then, as the anesthesiologist instructed him to do, Daddy started counting backwards from one hundred. By the time he got to sixty-two, the drugs had begun to take effect. He drifted away. Maybe that's what it was that had me so shaken. Daddy went to sleep on the number sixty-two and he was to turn sixty-two years old in a matter of twenty-three days.

I sat in that waiting room for three and a half hours by myself thinking about that. Well, I was especially thinking about that and the fact that I was alone. The scene on this surgery day was vastly different than on the day of Mama's surgery. On her surgery day, the atmosphere was electric, communal and you could cut the anticipation with a knife. At every doctor's update, the room was abuzz waiting for him to speak.

Not on that day though. On that day, that waiting room was taciturn and frigid. I was in a daze up until the time the doctor tapped me on the shoulder. I heard him say my name. He started talking. He looked ashen and like he'd just been in a train wreck. A number of barely noticeable dried blood smudges and specks adorned his aqua blue scrubs and his eyes that were almost the same color had turned bloodshot. He was average height, bald, clean shaven and fair skinned. He looked tired. I took a good look at Dr. Morrison Edwards and he appeared as though he'd just been in a tango with Jason Voorhees or Freddy Krueger. I think that's when my mind just shut off. He was talking and the only thing I could make out was "Your dad's very sick," "Operation was a bear," and "We may have to take the leg."

I think I may have said, "Why?" or "How?" in response to his medical dissertation. He said something about dead muscle poisoning the rest of the body and the leg having to come off. He said Daddy's lungs were a mess and that his heart wasn't much better. He palavered about his liver and kidneys. Because of forty-seven years of alcohol abuse, forty-four years of nicotine abuse and about twenty years of that at a two-pack-a-day clip, his body had basically turned into a toxic dump. Maybe he mentioned dialysis as well. I don't know. I was too busy calling Mama.

Mama and Daddy were together again four days later before they took him to cut his leg off. The doctors did all they could, but they couldn't save it. He and Mama were in his room side by side for a long time in that intensive care unit at Roper. Mama had on her oxygen tank as she stood over Daddy, who was near death about to get his leg amputated. Daddy's women weren't there. There was not a liquor bottle, cigarette, or any of the residents from the Town of Hollywood anywhere in sight. It was just Mama, Daddy, the Bible and *Hallelujah! Oil* in that room. Linda and Herbert were together again. I'd like to tell you that I know for certain that my daddy's going to live, but I just don't know. The doctors don't even know because they say they've never seen a case like his. My hero is lying in a hospital bed in intensive care and there's nothing that I can do about it. This is between Daddy and God now.

Daddy was seriously ill. Doctors gave him a less than thirty percent chance of surviving the four surgeries they performed on him after the complications resulted from his amputation.

I took him to the hospital in August and I didn't bring him back home until December. He was dead. There were many days when only beeping and clicking machines kept him alive. Too many days to count his body temperature reached dangerously high levels. Doctors constantly pumped him full of antibiotics.

On those days when Daddy was suffering the most, Mama made her way to the hospital to pray with him and pour Hallelujah! Oil over his head. She also doused the remaining foot of her soul mate. And when she did, without fail, his temperature went down. The oil impressed the nurses so much that soon even they were using Hallelujah! on him. Mama conveniently, after some time, "forgot" that she'd left a bottle of it right by his bed, and the nurses began using it on him around the clock. After that, Daddy's temperature remained at 98.6 degrees until he was released.

Today, if you see a three-wheeled magenta and pearl moped anywhere in Charleston, honk your horn at the driver. More than likely, that's my daddy. He's got his prosthesis now. Dead man walking. And riding. And he's happy.

I am a Geechie boy. I am a 'bama and a country bumpkin. I like any combination of grits, fish, raccoon, squirrel or opossum. All of those varmints taste pretty good to me. I'm a fan of Michael McDonald, Lynyrd Skynyrd and Marley Mar. *Takin' It to the Streets*, *Sweet Home Alabama* and *Act A Donkey* are watershed moments in music if you ask me. I say that because these artists were not afraid to represent their reality as they saw it. They told their truth as they understood it to be. Michael was white, but he was unabashed about his love for soul music and on *Takin' It to the Streets*, he truly bore his. Not coincidentally, The Doobie Brothers just weren't the same band after he went solo. Lynyrd Skynyrd wasn't afraid to represent Alabama. They spoke with a drawl and their mentality was backwater and backwoods. They loved where they were from and you could hear it in each note of *Sweet Home Alabama*. Marley Mar is the total embodiment of a Geechie. We call him the "Mount Millionaire" because he hails from Remount Road in North Charleston. Now, I don't know if he has a million dollars, but he most certainly has a million dollars worth of talent. As adept as Bill Sharpe is at reporting the news of the day, Marley Mar is light years better at reporting the news of the Charleston streets. By any parameter that one would use to measure an emcee, whether its lyricism, delivery, metaphoric clarity or just sheer *swagger*, Marley Mar is our Jay-Z, our Lil' Wayne, our Eminem. He says he's, "The King of The Chuck [Charleston]." If you listen to *Act A Donkey*, you'd be hard pressed to dispute the claim. Try *not* singing and rapping along with the song. Resistance is futile. He exudes North Charleston from every pore of his body. His music and attitude express the rugged individualism, can-do attitude and against-all-odds-but-still- I-rise ethic that North Charleston is known for. *Act A Donkey* has become an anthem in The Holy City because this guy is SO North Charleston. And I'm *so* Hollywood.

I am also an alcoholic. I love to drink. I can't deny it. Now, I only drink during Thanksgiving and Christmastime. When I do, I drink to the point of blacking out and throwing up. Alcohol in my system makes me feel invincible. I love that feeling.

Or maybe it's more the case that the Crown Royal, Jack Daniels and Canadian Mist make me numb and deaf. When they calm my constantly frayed and anxiety riddled nerves, the pang of Victor's voice and, for that matter, the voices of the sixth through eighth graders at Sky High and the ninth through twelfth graders at Baptist Hill from the early to the mid '90s, isn't as shrill or omniscient. Oh, don't get me wrong. It wasn't all of the kids. But, it was just enough of them to produce the kind of emotional migraine that no medication can truly cure. I can't say I blame them. I was classified as a lame. And in middle and high school, if you're a lame, you're going to get harassed. Bullied. Perhaps, even beat the fuck up. This mandate is written in *The Great Handbook of Teenager Bullshit. Rule #4,080.* I hate that it's this way. I wish there was some way that we could scrub the word *bully* from our vernacular. When I drink, I can still hear them telling me that my head is actually bigger than Marvin The Martian's and more oblong than Mr. Potato Head's. I can still eavesdrop on the conversations that alluded to the facts that beastliness had somehow latched hold to my face and the ugliness was going to leave me as virginal and pure as the driven snow, for the rest of my days, as *Heidi*. I do still hear them clearly. But when I'm drinking or drunk, I just don't give a fuck. My senses are deadened. When I'm sober and walk into a room for the first time, I'm sure everyone is thinking, "*He sure has a big head,*" and if I make eye contact with an attractive woman in Wal-Mart I wonder if she would laugh in my face if I were to walk up to her and ask for her number. I don't do that, though. Instead, I look away quickly after the eye contact.

So, because on a day-to-day basis I'm as dry as a bone, I'm forced to cope with the voices the best way I know how. My head thrums and my ears ring almost constantly. I'm so damaged that even when the most honest people on planet earth tell me that I may in fact not be totally repulsive, I'm forced to question their integrity. I was helping the girls do homework not very long ago as we sat at their little Hello Kitty table in the den, and out of the clear blue Quati said, "Daddy, you're so handsome; I love you." Not to be outdone, Qynn said, "Daddy, I wanna marry a handsome man like you when I grow up." On the double, the ghosts of my middle and high school past told me that even if I looked like the Toxic Crusader, my kids would still say those things. Maybe, they wouldn't. Who knows? I think I replied with something like, "I love you too, girls; but come on now, we gotta finish our homework." Those other voices will always drown out my kids' when it comes to those kinds of things. I don't think I'll ever believe, with any fervor, that I'm worth a damn. I think I miss getting tore down every day. Now that I mention it, I know that I do. Daily, I have to fight the urge to drink. If not for my children and my mother, whom I have been charged with looking after, I would get fucked up regularly.

And speaking of the girls, they're doing just fine. They're not so little anymore and they seem to grow at least a foot per month. And would you believe that for a man, who motivated by cowardice once questioned their paternity, I now couldn't imagine life without them. I even learned how to braid their hair. I've got Qynn's "first day of school" pictures to prove it.

You know that old saying, "God never closes a door without opening a window," well, it's a fact. The day after Felicia sent me packing, I got a call for a substitute assignment and by His grace I've worked more often than not ever since. This was a blessing because the day after she was arrested, the kids came to stay with Mama and me and they never left.

That was a few years ago. The days have not been easy, but we've managed to stay afloat. When the kids started school and I had an assignment to go on, I'd wake up at 5 in the morning. I'd go in the prayer room and pray with Mama until 6. I'd wake the kids up at 6:30, take them in the prayer room and Mama and I would pray with them until 7. I'd brush their teeth and then we'd shower. To expedite time, I'd brush their teeth and bathe them together. I'd line them up in the tub and administer an A-1 Simoniz to them until they sparkled and gleamed like a Mercedes-Benz off of Baker Motor Company's showroom floor. My girls were *so fresh and so clean.* Most mornings after I'd finished scrubbing them, we'd sing at the top of our lungs our Hollywoodized version of the OutKast classic. *Aint nobody dope aaas us/ Weee're just so fresh, so clean/ So fresh and so clean, clean*! Our bathtub/ stage name was Daddy featuring 2 Live Q's. When the curtains closed on our morning gigs, I'd brush my teeth, shower and dress. It was then off to work and school.

I'd drop Qynn off at St. Luke Headstart and then drop Quati off at C.C. Blaney. I'd leave C.C. Blaney between 8 and 8:10. I'd have to be in North Charleston, where most of my assignments were, at 9. The drive from Hollywood to North Charleston is normally about forty-five minutes, but when you factor in the morning traffic the trip took a solid hour. God was always with me because the schools always worked with me. They compromised with me because I trusted Him to touch their hearts to allow me to continue to work. From the day the girls came to live with us, the Lord's made a way for me to be able to provide for them. The girls love school! They are doing quite well and they prove to me each day, by the myriad of questions they ask, that I'm not as smart as they are.

After years of bitter feelings, resentment and the pain that a tumultuous break-up almost always leaves, my relationship with Felicia is finally back to where it started: close friends. J. Kevin Holmes, the same attorney that was going to represent Daddy in his case had it gone to trial, ended up representing Felicia. He is the archetypal Broad Street lawyer. He is one of the best criminal defense attorneys in Charleston and he got her off an embezzlement charge with just five years probation. I was so relieved when the judge sentenced her that day in the Charleston County Judicial Center on Broad Street. I was sitting there in that tribunal with her in the heart of the Four Corners of Law. I was about to shout *"Hallelujah!"* when the judge banged that gavel. If I had, and he held me in contempt of court and sentenced me to thirty days in jail, I would not have cared. Even though we hadn't been together in years, I shuttled Felicia around to all of her appointments with her Broad Street lawyer. During her short jail stint, she'd lost her apartment and both cars. When she had her day in court, I was the only family member, friend or prayer warrior in that courtroom on Team Felicia. Shaytee and Felicia were together again. And I'd play it again, Sam. No questions asked. No hesitation. I was going into battle with Felicia because of all of the good and bad times we had. I held her hand that day, quite simply, because of each kiss that pursed our lips and the tears that dried on our cheeks. I was in that foxhole with her for what we were; and because of those two phenomenal little women, what we would always be. It didn't matter what we had become. My girls were not going to lose their mommy!

Felicia has had a long and arduous road back since her Hunter's Point days. I've tried to give her as much love and support as I could. Quati and Qynn have kept her going through some pretty dark moments. We've realized that those two beautiful little girls are far more important than the grudges and the raw emotions that created the huge gulf between us. Somewhere along the line, the college sweethearts that became a baby mama and baby daddy long before they were supposed to, became parents. I guess while we weren't looking, we grew up.

I am clinically depressed. I should be on medication to control it. I've made myself comfortable on the leather couch, in the office of a psychiatrist, a time or two. I saw this one eight times before I decided that the shit he was telling me I either didn't want to hear or already knew. Do you honestly think that I don't know that I'm batshit crazy? Who amongst us doesn't believe that antidepressants wouldn't quell the "bucking damn fool" in me? However, I don't want to be chained to a bottle of Prozac or Zoloft. I know me; I'll matriculate from clinical depression to prescription drug addiction in a New York minute. No thanks. I guess I have been fighting depression since the day Mama Clay died, maybe even before then. I have *seriously* contemplated suicide more times than I can tell you. I have had sex with more women than I can remember. More than likely, they probably don't care to dredge up the experience with my ratchet ass, either. To be perfectly candid, I really can't seriously comprehend why any of those women took the slightest interest in me. I mean, I'm a realist; I'm totally underwhelming and I'm most definitely nothing to write home about. That much is for certain.

I've always longed to be viewed by the world as something special. I am the living and breathing example of what a father can do to a son with both their eyes squeezed shut. I turned into Daddy. All of his insecurities, his pain, his lusts and his passions, I purloined them from the depths of his soul. Now they are mine. I don't even know if I am happy or sad about my lot.

Herbert Gadson is the man from whom I extracted my example of manhood. The Mayor of Hollywood is my burden. I wear his legacy like a badge of honor. The blood of the awesome stain of that indelible mark he etched, on the soul of my town, is what I wear across my chest. It is imprinted on the walls of my heart. It is my scarlet letter and I am ashamed of it, but I wear it proudly. I'm the new Hester Prynne. Maybe one day I'll be somebody important like Daddy. Maybe I'll save humanity from its sins like Mama. Who knows what I'll become under this dim Hollywood spotlight? I guess, in the end, the only thing I really do know is that whatever I become, I'll become it right here. This is my home. Hollywood is where my heart is, scarlet letter and all.

The End

07-09-2007, 01:34 PM

movingtosouthcarolina
Junior Member

Hollywood, SC...anyone from there?

We are moving to SC soon. Hubby will work for the Navy. We are looking to find a rental in the country type setting. We have seen an ad for a place in Hollywood. Anyone have any ideas or thoughts on the area? Good, bad, indifferent? We just want a nice safe place to raise our family. Thanks so much and have a great day! 😊

[+] Rate this post positively

Quote

wesacat
Senior Member

Hi Moving,
Hollywood is a very small (one street) town about 30 to 40 min. south of Charleston. It is a poor town with a mostly black population. The schools in that area are not the best either. However, there is a lot of isolated country land there and very inexpensive.
Well, to tell ya the truth, Im not sure ANYone would be well received in Hollywood. LOL It's kind of a "you aint from around these parts, are ya?" kinda place.

/ww.city-data.com/forum/south-carolina/113071-hollywood-sc-anyone-there.html 12.

[+] Rate this post positively

Quote

07-09-2007, 07:48 PM

SCBeaches
Senior Member

Having taught in and commuted to Hollywood from James Island for 3 years (many years ago) I can vouch that newcomers, no matter what race, aren't well received. EVERYONE is related to EVERYONE else out there and they fight amongst themselves (a lot of shootings out there), but no one else had better step in or say anything about anyone else. Very tight community. On top of that there is a definite racial line in Hollywood, as illustrated with their recent mayoral/town council problems. There was a white mayor (first ever, I believe) but no one would go along with any of his decisions or work with him because of his race - police officers actually had to come to the council meetings to prevent violence, but there were still fights. There is a newly-elected black woman mayor but there are STILL problems making the news. Too much upheaval for me!

Articles, Letters, Pictures, Excerpts and Acknowledgements

John "Skip" Johnson – Editor
South Carolina State Historical Collections and Archives Department
Milller F. Whittaker Library
South Carolina State University
Orangeburg, South Carolina 29117
The Post and Courier
Imara Woman Magazine
House Calls Magazine
Charleston Magazine
South Carolina United Methodist Advocate
State of South Carolina Office of The Governor
The Island Connection Newspaper
City-Data.com
Jack Bass
Rural Mission, Inc.
Kenda Cooper
Claudelle Martin
Janie Hughes

Melissa Simmons-Stinnett
Isis Stinnett
Black Women In Sisterhood For Action
South Carolina African-American History Calendar

About the Author

Hallelujah! in Hollywood: A True Hollywood Story is Shaytee Gadson's first novel. He attended the College of Charleston and Morris College in South Carolina. Shaytee is a proud member of Omega Psi Phi Fraternity.He resides in Hollywood, South Carolina with his mother and two daughters.

"Grip your dreams tightly and nurture them with such ferocity that your determination forces your doubters to fall into a hate induced coma. As they sleep, they are compelled to dream right along with you,"
-Shaytee Herbert Abraham Gadson

Visit us at www.hallelujahinhollywood.com.

94548341R00165

Made in the USA
Columbia, SC
02 May 2018